Charles E.
Lindblom

Democracy
and Market System

Charles E. Lindblom

Democracy and Market System

Norwegian
University Press

Norwegian University Press (Universitetsforlaget AS), 0608 Oslo 6
Distributed world-wide excluding Scandinavia by
Oxford University Press, Walton Street, Oxford OX2 6DP

London New York Toronto
Delhi Bombay Calcutta Madras Karachi
Kuala Lumpur Singapore Hong Kong Tokyo
Nairobi Dar es Salaam Cape Town
Melbourne Auckland

and associated companies in
Beirut Berlin Ibadan Mexico City Nicosia

ISBN 82-00-02612-4
ISBN 82-00-18435-8 Pbk

British Library Cataloguing in Publication Data
Lindblom, Charles E.
Democracy and Market System.—(Scandinavia library)
1. United States. Economic policies
I. Title II. Series
330.973'0927

Printed in Denmark
by P. J. Schmidt A/S, Vojens

Contents

Acknowledgements

The Introduction (1987), Chapter 3: "Democratization in the U.S. and Its Problems" (1980), Chapter 5: "American Politics Since 1970" (1982), Chapter 6: "Democracy and the Economy" (1983), Chapter 7: "Bargaining: The Hidden Hand in Government" (1955), and Chapter 10: "New Decision-Making Procedures Governing Research on and Treatment of Catastrophic Diseases" (1970) have never been published before, at least not in English. (Chapters 3 and 6 have been published in Italian versions.) The remaining articles have appeared in various books, journals, and conference proceedings, and I should like to thank the publishers for their permission to reprint them here:

1. "Democracy and Economic Structure," from *Democracy Today: Problems and Prospects,* edited by William N. Chambers and Robert H. Salisbury, New York: Collier Books, 1962, pp. 80–121; copyright 1960 by Washington University, St. Louis, Missouri.
2. "The Rediscovery of the Market," from *The Public Interest,* No. 4, Summer 1966, pp. 89–101; copyright by National Affairs Inc.
4. "Changing Views on Conflict between Freedom and Equality," from *Freedom and Equality in Contemporary Society,* proceedings from "Japan and the World Tomorrow," International Conference, Tokyo: 1980, pp. 18–22.
8. "The Science of 'Muddling Through'," from *Public Administration Review,* Vol. 19, No. 2, Spring 1959, pp. 78–88.
9. "Economic Development, Research and Development, Policy Making: Some Converging Views," from *Behavioral Science,* Vol. 7, April 1962, pp. 211–222.
11. "Still Muddling, Not Yet Through," from *Public Administration Review,* Vol. 39, Nov./Dec. 1979, pp. 517–526.
12. "Integration of Economics and the Other Social Sciences

through Policy Analysis," from *Integration of the Social Sciences through Policy Analysis,* edited by James C. Charlesworth, Philadelphia: The American Academy of Political and Social Science (Monograph No. 14), 1972, pp. 1–14.

13. "Another State of Mind," from *The American Political Science Review,* Vol. 76, 1982, pp. 9–21.

14. "Who Needs What Social Research for Policy Making?" from Rockefeller Institute Conference Proceedings, Vol. 1, No. 2, May 1984, pp. 1–42.

Introduction[1]

Of the papers here collected, those in Part I, "Democracy and Market System," have sometimes appeared to past readers to be at odds with those of Part II, "Policy Making." Shortly after the publication of *Politics and Markets,* Albert Hirschman asked me how I had come, or could have come, from incremental policy making to the argument of that book, which accords with the papers of Part I. Realizing that I would have to give extended thought to the explanation, rather than ask for an answer he proposed that I write and publish a reconciliation of what appears to be two discordant lines of thought. I now have one to offer, marred as it will be by some of my failures to understand the pattern of my own work. I see now in retrospect that it has a pattern, but its development was not the fulfillment or implementation of a design. *Ex ante,* it never seemed clear to me what I should next study; only *ex post* do I see the pattern.

Why do Hirschman and others think there is a puzzle? My interest in incrementalism as a kind of politics and as a method of policy making seems to place me unambiguously in the pluralist camp. I appear to see politics as a contention among diverse groups each occupied with small objectives within an accepted social order. When I argue in addition that policy making through familiar small steps makes the most of man's limited cogitational capacities, I reveal skepticism about his capacity for ambitious or drastic planned social change. In accepting incremental change—indeed in endorsing it—as the normal pattern of policy making, I also appear to judge such progress as can be made in that way to be satisfactory. And from that it seems possible to infer that I believe the American and Western social and political world to be tolerably efficient,

1 My thanks to my colleague Barnett R. Rubin for helpful comments. At one point, I have appropriated, almost unchanged, several sentences from his comments.

just, and rational, even if not ideal. In the published critiques of disjointed incrementalism, a common point made was its conservatism.

But in *Politics and Markets* and the papers of Part I, I explicitly attack pluralism as a description of liberal democratic political practice. I also find in ostensibly democratic politics a disproportionate influence of business and other advantaged participants rather than a more genuine competition of diverse groups. I see policy making as enormously constrained by impairments in citizen capacities to probe the available alternatives, and I trace the impairments in some large part to business and class influences. That in turn suggests that man's cogitational capacities have not yet been given a good test rather than that we can now know them to be a low ceiling over the possibilities of intelligent policy making. I also argue the defects of the existing political and social order and the need for drastic alterations in it. Some reviewers go so far as to classify these lines of analysis as radical.

Two authors using the same name? A major career reorientation, such as seized some social scientists radicalized in the late '60s or early '70s? A wholly unintegrated mind? A clue to the answer is to be found in the dates of the various papers in this collection. They show that the two contrasting positions are stated both early and late. I did not move chronologically from the one position to the other. What I perceive, retrospectively, is two sets of research interests, each strikingly different from the other but less conflicted that first appears. I concede some lack of integration—I did not take care to resolve some marginal conflicts. But basically the sharp contrast above is more apparent than real.

I may add that it seems that many of my colleagues—Hirschman not included—would like to place me firmly in some one camp or other, for the urge to label, even among social scientists, is strong. When my first book, *Unions and Capitalism*, was published, a book in which I argued a deep conflict or mismatch between collective bargaining and capitalism without, however, pointing to a solution, some reviewers put me into the anticapitalist camp, one of them, for example, advising his audience to read both my book and Marx every year so that they would not forget who "the enemy" was. But others used the analysis of the very same book to classify me as a member of the Chicago School expressing its usual hostility to unions.

Do I believe that the political and social world is in such good shape that it needs only incremental improvement? Indeed not. Much of the world lives in sorry poverty, and those of us in the wealthy nations join them in living under the threat of nuclear annihilation, in addition to unacceptable economic and social inequalities that deprive many young people of life opportunities that should be theirs. Even in the ostensible democracies, political inequalities obstruct effective popular control over ostensibly democratic political institutions through which people might otherwise improve their situations. Among a long list of defects in the social order in the West, I would also give increasing weight to troubling evidence of the decline of education—not of training but of education—and the overwhelming commercial molding of culture.

Do we therefore need drastic change? Indeed we do. Given, however, the existing political structures of the ostensible democracies, there is little hope of getting it except through long glacial sequences of incremental changes. The rapidity of incremental steps can sometimes be accelerated; but societies seem incapable, except in emergencies, of acting more boldly than in increments. Proposals for more than incremental change, even so modest an increase in the size of the increment as represented by President Carter's ill-fated proposal for a comprehensive energy program, paralyze political decision making. The proposals have to be disassembled into smaller increments. Wars and other catastrophes aside, it looks as through anyone who wants drastic change will do best to promote rapid incremental change cumulating into drastic change. His prospects are poor, but ordinarily worse if he takes any other route.

Incremental policy making is weak, often inefficacious, inadequate to the problem at hand; and the control over it often falls into the wrong hands. It is also usually the best that can be done. Such a view of incrementalism, not the buoyant view of it that commentators often attribute to me, is not at all difficult to reconcile with the critical writing on democracy and market.

Why are the political systems ordinarily incapable of more

than incremental change? That is a question never asked nor answered in my writing on incrementalism, which was limited to two other points: that incrementalism is what we are usually limited to and that, given attitudes and institutions as they are, it is usually our best bet. But there is an answer. Thinking and discussing in liberal democratic societies, especially in the U.S., is narrow, even if far broader than in many authoritarian societies. There may be no "dominant ideology"; depending on what is meant, to say that there is goes too far. But the range of ideas entertained and discussed is constrained, as briefly outlined in *Politics and Markets*. Hence bold ideas die before they reach the political agenda, and only a timid set of alternatives is given serious consideration in policy making. And why so narrow a set? The answer to that requres a few words.

Anthropology and political science—the other social sciences less so—have rejoiced in the fundamental agreements that, according to anthropologists, constitute a culture and, according to many political scientists, make political peace possible within a society and, when sufficiently developed, make political democracy viable. In the course of their rejoicing—or, to put it more dispassionately, in the course of their finding a functional necessity for social agreement—they have neglected to ask how this happy or necessary agreement or narrowing of conflict is brought about. That it is desirable or necessary does not at all explain its origin.

Explanation of origins or sources has been either wholly absent or careless when attempted, the latter, for example, when agreement is attributed to tradition. For a society can have a tradition either of agreement or dissensus. The magic word "tradition" explains neither; it simply denotes a process by which some feature of the social order is transmitted from one generation to the next and leaves unexplained the source or origin of that feature.

For reasons that I cannot wholly develop here, but which are briefly laid out in *Politics and Markets* and worked out in much more detail with appropriate documentation in a forthcoming book on the uses of knowledge in social problem solving, I argue that the reason for the narrow diversity of opinion and discussion, hence the main reason we are limited to incremental politics, is a historical and continuing process of impairment of thought and discussion by indoctrination, as well as impositions that range from gentle intimidation to coercion, through which advantaged segments of society have sought, though usually not conspiratorially, to protect their advantages against slow erosion. Through subtle social processes, into which have been co-opted teachers and parents (and on the point no one is more impressive than John Locke), they have inculcated attitudes favorable to respect for established authority, patriotism, loyalty, faith rather than critical reason, belief in the inevitability and desirability of a wide variety of severe inequalities, antagonism to "agitators" (who on another view might be thought of as our heroes), obligations to "go along," responsibilities to adjust one's self to the institutional order rather than adjust the order itself, existing institutions that protect traditional advantages, and overestimating the dangers of experiment change. It is a complex argument, but it joins the analysis of incrementalism with the analysis of failures of democracy and obstructions to rationality, leaving them harmonious rather than conflicted.

But did my argument in "The Science of Muddling Through" (Chapter 8) and other articles on incrementalism not claim that holding policy making to small steps that only marginally alter existing institutions is a method of making the most of knowledge and intelligence? That it is a way of analyzing familiar alternatives and, what is more, of pursuing reversible policies that can be amended or abandoned if they prove to be mistaken, which is a possibility of correction much more difficult for drastic changes? That is correct. If so, then would I advocate drastic rather than incremental change if the political system and its narrow-thinking citizens were politically capable of it? The question poses a trade-off. Analysis and prediction of consequences of incremental change, as well as correction of error, are probably all more secure for incremental than for drastic changes (though the generalization will not hold without many exceptions), while drastic change, if it were possible, would, if competent, bring about needed results sooner. I would welcome the possibilities of various trade-offs of the two values, accuracy and movement; and I would not hold to the incremental method in all cases of trade-off.

What of conflict between the implicit pluralism of incremental thought, on one hand, and the argument elsewhere that the pluralist struggle is stacked, thus to a significant degree fraudulent, because of business and class influences in policy making on the other? The reconciliation, I suggest, is that although there is indeed pluralist contention, a competition of diverse groups seeking to influence policy, the contention over policy is within the constraints of narrowed thought and discussion just described. And within those constraints it is by no means a competition among equals. And sometimes it becomes largely a competition of business groups, other groups rendered ineffective.

If pluralist contention could break out of its constraints and if it could be structured to be more consistent with political equality, it is hard to see how any society prizing liberty and democracy and the application of intelligence to social problems could fail to prize it. For only in such diverse social interchanges as are possible only in a pluralist society can people reflect, debate, and mutually adapt their needs and wants to each other. Pluralism, whether achievable or not, is a fundamental requirement, for this reason, of the good society.

On the prospects that human beings can use their brains effectively to improve the social world, one will find strong notes of caution in both the articles on incrementalism and those on democracy and markets. Man faces a discrepancy—it has been tragic in the past and will probably be so again in the future—between the difficulty of his social problems and his cognitive capacities to deal with them. One of the appeals of incremental policy making is that it simplifies problems, brings them down to a size and character that fit man's limited intellect. On the other hand, for reasons already given, it is the case that his cognitive limitations are not all biologically imprinted and consequently irremediable. He is crippled in his capacity to think about social problems because he is socially impaired in the ways outlined above which narrow the alternatives that he considers and the clarity with which he thinks. If, then, on the one hand, his problems ought to be formulated in shapes with which his brain can somewhat successfully cope, on the other hand, it is urgently necessary that what brain power he has be given some freedom from its socially produced impairments; and that requires substantial alterations in social institutions, especially those of education, press, and broadcasting. Again the case for incrementalism is not in conflict with the case for major institutional changes that follow from *Politics and Markets* and the related papers in this volume on democracy and market system.

Some of the apparent contradiction between the two directions of my writing arises from the tendency to conclude that a radical diagnosis must lead to a radical prescription: Where there is a problem there must be a commensurate solution. This attitude seems to be a legacy of the Enlightenment's extreme faith in reason which found expression in the French Revolution. If the difficulty of change does not prove the worth of what exists, neither does the radical wrongness of "what is" endowed us with the knowledge and wisdom to improve it. This potentially tragic vision perhaps stands somewhat aside from the dominant debate of our society and may be alien to most Americans.

Beneath That Explanation Another

I have answered Hirschman's question only up to a point. The apparently conflicting elements in my publications can be on the whole reconciled. But why the predominant emphasis in earlier publications on the usefulness—even the virtue—of incrementalism and the reverse emphasis in later years on such defects in social institutions as obstacles to democracy and rationality?

A first answer is that I owe to an extraordinary economist, philosopher, and teacher, Frank Knight, an appreciation of— that turned into a fascination with—the hidden intricacies, but especially the hidden rationalities, of complex social institutions. For him, these hidden rationalities lay largely in the market system; but what I learned from him encouraged me to look for them in the political system as well, thus leading me to key aspects of incrementalism such as partisan mutual adjustment in politics with its marketlike characteristics. Recognizing the ills of the social system and the many defects of social institutions, it nevertheless seemed important to me to write about and to teach to my students the existence of social processes that achieved useful or in some sense rational outcomes despite their superficial appearances of disorder. The alleged "chaos" of the market system is no chaos at all, nor is the chaos of wheeling and dealing in politics. The obscured systemic consequences of superficially unattractive social processes are not optimal or ideal but they are often desirable outcomes.

This strong interest in useful though ugly social process was always at war in my thinking with a desire to understand and examine remedies for the major defects of social organization. In this very conflict of interests in writing and teaching, I was probably again heavily influenced by Knight, for despite his firm attachment to the competitive economic order he could write a devastating critique of it, as he did in his classic essay "The Ethics of Competition."[2] (I may add, perhaps unkindly, that many of his distinguished students have lost his capacity to combine appreciation with profound criticism.)

Why, then, were these two diverse interests not nicely balanced throughout my years? Why the emphasis on hidden rationalities in earlier years and on defects in later years? The answer to that question leads me to some criticism of myself, of the universities in which I have taught, and of the disciplines I have followed. They, the universities and the disciplines, constrained me; and I yielded to the constraints. It was in my younger years much safer to study and teach the hidden rationalities of the social order than to explore its major defects. I could save the latter for later. I will not admit to being craven in those years, for I did keep alive both interests in my publications and teaching. I did, however, give the one interest more emphasis earlier, the other later.

We now have in our universities and as successes in the disciplines scholars of great diversity of opinion, including, of course, Marxists. In my earlier years, they were also to be found, though less often, especially in the United States. That they were always present might be argued to say that such cautious criticism of social institutions as I might have given more emphasis I could have pursued without constraint. But the fact is, I suggest, that though the constraints left some social scientists untouched, it limited many more others, of which I

2 *Quarterly Journal of Economics* (May, 1922).

was one. That the constraints were sometimes gentle and subtle does not deny their effectiveness in shaping a career.

In my case, I had hardly begun teaching at the University of Minnesota in 1939 when the head of my department rebuked me for giving a talk to an undergraduate club on "Socialism and the Dollar Sign," in which I discussed Oskar Lange's concept of market socialism. I met with many other sharp intolerances of the economics faculty as it was then constituted, though none so threatening as from the department head. Eventually I was "let go" rather than promoted. I must be careful to say that I do not wholly know why, and the reasons may have been good ones unrelated to my interest in defects of the social order. Nevertheless, I had been chastened, and I decided that more caution was called for with respect to the kinds of scholarly interests I pursued.

Taking a position in economics at Yale, I found greater diversity of thought, consequently more tolerance (as I would have even if I had remained at Minnesota, so great were the changes in the next few years among the Minnesota economists). Yet the direction of my work was heavily influenced by the intolerances of the discipline of economics both generally and as represented among my Yale colleagues.

This is not surprising. An academic specialization like economics or any other is well named when it is called a discipline. What does it mean to discipline, say, a horse or a child? To inculcate in it certain habits of behavior, presumably desirable ones. Thus economics tries to make useful and good economists out of the undisciplined minds that come to the profession. But to discipline a horse or child also means to curb it, constrain the directions of its activity, and break its spirit if necessary. Given the impressive theoretical inheritance of economics, especially the elegance and precision of its methods, economics becomes perhaps the most intolerant of the social sciences and perhaps also the narrowest in that it restricts its inquiries to questions for which its formidable techniques are productive, refusing to venture into other no less important questions about economic life. Where, for example, political scientists range over every imaginable question about power, government, and politics and sociologists roam freely over the whole terrain of social life, each lacking a core of techniques that holds them to a set of questions for which those techniques are powerful, economics cultivates its fenced garden. Economists like to say that economics is defined by what economists do, thus hiding from their own eyes a large economic world into which they make only limited excursions.

At Yale my interest in large questions about basic economic institutions brought me into joint teaching with R. A. Dahl of the Political Science Department; and out of that came our *Politics, Economics, and Welfare*. It was given a poor rating by most of my colleagues in economics at Yale. Although I was already tenured as an associate professor, my department chairman urged me to resign, assuring me that I would "die on the vine" if I remained at Yale and would never advance from associate to full professor. A sophisticated group of economists such as constituted the department at Yale could not possibly have permitted themselves—they would not even be tempted— to downgrade the book because of its ideology or political philosophy. In any case, it was not ideologically objectionable to them, for though it dealt with basic institutions, it did so with much more approval than criticism of them.[3] Their opinion was simply that it was not a good book or that my presumed contributions to it were not up to quality. I cannot say they were wrong, but the place that the book has earned in social science might indicate a disciplinary narrowness or intolerance. In any case, I was again discouraged, as at my exit from Minnesota, and decided to follow safer interests, such as in the hidden rationalities of incrementalism.

That course of action did not wholly succeed with my economics colleagues. I thought they might be interested in market-like characteristics of the political process and the use of some economic concepts to analyze political processes. But though such studies later became important in both economics and

---

3 Yet some colleagues accepted philosophical or ideological constraints that they would not themselves endorse. When, for example, Dahl and I proposed giving our course the title of "Economic Planning," we were asked to change it to "Critique of Economic Planning" to avoid "misunderstanding." And of course there were—and always are—islands of special intolerance, such as the editor of one of the university presses to which I submitted the manuscript of *Unions and Capitalism* for publication, who asked me to delete certain passages he thought too radical. Another (commercial) press rejected the manuscript outright for the same reason.

political science, they did not much approve of my questions or methods; and, when I finally was given a professorship, my then chairman explained that it was warranted by my reputation "elsewhere." Again I must say that no issue was ever made of ideology or political philosophy. My colleagues intended to appraise only my competence as an economist. That they constrained the directions of my studies they never intended, except that each discipline requires some degree of methodological orthodoxy that defines the discipline, and I did not satisfy them on that score. As economists subsequently moved into the study of public choice and other political phenomena, they have on the whole insisted that the questions to be asked be those that can be answered by their techniques and that techniques developed for the analysis of market systems be the chosen techniques for the new inquiries.

My engagement with the economics department then continued in a gradual decline offset by increasing engagement with the political science department. By the time of publication of *Politics and Markets,* very few economics colleagues were interested in the book, and my graduate students were drawn almost entirely from political science and social sciences other than economics. But by then having a firm attachment to the department of political science, I could weather the discontent of my economics colleagues with the character of my work. Had I not been at Yale or at some other university with such flexibility in departmental attachment as Yale showed, the constraints of economics, from which I in fact escaped, would have been severe.

As you see, mine is no chronicle of a conspicuous dissenter bravely fighting the constraints of bigots. It is an ordinary story of a conventional career, some prudent adaptation to its milieu, a confining set of disciplinary traditions, and a willingness to disregard them growing only slowly with age and security.

The Study of Social Science Itself

The papers collected in this volume have been classified under three headings: democracy and market system, policy making, and social science. I may already have said enough to make clear that these are not three independent lines of work. The first category represents my interest in basic social institutions. Much, though not all, of my motivation to study them derives from a desire to compare them as alternative machineries for a "rational," efficient, functional, or productive social order (in social science circles one still loses points for saying "good," although that is what all these terms are substituted for).[4] That concern leads into comparison of market and democratic politics as instruments for policy making, the market being an alternative to politics (up to a point) for making decisions, or an alternative for reaching outcomes as by-products or "as though by a hidden hand" instead of as decisions. A study of basic institutions as components of the study of policy making also illuminates, as already noted above, market-like characteristics of political bargaining and other forms of mutual adjustment in the policy-making process.

The third category of papers—on social science—belongs with the other two for several reasons. First, achieving desirable outcomes requires ordinary and professional social science knowledge, but the kinds of knowledge needed by market participants is different from the kinds needed by participants in explicit policy making through the state. Hayek has insightfully made much of the distinction, possibly going too far in arguing that social science is little needed by policy makers when outcomes are the immediate objectives of explicit decisions to reach them. It is, he says, the indirections of market processes and the often unperceived connections between individual decisions and distant outcomes that call for social science, in that belief perhaps agreeing with Marx. Second, the narrowness and intolerance of each discipline, especially economics, raises questions about their capacities to make effective contributions to the knowledge required for good social organization and good policy making. Third, social science and social research have become an institution. Like the institutions of state and market, this now prominent great new institution needs broad and systematic study of its consequences for social organization, social change, and policy making. In recent times, it is sometimes called a new "industry," which it is. But it is more than that,

4 For an interesting analysis in this connection, see Charles W. Anderson, "The Political Economy of Charles E. Lindblom," 72 *American Political Science Review* (September, 1978).

and we have many clues to how much more as, for example, in the hypothesis that the knowledgeable are becoming a new ruling class, countered by the hypothesis that they continue to be "staff" for traditional ruling classes.

Among the "knowledgeables," social scientists are only one group. Their distinctive contribution to a better social order or better policy making is not obvious. Nor is it even obvious that they have ever made a distinctive contribution. That troubling thought has been another factor in turning me from the study of basic social institutions and the policy-making process back to studying what I am myself engaged in. It seems clear that without mathematics and the natural sciences no one would ever have stepped on the moon. Nor without the biological sciences would contagious diseases have been as well curbed as they are. I cannot think of any human accomplishment that unambiguously and undeniably could not have been achieved without social science. I expect we social scientists have been helpful; but that I cannot say that we have ever been indispensable leaves even the claim of helpfulness vulnerable to challenge.

Consequently we social scientists have a great task on our hands that we have hardly begun: to ask just what it is, if anything, that social science has accomplished and whether our lines of inquiry and our methods are well suited to such accomplishments as are within our competence. Like all other industries, ours produces waste. Reducing waste and increasing the product is difficult in this industry because we are uncertain which is which.

Part One
Democracy and Market System

1

Democracy and Economic Structure
(1962)

The dazzling productivity of the American economy since World War II has blinded some of its erstwhile critics. Even in 1958, when job hunters outnumbered jobs and, most dramatically, a slump in automobile sales proved that all that glitters is not sold, the mood of economic euphoria was only mildly dampened. We have been congratulating ourselves, however, largely on the economy's output; how the output is achieved exictes no special admiration and, on the contrary, stirs a few anxieties. Large national product, a bounteous flow of richly varied consumer goods, and a high rate of new investment—these we applaud. The possibilities that we are the dupes of conning admen, that big business is overly influential in Washington, that trade union power is neither harnessed nor sufficiently self-disciplined, and that continued prosperity rests on military spending all trouble us; and we do not know whether these and other possibilities like them represent minor skin infections or deep malignancies in democratic politics.

It is therefore appropriate that we reflect not only on the efficiency of the American economy but also on the lines of control that run through it and connect it with government. Who runs the economy and how? What are the relations between power holders in the economy and power holders in government? In asking such questions as these, we shall be examining economic structure not in the economist's language of calculation but in the political scientist's language of power.

Some characterizations of certain power relations in politico-economic life like James Burnham's thesis of the managerial elite or C. Wright Mills' thesis of business-military power are developed without any reference at all to certain other obviously important opposing lines of control, such as consumer control over sellers.[1] If read as comprehensive analyses of power in the economy, they are constantly misleading. If read as partial analyses, they do not identify the larger context of power relations into which the analyzed relations are supposed to fit and thus cannot be integrated into a larger organized knowledge of power in the economy. In neither case, therefore, do they make a substantial contribution to the cumulation of knowledge. Hence the frequency with which such theses come and go without leaving a lasting imprint.

It is all the more important to be comprehensive in examining power in politico-economic life because the central institution of economic life, the market or price system, typically drops out of analyses as though it were irrelevant to the study of power. Even if economists did not prove the point by using terms like "purchasing power," "bargaining power," and "monopoly power," it ought to be obvious that the market or price system is a power system; it is a system for controlling behavior; within it are to be found leaders or elites as well as a rank-and-file; and it embraces a variety of interpersonal controls, including coercion.

I. Power in the Price System

To use Hartz's term, there is one common "image" of the price system that leads those who hold it to assert a fundamental incompatibility between economy and democracy. In broadest terms, efficiency and democracy are viewed as in conflict. More precisely it is argued that the price system, or market economic organizations, is inherently undemocratic in its concentration of power in the hands of businessmen—managers and entrepreneurs—who are neither themselves popularly elected nor appointed by popularly elected officials and whose businesses are "their own business" rather than a public trust.

But professional economists have produced at least two other images of the price system that have come to be widely held in society. The first is an image of what a price system might be

1 James Burnham, *The Managerial Revolution* (New York: John Day, 1941); C. Wright Mills, *The Power Elite* (New York: Oxford Univ. Press, 1956).

if its potential were more fully realized. It is the price system seen as a system of delegated authority in which leaders hold particular powers subject to a kind of vote, a system about which such questions can be asked as: Do the leaders have to satisfy the voters as a condition of staying "in office"? Do leaders compete for followings? Can an incumbent be removed by an unfavorable vote?

So conceived, the price system is a political system something like government in which certain powers lie in the hands of a small active decision-making elite called businessmen. It is for them to decide directly both how much is to be produced of each good and what combination of labor, equipment, and other factors of production is to be used. In large-scale business, they coordinate a cooperative productive process embracing many thousands of participants.

If this elite manipulates the economy, it is seen as doing so only in a responsible and responsive way. For when a consumer makes a purchase, his expenditure constitutes a vote for continuing the line of production on which his money is spent. A businessman can only sell what people will buy, which means that their refusal to buy will effectively veto his policies while their willingness to buy gives him a mandate to continue. The entrepreneurial elite cannot long go on producing anything that does not win the dollar votes of the market place.

Markets are of course tied together in long chains so that some businessmen look for votes from (sell to) other businessmen who look for votes among still others, and so forth, as, for example, in a series of markets connecting the extraction of iron ore with smelting, steel making, auto manufacturing, and auto retailing. In this respect this image of market democracy is a system of soviets.

A significant characteristic of voting in the market, so envisaged, is that voters usually cannot vote for a particular member of the governing elite whose personality or style of policy making they like; they must instead vote for or against his individual policies. One can not vote for the president of General Motors but can vote for a two-toned red and cream Chevrolet convertible hardtop with whitewalls, heater, radio and power steering.

Market voting is similar to voting in the democratic state in that the initiative in policy making lies in the hands of the governing elite rather than the voter. What leaders initiate is eventually controlled by reaction to their policies at the polls and, in the interim, by each leader's anticipation of electoral response.[2]

In the democratic state, political leaders control each other by exchanging favors, threatening and promising, organizing alliances, opposing or supporting each other's policies. These moves are understandable only against the background of the competition for votes; on the other hand, they are worth mentioning as methods by which leaders are controlled by other leaders rather than by voters. Similarly, in the present image of the market, businessmen control each other in a variety of ways that might escape our attention if we thought only of direct consumer and supplier control over market leadership. They buy from and sell to each other; beyond that they frustrate or assist each other's plans in various ways. Similarity between state and market in this respect is illustrated in the ubiquity of bargaining in both.

Given the two conflicting images—price system as authoritarian and price system as comparable to political democracy with respect to its internal power structure—how does the price system actually function? Although its actual functioning does not correspond closely to either of the two conflicting images, it corresponds well to still another image that economists have produced. This is an extremely complex and sophisticated image that takes account of a variety of specific discrepancies between what is ideal or potential and what has been so far achieved. Because the image is complex we cannot describe it with a few

2 Still other differences and similarities between market voting and balloting will quickly spring to mind. Of the differences, one most significant is that in the market the electorate is doubleheaded. Just as each member of the entrepreneurial elite is competing for the consumers' dollars, he is also competing for their productive services. Hence the same individuals who control the businessman through offering or denying him their consumer votes control him again by offering or denying him their labor, their capital, or other services and goods he needs as factors of production. When we speak, as is commonplace, of *consumer sovereignty* in the market economy, we sometimes forget about this equivalent supplier soverignty; but the businessman is constrained in some decisions just as surely by the preferences of his suppliers as he is in other decisions by the preferences of those who buy from him. Because almost every member of the businessman's electorate is both a demander and a supplier, each "voter" has two heads.

words but will instead suggest how it takes account of various troublesome features of real world economic organization not recognized in the economist's first image.

A. *Business Response to Consumer Preferences*

In this second image, it is acknowledged that business management is not invariably responsive to expressed consumer preferences. Just as in government votes can be incorrectly counted, so also in the market the vote can be misrepresented through price manipulation. And just as in government a well-entrenched machine may show indifference to the electorate so also in the market a well-entrenched cartel may similarly show indifference to its consumer electorate. Where in government an incumbent may be secure against an effective challenge from another party or candidate, so also in the market the competitor may also be unchallenged. In short, the image recognizes monopoly.

But the image, being sophisticated and close to the facts, also perceives limits on monopoly. No firm can charge any price it wants or even approximate such power; consequently no firm's monopoly power is ever absolute. One of the most important foundation principles of economics is that *all* goods compete with one another for the consumer's dollars; hence, as the price of any one good rises, at least some buyers turn from it to others, and the seller is consequently constrained. All goods compete, whether peanuts and wrist watches or carpets and bobby pins, simply because in allocating his income a consumer will move away from items whose prices are too high even if he cannot find a close substitute.

Monopoly is also everywhere constrained by forces more powerful than the very general competition of all goods with one another. In advanced societies technology has made close substitutes of steel, copper, aluminum, glass, rubber and plastic. While they cannot in each of their uses be substituted one for the other, in many uses at least one can be substituted for another. Hence the attempt to manipulate price or restrict output for any one of them is restricted by the certainty that at least some part of the market will be lost. Moreover, in a wealthy economy in which consumer income goes into durable goods like autos and refrigerators, monopolistic exploitation of the consumer is greatly restrained by the consumer's ability to use what he has for another few years rather than buy a new model. For some consumer durables this control is supplemented by highly organized second-hand markets to which consumers can always turn to escape monopoly over new products.

B. *Manipulation of the Consumer*

The image also takes account of the fact that businessmen manipulate the preferences of the consumer electorate. Everywhere at hand is evidence—the renaissance of cigar smoking, for example—of the success with which the economic governing elite manipulates the preferences of the consumer electorate rather than simply responding to existing preferences. On the other hand, in this image it is recognized that what the elite does not attempt to do, as well as their conspicuous failure—the Continental and Edsel fiascos, for example—satisfies us that their manipulative powers are not unlimited. Still, if it were true, as is sometimes naively believed, that the more the manipulation, the less the democracy, it would be clear that democracy in the market was in poor health. But, just as we ask for some disclosure of record and program from each candidate for governmental office, we want information from businessmen about their products, and we want it *because* we expect it to influence our preferences. Without much doubt, therefore, some kinds of manipulationof preferences by governing elites are not inconsistent with democratic ideas.

C. *Income Inequality*

In the image under discussion, it is recognized that incomes are unequally distributed, and those who hold this image concede that at least some forms of income inequality are not consistent with a view of the price system as democratic. But does the one-man-one-vote rule in political democracy require by analogy an equal distribution of money votes?

Political democracy does not require equality of the vote in all decision-making situations. On the grounds of expediency and of their special concerns, we give to the inhabitants of certain areas—a town, for example—voting powers denied to all nonresidents, even though nonresidents have a stake in the decisions reached, as is the case with local street maintenance and traffic control. For some decisions on agricultural policy, we poll limited groups of farmers. For determination of bargaining units in industry, we poll limited groups of wage earners.

Sometimes, however, it is said that democracy requires, not equal power and not equal votes, but equal votes at the point at which the decisions are made on who will have specialized powers and unequal voting power. In other words, the argument runs, the democratic ideal does not require that you and I be equally powered generally but only that you and I have an equal vote in the determination (directly, or through election of officials) of when and where you or I shall have greater power than the other. But even this "last say" equality of the vote can be challenged as a requisite of democracy. We neither practice it in the United States nor agree that we should, as is illustrated in practices and attitudes on constitutional amendment. Moreover, it can be powerfully argued that democracy is better characterized as government resting on consent than as government resting on "last say" voting equality; and consent is won by conceding disproportionate powers to groups who must be wooed. Thus, in the United States, behind a superficial appearance of one-man-one-vote, lies a variety of arrangements, including the bicameral legislature and the electoral college, that in effect give some citizens a voting power far in excess of that of others.

To be sure, not all the inequalities in voting power in our government are the product of the search for consent; and, even for those that are, some observers would argue that they represent imperfections in democracy which can be avoided only in the ideal democracy in which consent can be won without sacrificing "last say" equality. I simply record that political democracy is not *agreed* to require equality of the vote and that we practice extreme inequality in "last say" voting power in the United States.

Analogy will therefore not prove equality of the dollar vote to be a requirement of market democracy. Is there, then, some other ground on which equality of the dollar vote is required for market democracy? If we consider the equalitarian tradition that has developed in Western civilization, we see that, powerful as it is, it is nevertheless severely limited by the acknowledged need, as in the case of political equality in particular, for function specialization, as well as by the desirability of certain other kinds of inequality. On close examination, the tradition is not so well characterized as a belief in equality as in opposition to certain specific kinds of inequality. Especially when the tradition is articulated in a politically effective movement does it appear not as a generalized push to more equality but as an attack on specific troublemaking inequalities: legal privilege at one stage, racial discrimination at another, for example.

The inequalities we have held to be intolerable are those that make one man an instrument of another; foster personal traits of arrogance, insensitivity, harshness and defensiveness, on one hand, and obsequiousness, apathy and hostility, on the other; create arbitrary marks of superiority and inferiority and proliferate other individious distinctions; leave the individual without minimum requirements of food, shelter, health and education; obstruct functional specialization; or create disruptive social cleavages. The list covers a great deal; nevertheless, it does specify. Some differences in "who gets what" create these problems, but some do not.

D. *Undemocratic Employee Relations*
The image also takes account common failures in the achievement of "industrial democracy" in the market. Many people, who, never having conceived of the price system as a potentially democratic system for the consumer, will raise no questions about consumer democracy, but will nevertheless question the authoritarian character of the employer-employee relationship. If democracy exists in the economy, they will say, it exists because it is to be found in the employer-employee relationship; if the market is undemocratic, it is simply because the employer-employee relationship is undemocratic. In the present image of the price system, however, are some grounds for claiming that the system is not fundamentally undemocratic even in the employment relation.

1. *The price system is itself a method of achieving industrial democracy.* This falls strangely on ears accustomed to hearing

of the market as the great barrier to industrial democracy. But if we think of higher wages as one of the major demands made by employees on businessmen ever since the development of the factory system in the United States, the fact is that this demand has repeatedly been made effective through the market. The explanation of rising wage rates in the history of the United States—or in any other country—does not turn on the labor union, for unionism has been shown to have had only a marginal influence on the historical course of wages. Wage increases in pre-union times are large, repeated and not demonstrably less impressive than under unionism.[3] The explanation, of course, is that, just as businessmen compete for the consumers' dollars, they also compete for labor; hence workers do in fact, all dogma to the contrary, exercise enormous control over employer decisions on wage rates even in the absence of a union.

The market, however, does not by any means give employees all they want in wages; and it is less satisfactory in its mechanisms for democratic control over working conditions, discipline, and individual rights and privileges on the job. If the beginning of wisdom is the recognition of the price system's limited but significant democratic accomplishments for the employee, the next step is the identification of inevitable limitations on democratic worker control, with which the next propositions deal.

2. *Many limitations on worker control of employer are attributable to the employer's responsiveness to democratic consumer controls over him.* Why does an employer resist high wage demands? Because beyond some point he can collect the funds for wage disbursements only by accomplishing a monopolistic control over prices charged his customers. Why does he resist demands to maintain obsolete skills, keep his employees on the payroll in depression, or make expansive improvements in working conditions? Often because competitive controls in the hands of consumers press him to cut prices and costs. The problem here is not that the employer is undemocratic, but that his electorate is, as we said, doubleheaded; and he cannot satisfy both heads at once.

3 Clark Kerr, "Wage Relationships—the Comparative Impact of Market and Power Forces," Reprint of Institute of Industrial Relations, University of California at Berkeley. Reprinted from John T. Dunlop, ed., *The Theory of Wage Determination* (New York: St. Martin's Press, 1957).

This fact calls for a reorientation of much policy discussion. Since what is at issue is not democratic control or none but conflicting demands made by an electorate working through two different channels upon the same leadership, the distribution of rights and controls between the consumer head and the employee head of the electorate cannot be decided by reference to traditional democratic criteria. It is possible, however, that study of this conflict might provide a basis for an extension of democratic criteria, to resolve problems of aggregating democratic demands upon leadership, when the demands are inconsistent. To make an example, can democratic theory be refined or extended to throw light on how to resolve conflict between consumer and employee interest in the employee demand for a guaranteed annual wage? Similar problems of aggregating arise in democratic control in government.

3. *Because of conflicts of interest among groups of workers many demands made in the name of industrial democracy are invalid.* It is argued, for example, that democracy requires the union shop. If the relevant electorate is taken to be the employees of a given plant and a majority of them wish a union shop, it can be argued that a union shop is democratic. If the relevant electorate is taken to be all wage earners who have an interest in employment in the plant and a majority of these do not want the union shop, the reverse could be argued. If it is held that the union shop issue is of such general importance that all wage earners in the economy are the relevant electorate, then whether the union shop is democratic or not depends on their wishes. Or if it is held that the union shop issue contains implications for efficiency or industrial peace such that consumers too—in fact, the whole governmental electorate—are the relevant electorate, then whether the union shop is democratic depends upon the decision reached by democratic governmental procedures.

While I am inclined to believe the union shop is generally desirable, my point here is that its merits cannot be argued by reference to the criteria of democracy, and we cannot say that an employer who resits the union shop is undemocratic. Similarly, demands for seniority and craft control of certain jobs cannot be argued on democratic criteria. Now again, as in the case of consumer-employee conflict, conflict among different groups of workers might be explored to see whether democratic criteria can be extended to resolve the issues. In the case of the union shop, for example, one might attack as a problem in theory the question of which of the various alternatives is the relevant electorate. Although some exploratory work of this kind would be worthwhile, the field may turn out to be a morass. It will probably be more profitable to analyze most worker demands upon the employer not in the language of democracy at all but as technical, administrative and organizational problems that have democratic solutions only in that their solutions are ultimately achieved within the framework of democratic government.

4. *Other than the market mechanism, the union has become the major instrument through which industrial democracy is strengthened or weakened.* This obvious proposition introduces some perplexing issues. We are all familiar with union accomplishments in protecting the employee against arbitrary, even whimsical, acts of the employer that impinge upon what almost everyone will agree are democratic rights, if not rights that are essential to minimum dignity and self-respect. Without deprecating these achievements, I pass them by simply because they are familiar. The perplexing issues arise out of other aspects of unionism.

The first issue is what powers unions should enjoy. Given what we have been saying about conflict between consumer and employee and between different groups of wage earners, the appropriate powers for unions cannot be derived, except on some minor issues, from democratic criteria. In other words, what powers to allocate to unions is a technical administrative question, and any one of a large number of alternative decisions on union powers is quite consistent with democratic criteria. Any one of many possible decisions about union power can be shown to satisfy the "democratic" demands of some group, but always at the expense of some other. Although this too presents a challenge to democratic theorists, they may, again, not be able to come up with any better answer, even after careful exploration of possibilities of extending and refining democratic formulae, than that whatever allocation of power to unions is sanctioned by democratic governmental processes is democratic.

Another group of issues is concerned with democracy within the union. Unionism has not solved the problem of protecting the individual against abuse by the leaders of a large organization of which he is a part. In trying to solve the problem in the case of the employer, unionism has created a similar problem in the case of the union leader himself. A somewhat different problem is union membership control over union policies, the immediate responsibility for which has to be delegated to leadership. Without characterizing unionism as generally deficient on these two scores, I am safe in saying that some large unions have been grossly deficient.

All this and more is familiar. Let me go on therefore to raise the question of whether the root of the evil, where it occurs, is rank-and-file apathy or nonparticipation, as is often believed. Apathy there is indeed; but governmental democracy survives in the face of it, and it has been argued that a large nonparticipating section of the electorate is desirable in governmental democracy.[4] Why then might union apathy be dangerous? One possible answer is that there is more of it; that is, the level of participation in unions is much lower than the level of voting in, say, a congressional election. If, however, we compare daily involvement in union and in governmental affairs or compare voting rates in union members are less participatory. Perhaps apathy in the union permits internal democracy to degenerate because there are no institutional devices, such as a two-party system, to keep the doors open for political activity within the union when the members wish it.[5] In government, a low level of participation is not a barrier to a high rate if the occasion demands it.

Such hypotheses suggest what a rich field for research lies at hand here, research not only to clarify the prerequisites for internal union democracy, which are not yet well understood, but also to contribute to a more general theory of the prerequisites of democracy. The study by Lipset, Trow and Coleman of the Typographical Union is an admirable and distinguished

---

4 E. Pendleton Herring, *The Politics of Democracy* (New York: Rinehart and Co., 1940), p. 32ff.
5 Joseph Goldstein, *The Government of British Trade Unions* (Glencoe, Illinois: Free Press, 1952).

beginning to what ought to be a thoroughly cultivated research field.[6]

As for achieving more vigorous union democracy, a straw in the wind is a shift in union attention from conflicts on which the union is homogenously set against employer to conflicts among groups within the union who differ in skill, rates of pay, seniority or other attributes. In the new responsibilities of unionism to achieve a democratic adjustment of internal group conflict lies a possibility that an internal political pluralism will flourish, bringing with it the rivalries that make democracy possible.

Union leaders will presumably be held responsible to their own members by a shifting combination of three major devices: democratic constitutionalism within the union, government restriction on union officials, and members' rights to withdraw. The third of these is, of course, presently declining. Some interesting though quite unfinished attempts have been made by union leaders themselves to argue the superiority of constitutional democracy over democracy through right of withdrawal;[7] the choice presents extremely interesting theoretical issues that ought to be explored by professional theorists. Similarly, government restrictions on trade union leaders designed to make internal democracy effective raise, in a context in which results can be observed, some traditional questions on the possibility of imposing democracy from above. Then too, insofar as government chooses to sanction the union shop and other restrictions on rights of withdrawal, the union moves from a status as voluntary organization into a yet undefined status as quasi-public agency. Here again are theoretical issues as well as possibilities for empirical study.

5. *Finally, industrial democracy is not correctly argued to be absent simply because production is large scale and bureaucratized, relations among participants impersonal, and responsible participation in decision making limited to a few.* Bureaucracy, impersonality, and nonparticipation are in large part products of technology. These phenomena are to be found in the econo-

6 Seymour M. Lipset, Martin A. Trow, and James S. Coleman, *Union Democracy* (Glencoe, Illinois: Free Press, 1956).
7 Clinton S. Golden and Harold J. Ruttenberg, *The Dynamics of Industrial Democracy* (New York: Harper & Brothers, 1942).

mies of all industrialized nations and are to be taken as describing the environment in which modern democracy is called upon to operate. They are not therefore evidence of the absence of democracy in industry.

For fear of going far afield, I pass these phenomena by with but one comment. It is not clear that employees wish to be responsible participants in decision making; their wish that some of the union representatives be so does not imply that they wish to be so themselves. Employee aspirations in this respect may differ greatly from period to period, depending upon the degree to which economic insecurity weights upon their minds and threatens them with family financial responsibilities they fear they cannot successfully bear. On the hypothesis that employee aspirations toward responsible participation are directly related to their responsibilities and opportunities off the job, I should like to see some research on the variables determining the desire for responsible participation. Its practical fruits would be to locate sources of unrest in industrial relations, as well as to determine how responsible participation can be had when needed, as, for example, to meet demands for supervisory and managerial personnel.

E. *Price System and Efficiency*
In the light of Beer's interest in the "efficiency" of democratic policy making, it may be worth asking: Is a price system an efficient policy-making system? In the depression of the 1930s, it was not, but in recent decades it would be difficult to argue that it has not achieved a tolerably high degree of both coherence and innovation. If opinions differ on this question, they will most probably reveal subtle differences in meanings attached to Beer's term. If I mean by *efficiency* the achievement of a set of policies—that is, for the price system, a set of outputs and a pattern of income distribution—that suits my particular preferences, I rate the system's achieved efficiency rather low. If, on the other hand, I mean by *efficiency* that the system has achieved the satisfaction of the expressed preferences of its electorate in a relatively systematic manner with a reasonable minimum inconsistency among policies, I must rate its efficiency tolerably high. Here *high* means high relative only to other complex

human attempts at efficient policy making rather than high relative to ideals toward which we might aspire.

And, it might be added for what light it throws on Beer's hopes for the achievement of efficiency in governmental affairs, such efficiency as is achieved in the direction of production and distribution in the price system is in large part, though by no means entirely, achieved without a central mind or direction that sees the interrelations of the economy as a coherent whole.

F. *Some Inferences about Democracy*

The upshot of this discussion of power in the price system is not that the system is or is not democratic. If we think of political democracy as an attribute of a "government" and play no tricks with the word *government*, then the price system is neither democratic nor undemocratic; it is simply a different kind of animal altogether. Our discussion of the image of the price system as a system of relations between leaders or officials, on one side, and a rank and file or electorate, on the other, has served only to show that, if one does wish to consider the price system in terms parallel to those in which we consider political democracy, several very important conclusions seem justified. First, it is not at all obvious that, so considered, the price system is an undemocratic element in conflict, because of its authoritarian character, with political democracy. Second, those who hold unusually large powers in the price system are invariably subject to some kind of "popular" controls, even if the effectiveness of these controls is in dispute. Third, the characteristic imperfections in popular control in a price system are analogous to the imperfections of popular control in government, and they include those that other essays in this volume [*Democracy Today: Problems and Prospects,* 1960] have thought important to mention as contemporary problems in democratic government, such as, for example, manipulation of the electorate by leadership and incoherence in policy making. Finally, the price system, so considered, is democratic or undemocratic depending upon one's standard of appraisal in the same way that our institutions for political democracy in government are or are not democratic, depending upon one's standard of appraisal.

We are justified, therefore, in continuing to discuss economic structure and democracy without yielding to the superficial view that economic structure is itself so undemocratic as to make such a discussion fruitless.

II. Impact of Economic Structure on Democracy in Government

Having explored democracy within the economic structure, we now consider the consequences of economic structure for democracy in government, beginning with the roles of business leadership and corporation executives in political democracy.

A. *Business Leadership and the Corporation*

It is hard to know where to begin in discussing corporate leadership and political democracy. We have such theses as Burnham's and Mills' to tell us that business leadership enjoys disproportionate power. But that we certainly already knew. Large-scale democracy requires and is marked by a high degree of specialization of leadership, and indeed one can even define a leader as one who has disproportionate power. We also know that there are at least some limits to the power of these leaders from the business elite. They do not suppress elections; they show dismay at the powers denied them, and they complain about the power of the union leader and professional politician.

Both Burnham and Mills neglect to analyze controls over business leadership.[8] They do not do so because they are both captives of the notion that power is fixed in amount; what the elite gains in power the non-elite loses. Believing in this lump-of-power fallacy, it is sufficient, if one wishes to prove the degeneration of democracy, to show new powers in the hands of the governing elite. We know this is too simple; it is possible at one and the same time both to increase the powers in the hands of the elite and to increase the controls held over them by the non-elite.[9]

8 Burnham, *op. cit.*; and Mills, *op. cit.*
9 Talcott Parsons, "The Distribution of Power in American Society," *World Politics,* 10 (October, 1957), 123–143; and Charles E. Lindblom, "In Praise of Political Science," *World Politics,* 9 (January, 1957), 240–253.

We are not at all interested, therefore, in whether the powers of corporate leaders are disproportionate. What we want to know is to what degree their powers are inconsistent with democracy in government. Not only do elitist theories fail us; what is worse, we have no adequate criteria by which to decide even if we could agree on the facts. For as we saw in discussing the business elite in the market, we lack an adequate theory of the appropiate functions of leadership in democracy. Failing such a theory, we do not know, for example, whether there was any valid ground for complaint on Eisenhower's "six millionaires and a plumber," as his early Cabinet was described.

The Corporate Executive in Non-elective Office

Let us see just what is required both in mastery of fact and theory beyond what has already been specified in the discussion of business manipulation of consumers. Consider, for example, the phenomenon of businessmen in non-elective office. Political scientists should find many challenges in the frequency with which high administrative positions in government are filled by corporate executives. Arnold A. Rogow has recently argued for the British economy that the tasks of economic regulation make it necessary for government to lean very heavily on the skills and experience of businessmen in high office.[10] This thesis generalized is itself worth investigation to determine in just what circumstances it holds. In a period of rapid nationalization and extension of other regulation it would seem more plausible than today in the United States, and it hardly explains the frequency of appointment of businessmen to Cabinet and other high posts in American government in one administration after another. Why so few appointments from executive positions in the union movement? Why not substantially more appointments both from slightly lower administrative positions in government and from the ranks of the politicos?

One can smile knowingly and say the answer is clear. But I doubt it. A relative consistency in frequency of recruitment from corporate circles running from a Hoover through a Truman

10 Arnold A. Rogow, *The Labour Government and British Industry 1945–1951* (Ithaca, New York: Cornell Univ. Press, 1955), p. 60 ff.

administration belies some of the obvious explanations, and not wholly absent variations in frequency belie others. I believe that research could help us disentangle and set out systematically the influence on recruitment of such factors as the use of appointments to repay campaign contributions, beliefs that business skills are required, public identification of union but not business leaders as partisan, unwillingness of some politicos to accept executive positions, and traditional distrust of abilities of civil servants.

It will be important to uncover the motives that lead prospective appointees from various groups to accept or decline. We may be able to document the hypothesis that far from grasping power, the corporate elite accepts government administrative duties somewhat reluctantly, being urged more insistently to do so because recruitment from the worlds of labor and of politics is difficult.

For the case of Britain, Rogow and others have also argued that businessmen are incapable of a sufficient change in role to avoid a very subtle sabotage of programs that they as businessmen disapprove of. Here certainly research is now merely scratching at the surface. How do businessmen see their role when they move into public office? What is their own testimony, and what are the objective indications of any change in attitudes, loyalties, and feelings of responsibility? In what terms do they conceive of the public interest before and after they move to government? How do they compare themselves in these respects with other public officials recruited from other circles?[11] For recruits from union circles or other interest groups, we should ask the same questions.

Roughly, the kind of hypothesis that research might verify is that in moving from business into high government administrative posts businessmen do drop some of their former organizational loyalties and pick up new ones, do act as "neutral" public servants in policies on which they can be unambiguously and explicitly directed, but nevertheless carry into and employ in their new positions previously held values and attitudes. Such findings as these could, of course, be made more precise.

11 For suggestions, see C. Addison Hickman and Manford H. Kuhn, *Individuals, Groups, and Economic Behavior* (New York: Dryden Press, 1956), Chs. 2 and 3.

If research produced such findings, it would then be important to try to achieve a systematic statement about the degree
to which the decisions of such officials are locked into position
by the political forces that surround them and, conversely,
the degree to which the officials hold important discretionary
authority in the exercise of which their business-oriented values
and attitudes are operative. Many scholars have a feel for
the facts on this point; but formalized, systematic statement is
required if this information is to be fitted into a larger comprehension of leadership in democracy.

To construct such a systematic statement, one might begin
from widespread agreement that there is no objective "public
interest." What values, whose interests, should then govern the
decisions of administrative officials? In the literature of political
science are conflicting answers that specify what the model must
cope with.[12] The administrator should be governed by the wishes
of the majority. But majority sentiment is simply not known on
countless problems, and citizens are dependent upon advice
from leadership where they are asked to express themselves.
The administrator should do what is best. But this requires him
to weigh and evaluate conflicting preferences in the light of his
own personal set of values. The administrator should be frankly
partisan. But this is defensible only to the degree that other
partisans can influence him. The administrator should follow
the directive of his superior. But the superior cannot avoid
leaving his subordinate some important discretion. The administrator should be guided by a party position worked out and
enforced through strongly disciplined parties. But, again, the
best worked out party line still leaves room for discretion.

The problem is not simply that there are alternative views
or images of democratic leadership, for we can build many
corresponding models. It is also that no one of the alternative
views on the administrator is well enough worked out in the
literature. What is required is a set of propositions, model,

---

12 For example, Luther Gulick and Lyndall Urwick, eds., *Papers on the Science
of Administration* (New York: Institute of Public Administration, Columbia
Univ., 1937); E. Pendleton Herring, *Public Administration and the Public Interest*
(New York: McGraw-Hill, 1936); Dwight Waldo, *The Administrative State*
(New York: Ronald Press Co., 1948); John D. Kingsley, *Representative Bureauc-
racy* (Yellow Springs, Ohio: Antioch Press, 1944); and others.

or—as Hartz might be willing to say—a professional analytical image that would lay out explicitly the relations most significant for democracy and place the administrator in them. Such a model or set of propositions must specify the preferences, interests or values; the discretionary range of choice; the constraints on choice; and the characteristic agenda for each of the following: voter, interest group, party leader, legislator, legislative group, various interdependent administrators, and president. The propositions must interrelate all these in an interaction process in which preferences and policy making act on each other.

Now, again, many political scientists have a feel for this set of interrelationships; some carry the required model in their heads in the form of beliefs that they have never wholly articulated; and others have gone quite far in the direction of writing it down.[13] So while constructing the explicit formal model is a big order, it is neither impossible nor uncongenial to the skills of political scientists. My emphasis on getting such models or images out in the open, making them formal, is that we have no adequate criteria, except very fragmentary ones, that permit us to record reasons for believing that businessmen (or any other recruits from an interest group) in high administrative office do or do not constitute a problem for democracy.

The Corporate Influence on the Social Preconditions of Democracy

Turning now to a quite different influence on democracy, we can distinguish several ways in which corporate policy seems consequential for democracy.

1. The Manipulation of Employees

In its discovery that an employee is an extremely complex machine whose output is sensitive to the most subtle changes

13 For example, Robert A. Dahl, *A Preface to Democratic Theory* (Chicago: Univ. of Chicago Press, 1956); E. Pendleton Herring, *The Politics of Democracy, op. cit.*; Earl Latham, *The Group Basis of Politics* (Ithaca, New York: Cornell Univ. Press, 1952); E. E. Schattschneider, *Party Government* (New York: Holt, Rinehart and Winston, 1942); and David B. Truman, *The Governmental Process* (New York: Knopf, 1951).

in handling, the corporation may have learned more than it ought to be allowed to know. The discovery pays off in increased output and more contented employees, but potentially it also strikes at what may be a precondition of democracy. For probably much of what we believe about democracy and its advantages rests on the assumption that the human personality is moulded by a wide variety of competing influences, including family, school, neighborhood, friends and acquaintances, books and newspapers. We would be hard pressed to make sense of democracy if any one homogeneous group of political leaders moulded our preferences to suit their needs, then turned around and conspicuously satisfied the demands they had taught us to make upon them. We would find it only slightly less troublesome to reconcile with traditional notions of democracy our indoctrination by a homogeneous group of leaders who held power to manipulate our personalities and preferences grossly disproportionate relative to other competing influences. Yet this disproportion is what the human relations movement may introduce. This is one aspect of the large problem of manipulation of the masses by a few.

Many critics of democracy have long been disturbed by the disproportionate influence of wealth and business enterprise on the mass media and other instruments of manipulation of the electorate. But the human relations movement makes the disproportion greater. Heretofore competitive appeals to our minds and emotions have been addressed to us as citizens not as employees. If business had disproportionate influence, it was when it sought either to influence our political activity or to encourage nonparticipation where we were thought dangerous to business interests. Whatever the degree of disproportion in influence, it was therefore to some significant degree limited by the competing appeals of unions, churches, farm organizations and various other special interest groups, as well as by internal conflict within business itself. The new appeal, to the employee not the citizens, is not equally constrained.

Three aspects of the new appeal to employees are significant. First, to a high degree employers agree among themselves, hence they reinforce each other's indoctrinations. Second, not even the union may be much disposed to counter the appeals because they do not ask for action that the union opposes. Third, since the businessman is motivated by the desire to make the individual an efficient instrument of production rather than a citizen ally, it may be that he will try to influence the individual more assiduously than ever before—more assiduously, because man as a tool is a better investment than man as a citizen. These, then, are three grounds for fearing that corporate indoctrination of large elements of the population may go much further than has ever before been possible, seriously violating the traditional democratic "competition of ideas."

But if these three aspects of the new appeals imply that they can be made more effectively than ever before, perhaps the appeals themselves are innocuous. This is what we do not know; for the time being the human relations movement does indeed appear to be more helpful in uncovering problems than in giving direction to a questionable program of indoctrination. It is the potential more than the present accomplishment that raises questions. For in a persistent desire to find how to make employees content and productive, the danger is that the appeals themselves will in effect encourage uncritical loyalty, obedience and passivity and will discourage independence, resourcefulness and responsibility.[14] In these respects it is feared that they undermine some of the social preconditions of democracy.

These misgivings about the human relations movement suggest several lines of research, not all of which are we yet equipped to undertake successfully. What kind of competition of ideas and of indoctrination does democracy require? What personality characteristics are required for democracy? Is the ideal employee a good citizen? What impact does the human relations movement have upon personalities of employees? Like other questions raised, these questions call for greater formalization of present knowledge as well as extension of empirical observation.

The possibility that indoctrination of the individual as an instrument of production will be more profitable than his indoctrination as a citizen raises a distantly related question so important for democracy that I mention it here somewhat out of

---

14 For discussion of possibilities, see Henry A. Landsberger, *Hawthorne Revisited* (Ithaca, New York: Cornell Univ. Press, 1958); and Harold L. Wilensky, "Human Relations in the Work-place: An Appraisal of Some Recent Research," in C. M. Arensberg, et al., eds., *Research in Industrial Human Relations* (New York: Harper, 1957).

context. As the businessman may find it more profitable to invest in instruments of production than in citizens, so in the larger political arena totalitarian rulers find it profitable to invest in their citizens as instruments of production where democratic rulers seem to think it unprofitable to invest in them as citizens. Hence, as we have discovered, the Soviets more rigorously pursue education than do the western democracies. Generalizing further, the time may come when on many scores totalitarian governments may do better for their populations than will the democracies. If this presents the democracies with the possibility of extinction, in the meantime it would be a not uninteresting theoretical problem to revise some traditional claims for democracy in the light of the possibility that an exploiting non-benevolent dictator may be more generous to the population than democratic leaders can afford to be.

2. Manipulation of the Consumer through Advertising
To say that advertising frustrates effective consumer control of the businessman, is not to say that it necessarily frustrates democratic government. But is there a connection? Hartz contends that contemporary developments have increased individuation, not submerged it; and the question can be raised both as to the importance of individuation to political democracy and as to whether advertising is one of the contemporary developments for which Hartz's hypothesis is true. The question has also been raised as to whether advertising conditions the electorate so that it can more easily be engineered, even if not by the advertisers themselves, in political affairs.

Economic theory will be of little help on this point, for economic theorists commonly employ a simplifying assumption of given wants or demands, raising no problems about where demands come from or by whom they are influenced. If this strikes a political scientist as an extraordinary defect in economics, its justification has been that the simplifying assumption is a lid on a Pandora's box.

Not only do economists thus turn their backs on the question of what manipulation might be tolerable, they do not even bother to set down the facts as to what kinds of manipulations are practiced and with what success. Voting studies as known in political science have no counterpart in economics, except in a kind of research underworld of advertisers and their staffs and a few scholars in the business schools. It is time to bring their material, which I do not mean to imply they always secrete, out into the open of academic discussion; and, if economists are prevented by an occupational habit from doing so, perhaps some students of democracy will see its relevance.

We already know, even if our knowledge is incomplete, that in many respects manipulation of consumer is like manipulation of voter. Leaders deliberately misinform and misrepresent, appeal to fears that they first arouse if not already present, and subtly strengthen some values and weaken others. On the other hand, they sometimes inform, sometimes play an important innovating role in calling attention to important neglected facts or values. Still again, in some circumstances they make appeals that divide the electorate and in other circumstances make appeals that unite them. Or they play upon desires for individuality in one case, upon desires for conformity in another.

A comparative study of political and economic manipulation of the electorate should be especially fruitful. The useful functions that a manipulating leader can perform ought not to be neglected; but useful or not, leaders' functions in the market need investigating. In political science, top governmental leadership sometimes is represented as a passive reconciler of conflicting interests, a resultant of vectors. Sometimes, on the contrary, it is represented as itself an interest group. Still again, though less commonly, it is represented in a vigorously creative role, like that of Schumpeter's entrepreneur, formulating issues and imaginatively integrating the conflicting groups in the society who never themselves rise to leadership's level of comprehension and innovation. And where some political scientists think of leadership's function in clarifying preferences, others have suggested that for democratic consensus leadership is required to gloss over differences, muddy the perception of preferences, sometimes alter them to make them more harmonious. Some of these views are relevant to analysis of leadership in the market.

If we can find out just what kinds of manipulation are attempted and what are successful, we shall achieve gains on two fronts. The observed facts will presumably contribute to an improved theoretical formulation of the desired democratic functions of leadership, a formulation which itself should be a major objective. They will also permit us to appraise leadership's actual behavior by the more explicit and defensible standards that will be formulated. In addition to clarifying leadership's role in the market, these studies should lead to more specific formalization of governmental processes generally.

Lacking both adequate facts and well-considered standards, we are presently able to look at manipulation of the consumer and agree with both calamity howler and complacent. Again, if we judge by sufficiently high or sufficiently low standards, the present situation can be agreed to be either disastrous or happy, even where no facts are disputed. The need for sophisticated standards for judging leadership's manipulation of the electorate is therefore especially pressing.

If we do not know enough about actual practices in manipulation of the economic electorate and lack standards for judgment, we are nevertheless able to draw a great distinction between possible adverse consequences of manipulation in economy and government. Manipulation in government is sometimes a prelude to revolution, to *coup d'état,* or to the slow atrophy of competitive politics. Manipulation of consumer preferences is none of these, nor, specifically, does it seek to stir dissatisfaction with the system or put one dominant clique into power. It is a highly fragmented and competitive manipulation, seeking only to influence the consumers' "policy" choices within an unchallanged institutional framework.

It might also be argued that no other great stakes are involved in such changes in expressed consumer preferences as are effected by manipulation. What does it really matter to market democracy if I buy one kind of car rather than another or if I am induced to try to raise my prestige by serving vodka to my guests instead of whisky? Especially in a wealthy society like ours, an original choice of car or liquor is already dominated by dubious motives of conformity, prestige, display, and other hasty and frivolous considerations. Hence a manipulated preference is no less satisfactory as the basis for a market vote than an earlier one. In short, the consumer is effectively manipulated only on kinds of choices that raise no serious problems for democracy in economic life.

I rather doubt that this line of argument deprecating consumer choice is correct; but it is worth investigating, both on its own account and because it raises a larger theoretical problem about democracy. Should our normative model of democracy postulate a process in which policy responds to electoral preferences generally or only to relatively more critical preferences? One can go far, I suggest, with the argument that for many categories of preference it is not at all important that policy be responsible.

The most persuasive objection to manipulation of the consumer is not, of course, that it actually challenges democracy in market or government but that it corrupts taste and values. On the ground that to examine this thesis would take us too far afield from our concern with democracy and that it is difficult to make headway on it in brief comment, I shall not discuss it.

3. *"Nul homme sans seigneur"*

Bertrand de Jouvenel has suggested that we are returning to the medieval "flight of individuals into the protection of lords" in an enlargement of the role of the corporation.[15] One aspect of this development is the rise of an expense-account elite, a group especially privileged because of their connections with business enterprise. Another is the growth around the business enterprise of services to employees, ranging from reading rooms to medical services or vacation accommodations. Still another is the corporate demand upon executives for maximum commitment to the corporation, including the commitment to stay within the corporate staff in after-hours social and recreational activity.

What is the extent of these phenomena and what are their consequences for the social preconditions of democracy? Despite recent attention to some of them, as in *The Organization Man*,[16] we are floundering. It may be that it does not much matter for democracy, but I should think it worth knowing, for example, whether sea and air travel first class is predominantly expense account, or becoming so, and whether some categories

15 Bertrand de Jouvenel, *The Ethics of Redistribution* (Cambridge, England: Cambridge Univ. Press, 1951), p. 67.
16 William H. Whyte, *The Organization Man* (New York: Simon and Schuster, 1956).

of Manhattan restaurants are now almost wholly supported by expense accounts. For a possible threat to the preconditions of democracy, I would put even more value on examining the degree to which corporate employee services and demands for loyalty are undermining community associations. On all counts, however, we need both facts, on one hand, and criteria from democratic theory, on the other.

The expense-account and the corporate provision of services to employees can both be attacked, if we wish, through tax laws. These phenomena rise from our giving corporations tax concessions quite different from those we give a family or neighborhood association bent on providing some of these privileges or services to its own members. Sometimes the difference on tax treatment is extreme. A corporation can reduce its taxes, for example, by building a swimming pool for its employees; but, should these same persons found a swimming club and build their own pool, each member would pay a federal tax on his payments to the club. In the field of taxation alone, therefore, are a number of interesting research problems that might be freshly approached as problems in the preconditions of democracy.

The problems suggested by *nul homme sans seigneur* are staggering; and, even when we limit ourselves to problems of the preconditions of democracy, they are too many, too amorphous, too imponderable. Their analysis will make little headway until we have achieved a better understanding of the requirements for personality and small group association in a democracy. But we are so far from having achieved even that understanding, so far from knowing what empirical observations would be critical in the development of understanding, that we shall only very slowly progress.

4. Privileges of Leadership

Around government leaders in a democracy are erected numerous barriers to the exercise of miscellaneous powers that fall easily into leaders' hands and that we wish them not to use. Although we are apparently willing to give high placed leaders both deference in certain limited respects and limited flattering privileges, we do draw a line. We do not permit, if we can help it, their taking a general and unspecified superior position in society. And, for specific examples, we do not want them to use their power to hire and fire for accomplishing certain private objectives, to enjoy special consideration at the hands of the police and courts, or to use their powers as buyers to win favors from those who sell to them. Presumably our attempts to restrict these high placed leaders reflect both a dislike of privilege and some fear that power is easily exploited for the purpose of winning more power.

In the case of the corporate leader, he is similarly placed to take advantage of various powers that fall to him as a member of a governing economic elite; but it appears that he is much less hedged about in using these powers. As explained above, consumer controls over business leadership can endorse or veto a product, an output, but not the methods by which the product was made. And even controls imposed from the other side of the market, by those who supply labor and other inputs, do not bear closely on details of business management. Hence, it can be argued that corporate leadership is a more personally privileged leadership than is governmental.

Not being at all confident that this is the whole story, I should like to see a comparative study of the privileges of leadership not essential to discharge of function in both government and corporation. If a significant difference is found, the next question to ask is whether it makes any difference to political democracy. At one extreme, an answer might be that we have overlooked a serious flaw in democracy in our toleration of privilege for business leaders; at the other extreme it might be discovered that our traditional fear that small powers beget large ones is unfounded. This is a line of research that responds to no generally felt public problem, but it need not be disqualified on that score. In the very long run it would throw light on, though not itself answer, such a question as one not yet seriously raised: Can we reconcile democratic aspirations with the inheritance of corporate position, as in the conspicuous case of Henry II? This is only an example of one of many possible applications.

Business Influence on Public Policy
Business influence on the pre-conditions of democracy already having been discussed, we now ask about its influence on the

political preferences of voters, legislators and other policy-makers. The subject has, however, been so much worked over that one hesitates to approach it. No doubt the business point of view on public policy is well represented in Washington, as well as in the mass media. The inevitable question is whether the competitive struggle between it and other points of view falls short of meeting any important requirement of democracy. A second question is whether reforms, such as publicly subsidized mass media, might improve the character of the competition. Important as these questions are, I shall not go over familiar ground and make instead only a few points.

In the competition of propagandas, what ought to be the limits of government propaganda to defend and implement its own policies in the face of attack by business or other propaganda? Government propaganda is often condemned by solid theoretical argument; on the other hand, presidential addresses and other public statements can hardly avoid it; and Rogow has in effect challenged traditional assumptions about the desirability of limiting it in his account of British difficulties with business propaganda.[17] Here again is a piece of the normative theory of democracy that needs working out, to which Pennock's essay makes substantial contribution.

On business propaganda itself and other business influences on policy, a distinction ought to be drawn between the twin influences of business and wealth in politics, even if the latter commonly supports the former.

Thus quite aside from the influence of money in politics, the significance of private enterprise in creating a homogeneous group of highly motivated partisans ought not to be missed. So tightly knit, so highly motivated are these partisans that Harold Laski's theses that businessmen will overthrow democratic government rather than yield on certain issues came to be widely accepted even in such relatively stable democracies as Great Britain and the United States. Although they did yield in Britain, Rogow has argued that in another sense they have not yet yielded.

The intensity of their partisan activities in the United States is nowhere better illustrated than in the doggedness with which

17 Rogow, *op. cit.*, p. 174ff.

business groups have sought to stultify the regulatory processes and capture the regulatory commissions. It has therefore been argued for the public utilities that the only way to make regulation effective in the face of partisan activities of business is to eliminate private ownership of the regulated industries. On the other hand, it has also been argued that, with the rise of a salaried managerial group in industry whose interests in and controls over their firms are not dependent upon their stock ownership, partisan activity will remain substantially the same in both private and public firms, since both business groups will take on narrow corporate goals in about the same way.

What then, a research project might ask, is the character and relative intensity of partisan political activity among owner-managers, non-owning managers of private corporations, and managers of publicly owned corporations? The findings may produce some surprises and, in any case, will throw light on some significant relations between business ownership and interest-group activity. To avoid confusing the issue, the influence of income and wealth ought to be removed from the findings; if a non-owning corporate executive is more intensely partisan than an owner-manager, we want to be sure that it is not simply because he has a higher income he wishes more intensely to protect.

A practical application of these researches would be in reconsidering regulation. But it ought not to be assumed that the less intense the partisan activity the better for democratic government. These researches would also point up the need for examining the functions performed by business partisanship, not all of which are disruptive to democratic government.

As to the influence of money in politics, inequality in income and wealth may so split a society as to make a democratic consensus impossible. But in the better established and not extremely inegalitarian societies of the western world, the problem of income and wealth in politics is that of its disproportionate influence on policy. Again, this is familiar. The threat of money is, however, presumably less serious if its influence is not linked tightly to that of a wealthy hereditary business elite. We ought to explore further, therefore, the relation between inherited wealth and membership in the business elite. It is probably just as correct to say of the United States that a man becomes rich because he is a corporate executive as to say that he becomes a corporate executive because he was born into a wealthy family. But how is business leadership recruited? Our information is fragmentary. Certainly corporations promote largely on merit, but how strong are other influences and how is merit appraised? And if corporations more solicitously woo Yale and Princeton graduates than they do the graduates of the state universities, they in effect recruit from wealth. To what extent is this the dominant pattern of recruitment?

In discussing the businessman in political office, I went into some detail on the need for explicit models of the democratic process for criteria by which the businessman's role could be appraised. In appraising the implications of the corporation for the social conditions of democracy, the need for criteria based on explicit and comprehensive theory was again apparent. Now once again, in appraising the consequences both of business partisanship and of inequality of income and wealth for the making of public policy, the need for theoretically derived criteria is no less pressing.

B. *The Union*

The consequences of the union for political democracy are in some respects like those of business in politics. For example, questions asked about the businessman's role as a partisan, about his capacity to adopt a new role when he becomes a public official, or about his demanding an excessive organizational loyalty can all be asked again about the union leader. Similarly the need for explicit models of the democratic process by which business activity in politics can be appraised is equally apparent for the appraisal of union activity.

The Leader's Role in Shaping Attitudes

Rather than repeat in the context of unionism what has been said in the context of business, let us instead move on to still other aspects of unionism significant for democracy. It is widely agreed that the rise of unionism diminished standing disproportions in the effective representation of group interests in making and administering public policy. Unionism achieved a somewhat improved organization of the potential electoral strength of wage earners, and union leaders came to be more effective representatives in policy making at all levels than wage earners had ever before been able to depend on. In speaking for wage-earners' interests in the continued debate on public policy that goes on in newspapers, magazines, and broadcasting; in legislative lobbying; and in representation both of wage-earner and consumer interests before regulatory bodies, union leadership presumably reduced the disproportionate strength of business and wealth. Unionism has probably also raised the level of political activity and improved the "circulation of elites." All this is familiar.

As an interest group, however, organized labor is different in important respects from other groups. Compared to business as an interest group, it is more formally organized, its members' political attitudes are probably less alike in the absence of organization efforts to make them alike, its members are less confident that they know what they want in politics, and they are consequently more dependent upon advice from organization leaders. Although these hypotheses themselves need to be tested, let me suggest some implications.

It may follow from the above differences between business and labor that labor's political activity is less well characterized as a pursuit of given objectives than as a process in which objectives are themselves examined and reconsidered in the process of pursuing them. Labor's political activity, more than business' political activity, is heavily influenced by a continuing interchange between leadership and rank-and-file, in which union leadership competes with other opinion leaders such as ministers, newspaper columnists, and even businessmen to whom the rank-and-file sometimes turns for advice on some issues. The competition puts leadership in a position in which it cannot depart too far from the preferences of its rank-and-file, but at the same time the rank-and-file demands information and advice from leadership as to what its interests are and what its demands ought to be.

Such an interchange between leader and follower, in which the leader himself both follows and leads, is to be found in microcosm among small groups of acquaintances some of whom make a bid for opinion leadership, and is to be found again in the relation between a newspaper editor and his readers or, even if in lesser degree, in the relation, say, between businessmen and the Committee on Economic Development. It is probably nowhere more obvious than within the union movement, nor is it anywhere more highly organized on an extremely large scale than in unionism. Chains of these relationships form an intricate network when a leader of one particular union group himself turns for leadership to some one higher in the union hierarchy.

As a universal phenomenon in democratic politics that is especially vigorous and easily observable in unionism, the process ought to be systemically studied. Who communicates with whom? What is the content of the interchange? To what degree is the leader constrained in what he says and what he does in the political arena by the beliefs of his constituents? To what degree do his followers depend upon him to tell them what to believe? How is the network constructed? At what points do union leaders themselves turn to leaders outside the union movement?

These studies would add to the richness of present research on attitude formation in that they would picture not selected aspects of attitude formation but a large integrated process, in which flows of information, impact of policy problems on leaders' attitudes, competition of leaders for followers, "shopping around" of followers for leaders imposed by followers' opinion on followers, and constraints upon leaders imposed by followers' opinions would be placed and clarified. Such studies would throw great light on a central and—I think—inadequately cultivated question: Is democracy to be construed as a political mechanism for satisfying demands on the citizenry, or is it better construed as a political mechanism for the discovering, adjusting, and only then satisfying demands of the citizenry? They would also illuminate the question imaginatively discussed in Berelson, Lazarsfeld, and McPhee:[18] In a democracy, what does the voter need to know about and what does he not need to know?

Still further, such studies would bridge a gap between some

---

18 Bernard R. Berelson, Paul F. Lazarsfeld, and William N. McPhee, *Voting* (Chicago: Univ. of Chicago Press, 1954).

older concepts of democracy in which the voter is envisaged as choosing among policies and the newer concept in which he simply chooses among candidates, for it would somewhat clarify the relation, for different kinds of political leaders, between the leader's success in competition for leadership and his role in forming and responding to policy demands. I would also expect such studies to contribute heavily to formalization of democratic theory on these and other points. Again, Pennock's essay carries these topics further.

Fragmentation of Policy Making

Conflict among interest groups has pushed political science a long way from the assumption of an objective public interest toward an appreciation of the multiplicity of publics and of interests. Although the multiplicity of interests is taken as evidence that policy will in fact finally be resolved in part by the power positions of conflicting groups, there remains in the profession a widespread feeling for an ideal in which at higher or highest levels of policy making some kind of overview of the conflict can be had and a reconciliation achieved through a reasoned adjustment of interests. The ideal raises a problem in democratic theory that, though introduced here in connection with the union as an interest group, pertains to interest group conflict generally.

I suggest that possibilities for reconciling conflict without a high-level overview and reasoned solution are greatly undervalued in social and political theory, excluding only economic theory. We in economics earn our livings theorizing about a complex social mechanism for achieving a resolution of conflicting demands upon resources and income which accomplishes no central overview, no centrally determined solution, no reasoned final reconcilation. Our preoccupation with this mechanism, the price system, makes us sensitive to the possibilities of achieving a high degree of coordination through wholly fragmented decision making. Similar possibilities of resolving conflict and achieving social coordination through political fragmentation, though by no means unknown to political theory, have not been exhaustively explored. I have myself been recently looking for counterparts in governmental processes to fragmented decision making in the market and find the search rewarding.[19]

Again, what is required is not scattered observation of phenomena but their comprehensive inter-linking so that the significance of fragmentation can be seen in the light of all the processes and requirements of democratic government. In short and again, we need large-scale models of democracy. And when we have them, we can deal much more surely and precisely with the impact on democratic policy making of such groups as unions.

Here, of course, I tend to challenge Beer's identification of group conflict with inefficiency in policy making. Conflict is of course a common source of inefficiency, but we shall misunderstand the mechanisms of democracy if we assume this always to be the case. That fragmented and generally disjointed rather than synoptic decision-making processes can achieve coherence as well as innovation is obscured by our habit of defining coherence as the product of a central overview of a policy problem. In actual fact, it is clear that some problems are too large, too complex, too imponderable to be grasped by any one man's mind or any committee's deliberations. Under such circumstances a series of incremental moves in policy achieved by mutual adjustments among shifting combinations of groups and individuals can, for all its imperfections, often achieve coherence superior to that achieved through a futile attempt to push the human mind beyond its limits. For it is a characteristic of such incremental mutual adjustments that they often focus attention and problem-solving capacity on such pieces of the larger problem as can be grasped, understood, and predictably controlled. And they represent also a sequential process of attending at one point to the corrections of errors—fortunately only incremental—made at other points, thus achieving a resultant coherence not through a super-human understanding beforehand but through a manageable mopping-up operation.[20]

Two kinds of coherence are, of course, not even to be desired in the real world. One is that kind of consistency in policy that

19 Charles E. Lindblom, *Bargaining: The Hidden Hand in Government.* pp. 137–168 in this volume; and Lindblom, *Decision-Making in Taxation and Expenditure* (Mimeograph, New York, 1959).
20 Lindblom, *Bargaining,* and Lindblom, *Decision-Making.*

is attainable only when the electorate is unanimous in its choice of values or objectives, as well as in its means or policies. I think none of us would tolerate so well ordered a society and would hope instead for the continued benefits of individual differences in values, attitudes, and proclivities. The second is a kind of consistency in which no social goal or policy is ever sacrificed for the achievement of some other. It is such a sacrifice that often prompts the complaint of incoherence, but clearly in a world in which even for like-minded people the achievement of any one of their aims is not wholly consistent with the possibility of achieving all others—where, in short, policies are costly in terms of each other—to aspire to coherence construed as "no sacrifice" is to be utopian in the worst sense.

Too Much Union Power?

If unionism has redressed a previous imbalance, it is often argued to have created a new one. If so, its excesses are not where they are alleged to be. The union in politics has not turned out to be the highly cohesive, intransigent, and intense voting bloc that was in some circles feared. Not so cohesive because of conflicts of interest among wage earners and among the allegiances within each wage earner. Not so intransigent because of two-way interchange between leaders and rank-and-file and again between policy and policy demands. Not so intense, because the wage earner is perhaps more citizen than union member. The union in the market place, however, may indeed post a threat to economic stability; the possibilities and probabilities are much debated.

Let us asume, for the sake of argument, either that unionism in the market is disruptive or that nevertheless we wish to take steps to ensure that it never becomes so. What to do? Thinking back on Adolph Sturmthal's demonstration of more than a decade ago that organized labor behaves one way as an interest group but quite another way when it becomes responsible for the electoral success of a political party,[21] it might be argued that a desirable development in American democracy would

21 Adolf Sturmthal, *The Tragedy of European Labour 1918–1939* (New York: Columbia Univ. Press, 1943).

be the assumption of party responsibility by unionism. The argument is that, once organized labor casts its lot permanently with one party rather than playing each against the other, its gains largely depend upon that party's becoming or remaining an effective competitor for the vote. Thus organized labor finds itself compelled to moderate both its political demands and its market behavior in order to find common cause with a potential electoral majority. It then finds it easier to attain its traditional segmental objectives through political means than through the market, for a potential majority can be organized around demands for social security and other welfare objectives, including income redistribution, while the pursuit of these same objectives through collective bargaining alienates the required allies. If all these hypotheses are correct, it would appear that deeper involvement of labor in the Democratic party and a consequently more predominantly political pursuit of labor's objectives might be a sufficient safeguard against excessive union demands in the market.

The hypotheses are plausible, and varying political roles of organized labor from country to country in the western world make it possible to test them by comparative analysis. Whether they are true or false, such research would add to our comprehension of the relation between interest groups and political parties, as well as clarify the processes by which potentially dangerous interest groups are curbed by their need for allies in competitive politics.

III. Private Enterprise, Price System and Regulation

Quite aside from the particular consequences of business and unionism, the structure of the economy in the large is itself consequential for political democracy. It is not, however, consequential in some of the ways traditionally alleged; and a good starting point for discussion is the consideration of two conflicting historical beliefs about economy and democracy that are in the process of being reformulated.

1. It is alleged that political democracy is impossible without the private-enterprise economy. Although political democracy and private enterprise arose historically in circumstances in which they appear to have supported each other, the proposition

has not had to depend on this evidence alone. It has been rather persuasively argued that the market economy, removing as it does many questions from the political arena, simplifies the tasks of government, lightens the load of decision making on political leaders, removes devisive issues from politics, minimizes the need for political authority—in all these respects easing strains on political democracy.

But the proposition fails to distinguish between the case for a price system and the case for private enterprise. Earlier the failure was unimportant, but we now know that publicly owned industries can be harnessed to a price system, and in every democracy some are now so harnessed. Today economists (whose opinions are not however conclusive on this issue) would probably largely agree that political democracy would require heavy use of a price system but would be divided on whether it required a wide scope for private enterprise.

More important, a growing number of social scientists will today declare that with the present resources of social science it cannot be known whether political democracy requires either price system or private enterprise. This I regard as a great gain, for it turns the attention of social scientists to questions of a form that can be researched and that have some relevance for the kinds of policy choices that democracies make. We now ask instead a question of the form: Will, in some specified circumstance, some specified alteration in price system, private enterprise, or government regulation be expected to strengthen or weaken democracy and, if so, in what respect? Thus we put an end to a traditional and sterile debate and turn instead to such a question as the appropriateness of public ownership for certain British industries or of certain American public utilities, or such a question as the impact of land-use planning on democracy and other values.

Pursuing this new line of questioning and suppressing the old, we find, for example, that governmentally sponsored old-age insurance, unemployment compensation, and relief have almost certainly at one time or another in different countries been a major underpinning for the consensus on which democracy rests. It is therefore clear that less price system or less private enterprise and more regulation can in some circumstances be essential to democracy.

Thus our research questions in this area are best stated when they permit us, first, to take account of variety in possible relations between price system or private enterprise and political democracy and, second, when they direct us toward *incremental* changes in economic structure so that we ask about the consequences not of the price system but of *more* price system or *less*, not of government regulation but of *more* governmental regulation or *less*.

2. It is alleged that socialism is required for democracy. Assuming "socialism" to refer to the public ownership of industry, it has never been well demonstrated that socialism is required for democracy in government. Inequality of income and wealth and the power of the business leader in politics can be argued to be inconsistent with political democracy, but corresponding threats to democracy in public ownership can also be argued. Although socialism may be necessary to a highly developed democracy (and not merely by definition), the resources of social science do not permit us to know; and, again, this kind of question has generally been replaced by researchable questions that have the additional merit of being relevant to actual policy choices open to the democracies, as illustrated in the discussion above of price system and democracy.

More often than not, this particular allegation does not specify that socialism is required for democracy in government but is to be read as claiming that economic democracy is impossible without socialism. But we have seen above that the market, even under the auspices of private enterprise or a mixture of private and public, is in many respects a democratic piece of machinery. Again, therefore, as indicated above, the relevant and researchable issues concern policy areas in which market democracy might be strengthened by specific alterations in structure, including the possibility of socialized enterprise. It is not obvious that choosing comprehensive socialist organization would strengthen economic democracy, nor do we in fact have such an option in democratic politics.

Leaving these issues aside, I finally come to a few hypotheses about economic organization and political democracy with which it seems both logically and rhetorically satisfying to bring this paper to a close. Some of these hypotheses are relevant but quite refractible to analysis; others point very directly to research.

1. *Specialization of function and the consequent hierarchical organization of skill and responsibility in all industrialized societies will appear increasingly to violate the prerequisites of political democracy.* This is a consequence both of the degree to which specialization and hierarchical development occurs and of our raising the standards for political democracy. Sooner or later, it would appear, we shall begin to be concerned with a pattern of specialization in which, say, two men make their careers out of saving time for a hierarchically superior third whom they would assist and whose talents are regarded as that much more valuable than theirs. Such a pattern is on some counts at odds with the democratic principle that one man is never the tool or instrument of another. The problem not having arisen yet with any force, we are in no position to begin research on how to solve it; but we might investigate the changing character of superior-subordinate relations in a society of increasingly specialized functions.

2. *Many of the beliefs that have grown up around our economic system threaten the survival of a democracy in its competition, with totalitarianism.* Fiscal orthodoxy, at one extreme, and a widespread reluctance to undertake collective expenditure on science and education are illustrative. That the Soviets are drawing close to us in many fields, surpassing us in some, everyone now knows; the degree to which the state of affairs is traceable to the folklore of our economic system is less well appreciated and well worth exploring.[22]

3. *In particular, the relative inviolability of private enterprise may cripple our efforts to meet the Soviets in trade rivalry and other forms of economic warfare.* The Soviets will not be constrained by constitutional prohibition and other effective political restraints on manipulation of production, prices, investment and foreign trade. So far, no such threat has arisen, but a Soviet attempt to outrival us in trade concessions or to disorganize certain existing patterns of world trade could very quickly make it major. This is a problem worth anticipating; and it raises

22 James Tobin, "The Eisenhower Economy and National Security: Two Views, Dollars, Defense, and Doctrines," 47 *The Yale Review* (1958), pp. 321–334.

certain technical economic problems that can be analyzed well in advance of the need for new policy making.

4. *To meet the above problems of rivalry with the Soviet Union, the role of government in economic life will be substantially increased.* Specifically, government activities will account for a substantially larger share of national product; collective expenditures will increase at the expense of private consumer expenditures; and government and business leadership may enter into a closer relationship in which, as in England, business associations and individual businesses take on certain functions we now think of as belonging to public administration.

5. *Democracy in local government may be strengthened by its increasing responsibilities for education, as well as for other community expenditures that will develop as we become wealthier.* This is much more a guess than an estimate of probabilities, but it suggests that we might take a new scholarly interest in emerging patterns of community demands for collective amenities and their consequences for local government. Assuming that national democracy survives, we may soon enjoy a renaissance of local government.

IV. Conclusion

Coming at the end of this essay, the above hypotheses might appear to be intended as a summary of issues. But they are not; they merely suggest research problems in one last area. Rather than attempt a summary, I shall merely point out that, of all the issues raised, the most persistently recurring have stressed the need for (1) formal comprehensive models of democracy, (2) special attention in model-building to the two-way interplay between leadership and electorate, (3) special attention also to the formalization of processes by which preferences are adjusted to each other and otherwise aggregated, and (4) reformulation of all-or-none issues into problems of incremental adjustment of institutions. Though these points constitute no summary at all, they have run like themes through much of the discussion.

Model-building, on which I have thrown so much emphasis, I see as a special form of image-building, to use Hartz's term. In his discussion of both the usefulness and the inappropriateness of images, his thoughts ran largely to those images of democratic processes that are widely held in a society and are part of the society's ideology as well as guides to conduct. A special class of images are those scholarly constructions known as models. They need not correspond to popular images, of course; nor is it even always necessary that they have ultimately some effect on lay images, for they are constructed for highly specialized analytical purposes. But just as Hartz pointed up the discrepancy between lay image and actual functioning of institutions, discrepancies between scholarly image or model and functioning have often loomed large. My repeated suggestion that students of democracy make their images formal, explicit, and precise is, of course, merely an appeal to some of the traditional aspects of the scientific method on which we count to minimize the discrepancy between the scholar's image and what can actually be observed.

2

The Rediscovery of the Market (1966)

What is the significance of the great debate, already several years old, on the appropriate role of profits in the planned economies of Communist Europe?

One interpretation of this change in Communist thinking is that Communism is turning capitalist. Since imitation is the sincerest form of flattery, many Americans are delighted to accept this interpretation. But the Communists do not see their reforms in this light; and Professor Lieberman, whose name is foremost in the Soviet debate over the profit motive, has explicitly denied that Communist use of the profit motive is capitalistic. On his side of the argument there is some weighty evidence: namely, the existence of profit-oriented *socialist* enterprises all over the world—e.g. municipally-owned public utilities in the U.S., the nationalized industries of Britain and Western Europe, and the socialized enterprises of many developing nations (like Hindustan, Machine Tools of India).

Indeed, the significance of the reforms has little to do with the antithesis capitalism-socialism. The new and growing use of profitability criteria in Communist enterprises can better be understood as a phase in *a worldwide rediscovery of the market mechanism.*

Now, capitalism and the market mechanism are not the same thing. Understandably, they are often confused with each other, because it was under capitalist auspices that the market mechanism first became, on a vast scale, the organizer of economic life. But the market mechanism is a device that can be employed for planned as well as unplanned economies, and for socialism and communism as well as capitalism. Today the market mechanism is a device both for the organization of the relatively unplanned sectors of the American economy and for such central planning as is practiced in the United States. In Britain and Scandinavia, it organizes both the private and the socialized sectors of the economy. In Yugoslavia it serves as an overall coordinator for an economy of publicly-owned enterprises. In many underdeveloped countries it is a powerful tool of development planning. It is this market mechanism rather than capitalism that the U.S.S.R. and its satellites are trying to employ—precisely to improve their planning.

Except for a convulsive attempt between 1918 and 1921, Soviet policy has never questioned the practical usefulness of money and prices. This does not mean, however, that the Soviet Union has heretofore made much use of the market mechanism. By the market mechanism, we mean the use of money and prices in a very particular way: Prices and price movements are employed—instead of targets, quotas, and administrative instructions—to give signals to producers with respect to what and how much they should produce; and prices on labor and materials consumed are set to reflect the relative value of these inputs in alternative uses to which they might be put.

It is the possibility of using a pricing process to evaluate alternative possibilities and to cue producers accordingly—whether to suit the preferences of individual consumers in the market or the preferences of central planners, whether to administer the resources of an advanced economy or to guide the developmental choices of an underdeveloped economy—that has struck a new note in Communist economic policy, in the economic reorganization of Western Europe, and in the economic development of the nations still in early stages of growth. The significance of the development, of which Communist reforms are only a part, can be appreciated in the light of its own history.

I. Adam Smith and *laissez faire*

Most people who know anything at all about the market mechanism seem not to have advanced beyond Adam Smith's view of it. He saw it as *an alternative* to government control of economic life. He was concerned about inefficiency and other defects of mercantilism; and, to speak anachronistically, he thought he had found in the market mechanism a substitute for incompetent planners. His specific insights were profound. He saw the possibility that resources could be systematically allocated in response to human needs as a by-product of "selfish" individual decisions simply to buy or to sell. He saw that prices established by consumers in their trading with producers could establish a set of signals that could direct the productive processes of the whole economy. He saw that competitive bidding for inputs would establish a market value for them that would make possible a comparison of their productivities in alternative uses. He saw that a comparison of input prices and output prices, that is, of the money cost of production with money receipts, could control the flow of resources into each of their alternative possible uses. Finally, he saw that the market mechanism was for all these reasons an extraordinarily powerful device for decentralizing economic decisions. In all this, however, his vision was limited: The market mechanism was always a private enterprise market and always an alternative to planning.

II. Market Socialism

It was not until the development, over a century and a half later, of the theory of market socialism that any significant number of people perceived the possibilities of using the market mechanism in a completely socialized economy. Even today the idea of market socialism remains esoteric. In 1920, Ludwig von Mises published his now famous challenge to the socialists to indicate whether they had any system in mind for the actual administration of economic affairs in a socialist order. It was a challenge that many socialists brushed aside, believing that they could cross that bridge when they came to it. But a few socialists, conspicuous among them the late Oskar Lange, turned back to the 1908 work of the Italian economist Barone, to construct a model of a socialist economy that would practice a systematic and decentralized evaluation and allocation of its resources. They showed that prices could be manipulated by government in such a way as to reflect the values that consumers put on consumer goods and services, and also to reflect the values of inputs in alternative uses. Their discussion of the pricing process under socialism clarified the useful functions that prices can perform. If, for goods and services in short supply, prices are systematically raised by government pricing authorities, the high prices can be taken as signals for increased production, while being at the same time at least temporary deterrents to consumption. Similarly, if prices are systematically lowered for goods in overabundant supply, the low prices can be taken as signals by producers to curtail supply, and by consumers to increase consumption.

Lange's 1936 exposition of these possibilities made it clear that prices could be systematically regulated to perform the signalling and evaluating functions even in the absence of those competing private sellers whose rivalry sets prices in a private enterprise economy. Moreover, his exposition demonstrated that prices so set permit a systematic comparison of alternative patterns of allocation, a comparison that would not be possible without prices of this kind.

If the development of the theory of market socialism made it clear that the market mechanism could serve socialism as well as capitalism, it nevertheless did not much interest the socialists of Western Europe or the planners of Communist Europe. For the market socialist had developed a model of a socialist economy that left very little room for central planning. Their socialist market mechanism was designed, as was the market mechanism of classical economics, to serve the preferences of individual consumers rather than the priorities of central planners. As in a capitalist economy, in this kind of market socialism the consumer remained sovereign—at a time when most socialists, planners, and Communists were looking for ways to effect collective purposes and national goals, rather than individual preferences. Although socialist theory considered harnessing the market mechanism to centrally determined priorities, it did not construct a persuasive case as to how it could be done.

In the Communist countries, the possibilities of market socialism were underrated for still other reasons. Communist ideology was antagonistic to the very idea of the market, hence inevitably to market socialism. Academic and professional Soviet economics was also antagonistic to the orthodox tradition in economic theory out of which the theory of market socialism sprang. Finally, with respect to formal planning and resource allocation, the overwhelming concern of Soviet policy was "balance" rather than what economists call "optimality." Optimality involves a careful evaluation of returns to production in alternative lines. To Soviet planners, however, the need for big allocations to steel, electric power production, and national defense seemed obvious. Speaking very roughly, all that remained to be done was to insure that allocations for the rest of the economy were roughly consistent with, or in balance with, the crudely calculated but obviously necessary allocations to these high-priority sectors. And even this formal interest in balance was secondary to their interest in the crude growth of physical output.

III. The Market Mechanism for Centrally Determined Objectives

If the market mechanism was ever to be of any use for central planning, it had to be shown that prices could be set to reflect centrally determined values, and not merely individual consumer values. In the economics of the West, it has in fact long been clear that they can do so. For example, a subsidy to maritime shipping lines or to airmail carriers is a way of raising the price received by those who provide these transport services, thus signalling them to increase their production of the services. Similarly, a tax on liquor is a way of depressing the price received by manufacturers and distributors, hence a way of signalling them to restrict output. The result of these interventions—either subsidies or taxes—is to achieve a price that reflects both individual consumer preference *and* the preferences of governmental authorities.

A government can go even further—and in wartime often does. It can completely eliminate the effect on price of individual consumer demands so that producers respond to a price set entirely by government. This can be done either through the imposition of a legal price or by exclusive government purchase of commodities and services, after which government agencies either consume the purchased goods and services themselves or, in the case of consumer goods, redistribute them in some way to consumers.

Using the market mechanism in this way is an alternative to direct administrative control—to targets, quotas, physical allocations, specific instructions, etc. It is not always a good alternative, but it often is, since it is a way of manipulating incentives powerfully while leaving the actual decision—to produce or consume more or less—in the hands of the agency or enterprise whose price has been altered. Hence, a general virtue of the market mechanism as an instrument of central direction is that it permits extraordinary decentralization of detailed decision making.

To understand the possibility of subordinating the market mechanism to governmental rather than to individual choice, it is essential to distinguish between actions in which governments signal their production targets through prices, and actions in which they intervene in the market mechanism to alter the results without, however, actually using prices systematically as such a signalling device. To raise agricultural prices, for example, in order to stimulate agricultural production is a way of employing the market mechanism for the achievement of a centrally-determined goal of high agricultural production. On the other hand, to raise agricultural prices as part of a complex process of restricting farm output (as in the U.S.) is an entirely different kind of operation, in which direct administrative controls (such as acreage quotas) replace the market mechanism. Or again: Depressing the price received by a manufacturer by imposing a tax on his output is a way of implementing a central decision to discourage consumption of the commodity, whereas the general imposition of legal maximum prices to control inflation has the effect of interfering with the market's ability to reflect either collective or individual choices and will ordinarily give rise to rationing, or to some other administrative device for the allocation of goods and services.

Perhaps it is the easy confusion of miscellaneous intervention in the pricing process (which the Communist economies have always practiced) with the skillful use of pricing to implement central planning of production that has contributed to Communist indifference to the latter. In any case, the Western demonstration that the market mechanism could be used to implement central priorities did not significantly affect Communist policy until certain other developments occurred. Even as late as 1950, the model of market socialism seemed to be consigned to a limbo of interesting irrelevancies. Ideological barriers were still strong; so also was the obstacle of fundamental ignorance in Soviet economies about the pricing process.

IV. Yugoslavia

The Yugoslav economy was the one sensational exception to Communist indifference to the market mechanism. Yugoslav Communism was indigenous, not imposed by the U.S.S.R. as in the satellites generally. Political relations with the Soviet Union were such that in Yugoslavia independence in economic policy came to be valued rather than feared. Moreover, Yugoslav intellectuals and politios had closer ties with their counterparts in the West than did any of the other Communist countries. Whatever the reason, in 1952, recoiling from the inefficiencies of detailed administrative control over the economy, Yugoslavia brought into being a greatly decentralized market socialism. The change of direction, taken together with the rapid growth that ensued, excited much interest in the Communist world. The significance for Communism of the Yugoslav venture was greatly diminished on one score, however. For when the Yugoslavs abandoned detailed administrative control over the market mechanism they also went a long way toward consumer sovereignty as a replacement for the central direction of the economy. Hence, in the eyes of Communists elsewhere, the Yugoslavs had largely abandoned central planning itself.

V. New Freedom for Economic Inquiry

New possibilities for economics were opened up by Stalin's death in 1953. Soviet economists, engineers, and administrators could finally look with some freedom at the lessons to be learned from foreign experience with the market mechanism. One especially noteworthy gain for economic analysis was the lifting of Stalin's capricous ban on mathematical economics (input-output analysis, and linear programming, etc.).

Soviet mathematical economics, reaching back to work originating in the 1930s but not then pursued further, demonstrated independently of Western economics that pricing can be made useful to the planning of resource allocation even in the absence of any actual exchange between a buyer and seller. If we consider all the alternative combinations of end products that an economy can choose from, and all the alternative combinations of inputs that might be used to produce any given output, we see that there are vast possibilities of substitution—of one end product for another, and of one input for another. These possibilities of substitution can be represented by "substitution ratios"—and these substitution ratios can be expressed as a system of prices. (In the absence of any actual transaction in which a real price would be set, they are often called "shadow prices.") *Pricing turns out, therefore, to be implicit in the very logic of rational choice among alternative uses of resources.*

This discovery clearly removes certain traditional ideological objections to market pricing for it makes clear that pricing is not a capitalist invention but a logical aid to rational calculation even in circumstances far removed from capitalist buying and selling. Whether in fact the discovery has yet achieved this consequence for Soviet thought is not certain, however, for Soviet mathematical economists have, on the whole, drawn the inference, not that the market mechanism might now be more openly examined, but that such pricing as might be achieved through the market mechanism can in principle now better be achieved through further mathematical analysis and electronic computation.

The "in principle" is crucial, since a prodigious amount of information needs to be gathered and processed in order to substitute computers for actual markets; and so far the accomplishment is beyond the capacity of economists, Soviet or Western. Nor can it be said with confidence that there is any way to gather and test the required information except by putting consumers or planners in the position of actual choice in a real market. Still, the exploration of the practical mathematics of resource allocation is far from its maturity.

VI. The Rising Concern for Allocative Efficiency

In any case, the discovery of "shadow pricing" did not of itself overcome Communist disinclination to exploit the market mechanism. A final consideration was the growing complexity of the Soviet economy, with complexity outstripping admittedly growing Soviet competence in planning. The economy became more complex for at least two reasons: With the rising standard in living, the demand of consumers for varied and higher quality consumer goods came to be more pressing; and with technological advance, alternative production possibilities became more numerous and complex. Soviet policy makers could no longer be satisfied with the simple mobilization of large quantities of capital, and the attendant mobilization of agricultural labor, for industry. As one student of the Soviet economy has written:

> The Soviet economy again appears to be at a turning point. It is clear, as the debate shows, that it is becoming more and more difficult to plan *everything* centrally. The Soviet economy has grown not only in size, but in sophistication in concern for the consumer. As a result, campaigns and storming can no longer solve all the problems that arise. There are simply too many sectors which need attention. They can not all be manipulated from the center. It has been estimated that, if the economy continues its present growth, by 1980 the planning force will have to be thirty-six times its pressent size.

It is especially noteworthy that the older Communist concern for "balance" is, in the face of this new complexity, no longer thought sufficient. It is increasingly, difficult to find some clear superiority of one pattern for a few key industries over another alternative pattern. And that being so, Communist countries can no longer be satisfied with merely balancing the outputs and inputs of all other industries to satisfy a prior commitment to a few key programs. In short, consistency in an economic plan is no longer enough; optimality in a plan is now becoming a pressing objective. Hence, finally, the new interest in the market mechanism.

In their forthcoming study, *The Soviet Capital Stock 1928–1962,* Raymond P. Powell and Richard Moorsteen will document still another hypothesis to explain the new Soviet interest in improved resource allocation ("optimality"). The Soviet Union, they suggest, has been exhausting the possibilities for rapid growth through indefinitely larger and larger capital investment; it must now either find an alternative source of growth—i.e., a better allocation of resources—or resign itself to a lower growth rate.

VII. Paradox of Planning

How far the Communist economies will go in employing the market mechanism of course remains to be seen. An ideological and traditional resistance to the market mechanism does not quickly evaporate and presumably will never wholly evaporate. Moreover, a market mechanism is not always and universally a serviceable instrument for economic organization. Even in an economy like that of the U.S., in which ideology is all on the side of the market mechanism, its use has to be constrained by the recognition of its limitations.

In the Communist case, there remains one conspicuous obstacle to extending the employment of the market mechanism, sometimes referred to as the *paradox of planning*. The problem can be posed this way: If the planners intend to use prices to signal production goals for the economy, they cannot set appropriate prices for end products until they first decide what quantities of various end products they desire. But they cannot intelligently decide on appropriate quantities of end products unless they know their costs, i.e., the resources used up in their production. Now, in a market mechanism, these costs are represented by prices; and this is to say that they cannot determine desired quantities of end products until they know prices. But we have just said that they cannot determine prices until they know what quantities of end products they desire!

This problem does not arise when the price mechanism is used to implement any single collective choice, as in a Western economy, because a decision, say, to expand the production of maritime transport services can take as given the relevant prices already prevailing on the market. Planning an increase in the production of no more than a few commodities or services does not so alter price relationships and production patterns for the entire economy as to invalidate prevailing prices as guidelines for the planners. But to plan, through pricing, a production pattern *for an entire economy* promises readjustments of prices that will invalidate the very set of prices that the planners depend upon for making their plans.

It follows that the fullest use of a market mechanism as an instrument for central planning would require that central planners actually operate, not directly through a master plan in which all major lines of production for the economy are simultaneously established, but through a large number of (and a series of) specific choices for each of all outputs or industries to be planned. When a choice is made for any output or industry, the outputs and prices for other industries need to be regarded—for planning purposes—as unchanged. To make the fullest use of the market mechanism, central planners need to work out a strategy for goal-setting and pricing (against a background of the overall general plan) that proceeds through many specific *and sequential* price and production decisions.

Such a procedure, it may be the case, is already in embryo in the Communist economies—even though, for lack of understanding of its utility, it is more often hidden than openly displayed. Given the complexity of the task of comprehensive, synoptic national economic planning, and given also the inevitable limits on man's intellectual capacities, even where these capacities are extended by electronic computation, planning all over the world tends to break down into clusters and sequences of specific decisions. The mere construction of detailed five-year plans does not prove that anyone or any organization has achieved an integrated synopsis of the elements of the plan; instead these plans are typically a collection of targets and policies from many sources.

VIII. The Rediscovery of the Market in the West

Outside the Communist orbit, an appreciation of the usefulness of the market mechanism has been most conspicuously on the rise since World War II. With good reason, the market was under great attack in the depression of the '30s, the severity of disillusionment with its usefulness nowhere more vivid than in the American NRA, an attempt at partial displacement of the market in favor of private and public administrative controls. But in the late '30s, Keynesian economies began to hold out the promise of ending depressions by improving rather than eliminating the market mechanism; and Western governments, learning the lesson, have in recent years sustained higher levels of employment than used to be thought possible. Similarly, taxation and transfer payments, as well as provision of subsidized public goods like education, have attacked problems of inequality in income distribution—such problems can therefore no longer motivate proposals to disestablish the market mechanism. The result is that, in the West, the market mechanism is in better repute than ever before, as is indicated in the decline of socialist opposition to the market mechanism both on the continent and in Britain, where after World War II socialists deliberately subjected their newly nationalized enterprises to market controls rather than to the battery of administrative controls they had once contemplated. And the great event in Western European development in recent decades has been a substantial move toward unification, not through common government, flag, army, or language, but through the Common Market.

IX. The Developing Nations

As a group, the underdeveloped nations of the world are lagging in their understanding of the usefulness of the market mechanism. Abstractly, they should be eager to exploit every possibility for economic advance; in fact, they stand in a kind of backwater.

One reason is that their leaders and intellectuals are often prisoners of a once exciting but now stifling orthodoxy. Some of them are prisoners of early Marxian doctrine on planning, the very orthodoxy from which European Communism is escaping. Others are prisoners of English socialism of the style and date of Harold Laski, or even of earlier versions of English socialism—in either case antagonistic to the market mechanism. But times change: Although Nehru was a prisoner of both, his daughter may turn out to be a prisoner of neither.

Another reason is, oddly enough, the insistence of the United States, the World Bank, and other lenders that underdeveloped countries formulate national economic plans in order to qualify for aid. They mean by a plan a balanced and consistent set of investment outlays. The effect is to divert some of the best brains in these countries away from high priority questions of growth strategy to the construction of reconciled investment programs reminiscent of those the Communist countries are trying to leave behind as inadequate. In India, for example, the question of the size and internal consistency of the five-year plans overshadows in public discussion, and in the attention it receives from experts in Indian government, many more rewarding questions of growth strategy, including such questions as how the market mechanism might be employed to hold out incentives to farmers to raise food production or how it might ration scarce foreign exchange in such a way as to substantially raise the level of economic achievement.

To be sure, just how much the underdeveloped economies should count on the market mechanism is subject to much dispute. The point being made here is only that the underdeveloped countries themselves do not well understand the issues, and have often not tumbled to the fact that, for many of the specific developmental problems they face, they can employ the market mechanism in tandem with other methods of controlling and planning economic development.

The prospect that the underdeveloped countries may take a new view of the market mechanisms as an instrument of development planning is, of course, greatly enlarged by what they now see developing in Communist Europe. For even if they do not intend to follow the Communist path to development, the evidence that Western and Communist economies alike are finding the market mechanism useful is certain to impress them.

How they can best employ the market mechanism depends upon the particulars of their circumstances. But on a few counts a general usefulness of the market mechanism for these economies can be predicted. First, they all suffer desperately from a shortage of administrative skills and organization: They are not very competent in executing *any* kind of plan, economic or otherwise. Even the best of their civil services have developed procedures and traditions more suitable to keeping the peace than to stimulating economic development. Hence, on this score alone, they need the market mechanism more than do the advanced countries of the world.

Secondly, most of them have accumulated a mixture of administrative interventions in the market mechanism, such as price controls and exchange allocations, which have undercut the servicability of the market mechanism without putting any positive administrative program in its place. To impose, for example, maximum prices on food grains in order to hold down the price of food in towns and cities saps the farmer's incentive to produce more. It takes away the monetary incentive and puts nothing in its place—it destroys one mechanism of development without substituting another.

Thirdly, while the development of an economy through administrative techniques furiously engages the energies of a planning elite, participation in development through the market mechanism is open to everyone and, indeed, typically engages most of the adult population. Cueing, signalling, rewarding, and penalizing through the market mechanism are methods of drawing on the largest possible number of responses—and, in addition, a method of extricating a traditional peasantry from older institutions and habits of life that retard development.

Fourthly—and here is a consideration of enormous importance to most underdeveloped countries—they need the market mechanism because they cannot take the route to rapid development that the Soviet Union took from the 1920s to the '60s. Foreswearing in the period any hope for skillful allocation of their resources, the Soviets instead counted on achieving growth through restricted consumption and massive investment. Their strategy worked because the restriction of consumption was in fact possible. It was possible for two reasons: The standard of living was high enough to permit forced savings, and the Soviet government was willing and able to use compulsion. In many underdeveloped countries, neither of these conditions holds; in some, only one does. In many cases, the surplus over and above what is essential to consumption is much smaller than in the Soviet case, where development proceeded from an already advanced stage of early industrialization and food availability. And in ever more cases neither effective systems for tax administration nor other instruments of compulsion are sufficient to gather the savings that are hypothetically available. Hence, except to the extent that capital assistance from abroad can take the place of forced savings and investment, these underdeveloped countries cannot successfully imitate the older Soviet pattern. They need to understand, as even the Soviet Union in its new condition is coming to understand, the indispensibility of a judicious use of the market mechanism for efficient use of the limited resources they can command.

X. No Paradox for Planning

That the non-Communist underdeveloped nations can use the market mechanism to satisfy the individual needs of consumers is of course clear. But what of the usefulness of the market mechanism for implementing centrally determined social priorities—to strengthen the industrial sector, for example, or to give a special push to agriculture, or to establish a steel-producing capacity? It follows from what was said above, about the paradox of planning, that it is just this kind of precise intervention for which the market mechanism is a demonstrably effective instrument of central planning. For this kind of *planning through selective intervention,* the paradox of planning does not arise; and no special techniques need to be devised to overcome it, as do need to be devised in the Communist countries of Europe. Hence, it turns out that the kind of "central planning" to which these underdeveloped economies are committed is the very kind for which the market mechanism is best suited.

XI. Conclusion

That the market mechanism can be serviceable to planned and unplanned economies alike, to public and private enterprise alike, to collective and individual choice alike, is a discovery the significance of which may soon dwarf what we have seen of its consequences so far. To say this is not to take sides in the many disputes in many countries in which, for particular purposes at hand, the question has to be settled as to how far and under what circumstances market organization ought to be pushed. It is only to take note of the fact that, although these disputes will remain, and although different countries will choose different combinations of the market and other forms of organization of economic life, the market mechanism is now everywhere coming to be recognized as a fundamental method of economic organization which no nation can ignore and which every nation can well afford to examine freshly. Even China, bent on its own course, may come to be caught up in the movement toward the market. For lack of experience with, and personnel for, direct administration, China has perhaps gone less far in disestablishing the market under Communism than its ideological claims would suggest. If so, we may be witnessing a race in China between an old-fashioned Marxian determination to undermine the market as soon as administrative competence permits and a growing sophistication about the market's usefulness—with the result unpredictable, if momentous.

3

Democratization in the U.S. and Its Problems (1980)

To talk about the transformation of the political and constitutional order of the United States has led me to try to organize my comments around one main theme, which is the gradual democratization of the American political system and the problems that are connected with it. I am going to deal very speculatively with its democratization, because when one tackles large and ill-defined issues it is difficult to be anything other than speculative. Perhaps in any case there is an inverse relationship in social science between the significance of what we say and its provability. We can demonstrate rather conclusively only insignificant propositions. To deal therefore with more significant and interesting propositions, we are forced into speculation.

With respect to the growth of democracy in the United States, or the democratization of the system—a word that I can use to refer to the trend toward democracy—some of you may be puzzled that one should talk about tendencies toward democracy in a country often characterized as an already highly developed democracy. Consequently, I first want to acquaint you with some features of the United States and its government that are undemocratic—or at least fail by far to achieve a high development of democracy. There are indeed a number of those features. Only in light of them can you appreciate the significance of the tendencies toward raising the level of democracy in the United States.

I. Obstructions to American Democracy

The first thing you must understand about the American democratic system is that it was designed to achieve or to protect a high degree of personal liberty, but not to achieve much democracy. Sometimes people do not distinguish between the two—

liberty and democracy. They assume that a system capable of protecting individual liberties is at the same time democratic—that is, subject to popular control. But it seems clear that it would be possible for a political system to afford its citizens a great deal of personal liberty—freedom to worship, speak, publish, read, think, talk as they wish—yet at the same time not give those people any high degree of control over their government. I repeat: The American system is designed to give citizens a high degree of personal liberty rather than a high degree of control over their government. This feature is to be found in the Constitution and in the judicial interpretation of that Constitution, which is the operating constitution.

Why such a system? Many of you know the answer. It is that the American system grew out of a commercial revolution, a revolution led by merchants and businessmen who wanted freedom from constraints on trade more than they wanted a popularly controlled government. They wanted freedom to make money. Some of you know some of the legends of the eighteenth century American revolution. One, for example, is the Boston Tea Party, in which American colonials dressed as Indians dumped a load of tea from a ship into the sea to protest a British tax on trade. Freedom to trade is built into our folklore.

The American libertarian constitutional tradition imposed severe restrictions on the popular vote. Originally, among other constraints, it levied property qualifications on voters, required indirect elections of senators, and set up a number of devices to keep the population from achieving any quick, direct, or massive control over government. Ours has been an imperfect and deliberately crippled system of popular government.

A number of other still surviving aspects of American government render it less democratic than it is conventionally thought to be. One, for example, is our complicated multiplicity of governmental units. As you know, we have states as well as a national government—and, of course, municipal governments. What some of you may not appreciate is the impressive degree of autonomy of the separate governmental units. In most European countries, provincial and municipal governments are creatures of the national government, their powers granted and revocable by the central government. This is not the case in the

United States, where states' prerogatives are written into the Constitution and have been made effective in a long-standing political and judicial tradition. Consequently, for an American to try to take part in government Fuller and achieve some control over it requires that he participate in three somewhat independent categories of government. It is a discouraging task, which most Americans are not interested in undertaking. Their level of political participation is relatively low. Their degree of effective political control over government is correspondingly reduced.

And then, too, the size of American government, the citizen's distance from Washington, and the impersonality of a vast bureaucracy also persuade American citizens that control over their government is an extremely time-consuming, laborious, and unpredictable task, hardly worth undertaking.

A further undemocratic feature of American government—I do not have time to discuss them all—is the effect of class on American politics. It is a common belief that America is a relatively classless society. You will see relatively less visible evidence of class conflict than in most European countries. But there is a mistake lodged in that perception. We do not see evidence of class conflict, I suggest, because the dominant classes in the United States have been more effective than their counterpart classes in European societies in teaching (or educating, indoctrinating, or persuading—use whatever verb you want) other elements in the society to accept their styles of life, their values, their political preferences. There is consequently less overt class *conflict* in the United States than in European countries. Yet one might argue that America has achieved a more successful class monopoly than the systems of Europe. I suggest that such an influence of class has constrained the scope of political discussions and the variety of alternatives in politics which Americans seriously consider when they vote. Political debate in the United States is narrow when compared to that of Europe. There is no sizeable audience for socialist or communist thought or for practical socialist or communist policy.

II. Movement toward a Fuller Democracy

I would now like to turn to a happier story, which is the evidence that the American system is moving toward more democracy.

In recent years it may have been moving with more vigour than has been the case for some time. The evidence is of many different kinds, each by itself inclusive yet all taken together indicating a profound restimulation and extension of democracy.

A. *New Popular Agitation*

The first evidence, I suggest, is the various liberation and agitational movements in American society and politics. I say society *and* politics because these movements have made demands for changes in social behaviour and in job opportunities, thus in a wide variety of aspects of life not limited to politics. I have in mind, of course, movements like women's liberation. Before that and still a more powerful movement is black liberation, representing an enormous change in the political efficacy of black participation in American politics.

These movements are many and diverse. They include, for example, political agitation by "welfare mothers," that is, women of broken families who live on public relief. They include gay liberation for homosexuals. Every manner of group in the United States today organizes to make demands effective in municipal, state, and national government. All indicates a new birth of popular activity in the American political system.

Another group I would call attention to—highly unstable, even fickle, one might say; but still a sizeable group—is composed of activist university students. As you may know, they were extremely active during the Vietnam War and are currently in a period of relative quiescence in the United States; but one should expect to hear from them again.

There have also arisen diverse, keenly felt, and activist movements for developing better control over energy use and over environment, two areas in which the nation is gradually becoming aroused.

B. *Reform of Political Parties*

A different evidence of democratization in American politics is the reform of the party system. The Democratic party especially has undergone a substantial change in its rules to permit small groups, through caucuses in their neighborhoods, to achieve a more immediate participation in and a more immediately effective control over nomination of candidates—taking the nomination of candidates out of the traditional smoke-filled room in which political leaders pick their favorite candidates, and moving it out into the open under popular control.

C. *New Attitudes toward Business in Politics*

Another evidence of growing democratization in the United States is, I suggest, a sharp, measured decline in the popular belief that what is good for business is good for America. That is a traditional old slogan increasingly in disrepute. Americans are challenging, finally, the long-established disproportional influence of commercial, merchant and business groups in American politics. The movement has not yet gone far; but it is a movement that has revealed a sharp disillusionment with business leadership in economic affairs and in American politics.

D. *Rising Educational Accomplishment*

Another evidence, less of increasing democratization than of a potential for democratization, is a significant phenomenon: that American society has slowly been transformed from a population of high-school graduates to a population of college graduates. There lies a potential for an explosive change in American politics. The primary and secondary school systems in America have been a profound source of complacent and self-satisfied attitudes toward the American system and toward its political policies. College education is of a different sort. In American colleges and universities, students are coming into contact as they did not before—with a wider range of thought, some of it highly critical of American institutions. Although it is still true that the universities are more given to perpetuating a political and cultural tradition than to upsetting it, the subversive function of the American university is more powerful than any such subversive function in primary and secondary education. The transformation of the educational background of the American population is a potentially revolutionary force in American political life.

III. Difficulties

I now want to discuss some of the consequences of the drive or drift toward democracy. Let me say that generally I rejoice in trends toward democratization. I also take some pride in a system that has a potential at this late date for further enlarging the area of effective democratic practice. Nevertheless, one of the oldest questions in politics has been the question of how far democracy can be pushed before it creates problems which are themselves insurmountable by democratic procedures. As society moves toward greater democracy, it incurs certain costs. These I want to talk about. Many of them, we hope, are transitional costs. Some of them seem fairly clearly to be so. But we cannot be so sure of some of the others. Some represent lasting problems that attend any attempt to achieve a substantially higher level of democracy than the American government has so far achieved.

A. *Economic Decline?*

One first possible difficulty is that the increase in the effectiveness of democracy undercuts the prosperity of business enterprise, asking us in effect to pay for increased democracy with economic decline.

Why economic decline? The fuller development of the argument would go back to my *Politics and Markets*, but I can suggest it somewhat briefly. In order to achieve a high degree of growth in a market system in which the responsibility for growth and for high employment rests on business management rather than on public officials, it is necessary that business managers be on the whole buoyant, pleased, or optimistic about their prospects. For if they are not, they will not invest, offer jobs, expand the economy. That is why, in all successful market systems, governments heavily engage in a wide variety of policies of benefit to business. Even in earlier periods of development, the governments of the market economies undertook costly development help to business, such as in creating transportation and communication systems. England did it, as the leader in the eighteenth century and nineteenth century. The continental countries picked it up, Germany later than France.

If we look at the case of an extraordinarily rapid development of a market system in Japan, we see that it was marked by an unusually generous set of benefits to business from government in the form of assistance to investment, protection of markets, and other devices.

In short, to make market systems successful, government has to pay disproportionate attention, be especially responsive to the business community, more so than to any other group in the society. Hence these governments cannot be genuinely democratic, in the sense of being responsive equally to all sections of the population.

In the rise of new democratic demands is implied a diminution of the political influence of business as a favored political group. And, consequently, there is a more frequent refusal of public policy to give business the incentives it needs to carry on its activity. As you know, we have had in the United States in recent years a relatively low rate of growth. We have therefore some reason to doubt that business enterprise is sufficiently favored to carry on at the level of vigour and growth that we want of it.

B. *Stagflation*

Closely connected with the problem of economic decline is another difficulty arising out of the increasing democratization of the American political system—and there are counterparts in Western Europe. It is the simultaneous appearance of unemployment and inflation. As most of you know, societies used to be able to choose between those evils; they did not have to suffer both at the same time. We now may be in a position in which the democratization of the American system, specifically the new demands put on the system and their undercutting of the privileged political position of business, makes growth possible only with a special business incentive in the form of rising prices. Inflationary price increases are turned to in order to provide the stimulation otherwise missing. This may be one of the factors accounting for the simultaneous appearance of inflation and unemployment.

C. *New Business Demands*

Another difficulty with increasing democratization is that businessmen are themselves making new demands. Looking about at the increasing tendency of all elements of the population to ask for benefits from government, businessmen decide to join the parade, to make comparable new demands. Consequently the welfare state, originally designed to take care of disadvantaged groups in the society is now enlarged in concept to include the disadvantaged corporation.

An early case was the much-debated request from the Lockheed Aircraft Corporation for substantial government underwriting of its losses some years ago, and its success in getting some underwriting. Some of you have seen that the issue has been raised again in the form of a request from the Chrysler Corporation for special help to enable it to cope with its losses. Now I understand this is an old story in Italy, that you have hundreds of firms which have been bailed out by your government and which are living on government subsidies decade after decade. That has not been the case in the United States; but we appear now, perhaps following Italian leadership, to be embarked on this same course. I would suggest that in possibilities for inefficiency through subsidization of businesses that ought to be allowed to fail we have promise of a great waste in American society, growing, curiously, in an indirect way, out of our tendencies toward democratization.

D. *Disorganization of Political Parties*

Now we come to more specifically political consequences of the growth of democracy in the United States these days. One is the decline in the usefulness and effectiveness of our political parties.

I must explain this with care because what you mean in Italy and in European countries by a political party is something different from what we mean by an American political party. The day before yesterday in Rome, as I was driving through the city, one of my hosts called my attention to the fact that we were driving past the main offices of the Christian Democratic Party. It was marked by a large sign. He thought it worthwhile calling my attention to the Party's headquarters. Not so in the

United States. Almost no one knows where the offices of any political party are in the United States and nobody cares.

Now, to be sure, there must be a main office of each of the major parties in Washington, even if I have never seen one, have never been in one. The active organizational units of our parties move about depending upon who the candidates are and what the election is. The parties have almost no permanence, have inconsequential staffs between elections; and there is no such thing as a formally established genuine party leadership. If a person is nominated at a Democratic political convention, it is assumed by most people that he is to be considered as head of the national party. But some people do not consider him so; he is not elected to such a position or formally appointed to it. If he loses the election, he is ordinarily no longer considered to be the head of the party; and whether there is any head of the party may not be determined until another campaign, in which another presidential candidate is nominated.

The party is a loose, diffuse, weak organization; and you must not attribute to it, therefore, more significance than it has. Nevertheless, as an organization for mobilizing, at least spasmodically, at election times, a number of somewhat cooperating activists, it achieves some effectiveness in inducing a group of political leaders to try to put together some kind of coherent program or bevy of candidates that will help attract enough voters to win an election.

One of the effects of the democratization of the party—the democratization to which I referred above—has been to take the party out of the hands of leadership and let party nominations depend upon the accident of primary elections and of local citizen groups. The result is that the possibility that once existed that a small group of experienced political leaders would take seriously the weighing and evaluation of alternative possible candidates and programs to appeal to a coalition of forces has eroded. The possibilities that relatively inexperienced people with a dramtic or charismatic appeal can win nominations both for the presidency and for minor or secondary offices has greatly increased.

The result, I suggest, is that the democratization of the political parties probably means we are going to have more incompetent political leadership than before. A great many people would say that President Carter may be an example of that trend.

The resulting incompetence is not, however, only the incompetence of candidates with insufficient political experience who are not tested by their political colleagues. The decline of the party system also threatens us with an institutional incompetence; a decline in the possibility of organizing systematically a coalition that knits together a variety of segmental interests into some kind of broad or overriding collective public interest.

E. *Collective and Segmental Interests*

This last point about segmental and collective interests needs explanation. We appear to be living in a time in which politics has to deal increasingly with what might be called collective rather than distributional issues. Consider two kinds of issues in politics. The distributional issue is the "who gets what" kind of issue. Distributional politics is a competition for benefits in the system. Distributional issues have been the principal concern of American politics for at least a century. The other kind of issue, the collective issue, is an issue in which I do not push for something at your expense, nor you for something at mine, but where we share an overriding collective concern. To some important degree, we all sink or swim together. Our growing problems of energy and environment are, in large part, problems of the collective health of the economy and the political system, in which we all, to some important degree, sink or swim together.

Thus, in short, at that very time in our history when we need a new political capacity to deal with the common good rather than segmental interests, the fragmentation of political leadership through the decline of the party leaves us with a reduced rather than with a heightened capacity to deal with those very collective issues.

F. *Government-Business Collusion*

The next consequence of democratization is the growth—again a highly speculative hypothesis—of government-business collusion at the public expanse. Why? For reasons given above in the discussion of the privileged position of business. Government leaders know that if they are to stay in office there must be a fairly high level of employment and other signs of economic health and growth. They know that they must consequently give with generosity the kinds of benefits, tax concessions, and other favorable policies that will induce the level of performance of business that the nation demands. Simultaneously, the new democratic forces demand a variety of reforms and regulations antagonistic to business. What is a public official going to do in a circumstance like that? He is in a difficult position. He knows that the more urgent and compelling demand is business prosperity. He can afford to thwart the public's electoral demands. In the confusions of politics, especially in a large politically fragmented system like that of the United States, it is extremely difficult for citizens to hold leaders closely responsible. Consequently, I suggest, increasing democratization paradoxically drives government and business into a high degree of collusion to see to it that the needs of business are met even at the expense of thwarting in various ways the electoral demands coming up through the new democratic pressures and organizations.

At an extreme, deliberate deceit of citizens by officials may be on the rise. Many Americans believe that deceit is reaching new levels. With President Lyndon Johnson came the new term, *credibility gap*. He was severely criticized for the extent to which he was thought to have deliberately misled the American public and Congress on the direction of public policy, especially with regard to Vietnam. Since then the concept of the credibility gap in American politics has become commonplace and has been used to express anxiety about deliberate deceit and secrecy on matters of public policy.

G. *Public Unwillingness to Bear Costs*

Finally, one last unhappy political consequence of the democratization of American politics is a widespread unwillingness of the population as a whole to bear the costs of what it demands of the political system. This is a problem for which we once had a solution and for which the solution may be now vanishing. The disproportion of political influence in American government in favor of wealth and business used to make it relatively easy for politically strong groups to impose costs on the great mass of weaker citizens. The rise of egalitarian and more democratic participation in the system puts increasing numbers of people in the position where they can effectively resist what they used to bear. Hence our wave of tax revolts. Hence also the public's refusal to share the costs of and to bear the disadvantages of energy conservation. Democratization also makes all groups potentially effective in insisting that they not be made to pay the cost of environmental cleanup. The consequence is paralysis.

4

Changing Views on Conflict between Freedom and Equality (1980)

I. Growing Discontent with Equality of Opportunity

The conflict between freedom and equality has long been embarrasing to many thoughtful men who wish to advocate both and who wish therefore to deny that either one can be had only at some cost to the other. As early as the first half of the nineteenth century, a major innovation in social thought—and ever since then a widely accepted one—sought to deny conflict between the two values by asserting that the only equality that men should prize is equality of opportunity. If men use their opportunities differently, their resulting inequalities are wholly acceptable. Ergo: no conflict between equality and liberty as values.

The conclusion is now gradually being discredited. In 1931, in *Equality,* R. H. Tawney exposed the inadequacy of the doctrine. In the world of tadpoles, he wrote, all tadpoles in a pond enjoy equal opportunity to lose their tails and grow up as frogs. But most tadpoles die. Many thoughtful people now believe that equality of opportunity is not at all sufficient. They indeed value opportunity, but they also value the character of the competition and the relation between winners and losers. Above all, in any society in which the great mass of people are valued enough so that we prize their freedom, we cannot be indifferent to the distribution to them of the pleasures and benefits of life, even if most people are losers, or at least not front-runners, in the competitions opened up by equality of opportunity. I see the decline of the doctrine of equality of opportunity as one of the great intellectual transitions of our time.

Professor Hayek is probably correct in telling us that the pursuit of equality in the broader sense is incompatible with certain important kinds of equality before the law. Yet it is a major feature of contemporary society that the pursuit is on.

II. Rise and Fall of Meritocracy as a Form of Equality

A second development, closely associated with the first, is the rise and decline—the decline already having begun—of the idea of a meritocracy. Egalitarian thought led most of us to believe that it was wrong for men to hold high position by inheritance, or because of wealth or family position or old-boy network. Leaving aside certain special positions to be filled by democratic elections, the new doctrine was that positions should be awarded in accordance with ability. The best to the top. Only in a condition of equality of opportunity could and would the best rise to the top. Meritocracy seemed to promise a much fairer, as well as a much more efficient, allocation of powers and responsibilities, together with the perquisites, like income, prestige, and deference that go with power and responsibility.

Many thoughtful people are now frightened by the possibility of meritocracy. Assume that the best rise to the top. The best what? The best climbers? The most skillful manipulators? The most aggressive? No doubt, advocates of a meritocracy *intend* that the brightest or the most able—most able to do the world's work—rise to the top. But that thought too is frightening. For in the world's many and long struggles between the rulers and the ruled, much of mankind's hope has rested in the knowledge that ability was not monopolized by the rulers. Among the reformers and revolutionists, there have always been great pools of ability. A more ominous trend can hardly be imagined than one in which the world is divided into two groups: rulers who are the able, and the ruled who are not. Who then will be able to guard the guardians?

And even if the rulers can be constrained, even if the combination of rule and ability does not constitute a foundation for despotism, meritocracy remains frightening because it promises that honor, authority, deference, and the other perquisites of office are awarded to the biologically lucky, thus, like heaven to a Calvinist, to a predetermined elite. They become rewards in life for which most men know they cannot successfully compete, for all the ostensible equality of opportunity. That positions are *earned* is not a sufficient justification for calling meritocracy egalitarian.

In short, the competitive egalitarianism of a meritocracy,

however much we once praised it, is already generally unacceptable because of its implications for other kinds of equality and
more specifically because it threatens the destruction of freedom
when joining brains with power too tightly.

III. Renewed Understanding of Market Coercion

The conventional liberal doctrine is that the market system,
and only the market system, can organize large-scale social
cooperation consistent with freedom. No man engages in a
market transaction unless it is to his advantage to do so; hence
he voluntarily, freely, uncoercedly cooperates. In rough and
simple argument, so long as there are many buyers and sellers
in each market, no buyer and no seller can coerce any other
market participant. It is an important argument because there
is much truth in it.

Liberals forget, however, that many early English advocates
of the market system thought it good because it coerced, because
it did not leave men free. Society, they believe, must coerce men
to work—either by law or by the "silent, unremitting pressure"
of hunger.[1] Market coercion is of course impersonal. No particular A coerces a particular B. But like any system that denies
livelihood to those who will not work, it reduces options; it
compels man to work. Even if you and I believe that men ought
to work, we cannot deny that the market coerces men to do so
(in a way that it does not coerce them to work in a particular
job or for a particular employer).

Thanks to contemporary critics of liberal doctrine, thoughtful
men everywhere are becoming increasingly sensitive to the many
other ways that market systems coerce. They put enormous
pressure on the individual to play the game of life by market
rules and to compete for those values that loom especially
large in market societies. Most thoughtful men now give some
significant credence to Marx's argument that life in market
societies powerfully affects the kind of personalities formed.
Hence, if a man feels free, it is often because he has been shaped
into just such a personality as he wishes to have and do what
the market system permits him to have and do.

[1] William Townsend, *Dissertation on the Poor Laws* (1785).

IV. Equality in the Distribution of Freedoms

The three developments in thought so far identified lead many men to a fourth. A clue to the relation between equality and liberty is to be found in the idea that liberty is achieved by equality before the law. Most people probably do not believe that legal equality is enough. That aside, note the point: Men are free if they equally enjoy or possess something of great value. Look at the same point from a different perspective: Would men be free, would a society be a free society, if some few men enjoyed many options or choices but most men did not? I think we would answer no. Next step: What choices or options need to be widely shared before we say each man, or a society, is free? Clearly nontrivial choices. Certainly choices about life styles, about what one thinks, about where one lives or moves. Men are not free if these choices are not widely distributed.

We come, then, to the conclusion that liberty as a value is not defined unless the distribution of liberties is specified. Equality as a value, in many minds today, denotes the value placed on an equal, or at least much more equal, distribution of liberties. In these minds, the conflict between equality and liberty has varnished, for the liberty they seek is an equally distributed set of liberties; and the equality they seek is an equality of liberties. It is also an equality of opportunities, but no longer of opportunities narrowly considered. No longer solely opportunities to enter a race, to begin a struggle; but instead opportunities at every moment in life to make choices, to choose among life's pleasures, benefits, challenges, rewards, responsibilities. Liberty, so conceived, thus calls for a high degree of equality in income and wealth, perhaps also in the distribution of authority and other power.

V. The Unfree and the Unequal

A final observation. One of the great puzzles of twentieth-century history is that masses of voters in essentially free democratic societies do not use their votes to achieve a significantly more equal distribution of income and wealth, as well as of many of the other values to which men aspire. Whether they would be wise or foolish to do so is beside the point. What needs explaining is why they do not try.

The most plausible explanation, I suggest, is that they respond to leaders—political, social, religious, and intellectual—who have no passion, despite their frequent rhetoric, for equality. They are successfully led by these leaders because ideology and indoctrination are passed on from parent to child and are reinforced by public education and the press.

One can then say of them that they do not try because they are unfree. For all their nominal democratic rights, their minds are not free to choose differently. But one can also say they are not equal; they are controlled by elites with greater power than theirs: greater authority, greater knowledge, greater voice, thus greater influence. But if we can say, while meaning the same thing, either that they are unfree or that they are unequal, then the affinity between freedom and equality in which equality is seen as a distribution of liberties is given dramatic illustration.

5

American Politics Since 1970 (1982)

Since politics is all around us—we live in it—each of you is as competent as I to characterize the American political world of the 1970s. My paper cannot therefore be intended to instruct you. Its purpose is presumably to stimulate an insightful discussion. Fair enough. I shall not instruct you, nor will I carefully balance, for fear of seeming to fail in objectivity, a pro with a con, or even a favorable view of American politics with a critical one. I shall instead lay out a frankly subjective characterization of American politics in the '70s with all the distress that I feel about it.

One of the suggestions given to me for getting a grasp on the American polity since about 1970 was that I identify the big shocks to the polity, after which I could discuss the political response to each. My subsequent difficulties with the concept of shocks may be instructive.

Consider first the oil shocks. Shocks indeed, but to the economy rather than the polity. They posed some problems to the U.S. government; stimulated briefly, for example, some interest in a comprehensive federal energy policy, threatened gasoline rationing, stirred some debate on administrative versus price rationing, raised anxieties about national security, and so on; but the shocks never produced a major political crisis or watershed, failed to change the practice of politics as usual, and on the whole upset various markets a good deal more than they upset the American political system.

The lasting political effects of the oil shocks may include one more lesson that Americans are not masters of the world. Another effect may be to push Americans in the same direction that higher local phone rates are pushing (as a result of AT&T divestiture). High fuel prices and high phone charges for low-income groups have both renewed in a practical way an old theoretical issue: Can a modern ostensibly humane society permit necessities to be rationed through the inequalities of the market system? Effects like these suggest that the oil shocks carry long-term consequences even if not through shocks to the polity.

The oil shocks shocked not the government but the people, who as a result altered their market behavior, although continuing the same old political behavior for the most part. Another shock to the American people was the illegality, immorality, and vulgarity of Nixon and his close high-level associates disclosed as a result of the Watergate break-in. Again, the events seem not to have shaken the political system greatly. Presidential candidate George McGovern could not arouse an electorate over it in his campaign against Nixon; and even as one revelation after another disclosed a conspiracy to break the rules of the democratic political game, leadership and nation remained, though titillated, passive. Had Nixon not displayed a smoking gun, it seems likely that he would never have been deposed.

The American political system thus displayed an incapacity—rooted partly in the Constitution and partly in Congressional timidity and disorganization—to cope with a serious threat to the continuation of political democracy. Specifically, Congressional and other political leadership abdicated its leadership function until its hand was forced by the evidence of the smoking gun, pretending that sufficient evidence had not been available until that juncture. And subsequently, despite some announced resolves to prevent a recurrence of such conduct by the President and his associates, almost nothing has been changed to forestall a recurrence.

The American intervention and failure in Vietnam were more clearly shocks to the political system than either the oil shocks or Watergate. But neither intervention nor failure was an exogenous blow to the system; it is the system itself that produced both and not simply through an aberation, as some would characterize Watergate, but through the ordinary and usual processes of American politics, the same politics that had taken the U.S. into Korea years earlier. That the events were indeed a shock to the political system is evidenced by voiced opposition to the war, opposition of a character that would in any other war have been declared subversive, by the flight to Canada of draft-age young men, by disorder in the streets, and by President Johnson's inability to run for another term.

The response to the shock was and is not reassuring. Although many non-Americans will rejoice that Americans learned from it something about the limitations of military power, the American government has shown little sign of learning anything beyond that. The U.S. government, whether Republican or Democrat, seems not to have thought through the long-term implications of allying itself throughout the world with authoritarian governments and against popular and revolutionary movements. Even more specifically, critics today ask whether El Salvador is to be another Vietnam. To many thoughtful people throughout the world, American foreign policy toward third-world enemies of democracy seems either incompetent or systematically and deliberately anti-democratic.

And that brings us to a development far more important than any shock: the decline of the U.S. as a leading moral, political, and military force on the side of democracy. I believe that there are two thoughtful explanations for American support of authoritarian third-world governments. One is that the U.S. is so obsessed with its fear of Soviet power that it has simply abandoned a democratic mission. The other is that the U.S. is choosing capitalism over democracy, thus opposing any popular or revolutionary movements that threaten socialism no matter how undemocratic the forces arrayed against them. Either way, the U.S. comes to be looked at—increasingly?—as an international criminal. The consequences of American hostility to third-world democracy for the actual development of democracy in the third-world are potentially catastrophic. So also might be the public identification abroad of the U.S. as hostile to democracy. Either could shrink the democratic world.

Another shock is of a still different kind, suggesting again that the term is of dubious help to our purposes. It is the U.S. government's loss—a loss suffered by other nations as well—of a competent body of economic knowledge to guide macroeconomic policy. I suggest that it is not only clear that the U.S. government cannot cope with unemployment and inflation as well as it once could but also that the professional economics base for monetary and fiscal policy is in disarray. The world has changed, economic institutions and behavior have altered, in ways that have not been sufficiently grasped by the economics profession. Perhaps I should simply have said the shock is the loss of capacity to stabilize the economy, but I wish to point to the state of economics as a major source of that new incapacity.

What has the response been? Inflation and unemployment and slow growth. Has this unhappy situation stimulated the nation to undertake a special effort to study the institutional changes that render the old macro theory defective? On the whole, not. Instead, though left to themselves, economists are making some headway to grasp the institutional changes and incorporate them into useful new theory, economic discourse has tended to become more theological, ideological, and rigid, which makes a bad situation worse.

Some people see governmental failure to grapple successfully with economic stability and growth as part of a larger versatile failure in problem-solving capacity in government. They see the beginning of the failure in the shortcomings of President Johnson's war on poverty, and they are understandably alarmed as they see government falling short across the board: Public education that fails to teach children to read and is often mired down in maintaining no more than classroom discipline, drug importation and use that escapes control, toxic wastes that proliferate faster than they are cleaned up, environmental decay that continues apace despite some gains in clean air and water, school desegregation still obstructed, highways and bridges falling into decay, extraordinary waste in the military, anxieties about the finance of old-age pensions, welfare abuses, street crime, tax inequities and evasions, and, above all, international tension that threatens nuclear war.

The response to these fears? New ideas for reform of the policy-making process? Almost none. Agitation for discussion and action on reform? Almost none. Loss, so the polls tell us, of confidence in leadership, both in government and business. And not much incentive even to vote. Quiessence. Disillusionment.

A related feature of American politics these days is the thinness and incompetence of political debate, all the more remarkable in a nation that produced the *Federalist Papers*, and the Lincoln-Douglas debates. If these are critical times, domestically and internationally, debate does not rise to the occasion. In

Watergate, almost no one formulated any standards by which a president might be judged, acquiescing thus by default to the inappropriate notion that a president, like any other person, must be judged innocent until proved guilty—a principle that none of us would use in deciding whether to change physician or even television repairman. That a public official must meet a more severe test was rarely articulated and even more rarely discussed. In economic affairs, the Right offers not much more than the old liberal case for the self-regulating market; and the Center and Left seem to have found nothing even that consequential to preach. In international affairs, an American foreign policy that seems, as noted above, to have abandoned democracy is not persuasively defended; nor are its critics eloquent in their attack on it. The most searching attacks on it, like Chomsky and Herman's *Political Economy of Human Rights*, are labelled as too radical to warrant repeating or discussing; and, indeed, there is some, at least small, cause for suspecting that American society is boxed into a situation in which, given the homogeneity of American political opinion, any fresh idea worth discussing is by definition too radical to discuss.

Amidst all these notes of despair I see one cause for optimism, not for tomorrow but for a distant future, if we live that long. It is—I think I see—an emerging heterogeneity in American political opinion, a new skepticism, an irreverance long overdue toward American political and economic instututions. Now and for the immediate future, we appear to be in the grip of a new passion for old orthodoxies, thus the Right is ascendant. But I suggest that the underlying movement is toward questioning, diversity, challenge to old ideas: Thus the Left is growing in strength. Some of the evidence I find among my students. Doctrinaire free marketers edit undergraduate newspapers and journals these days, and their enthusiasms are conspicuous in undergraduate life. But among undergraduates, who continue to identify themselves as liberals, conservatives, and radicals in much the same proportions as before, many who call themselves liberal are radical just as many who used to call themselves liberal were conservative. The whole spectrum may be shifting to the left.

The radicalization of 1967 to 1971 has subsided; but a legacy remains and is not wholly wiped out by backsliding.

With larger numbers of young people going through college and eventually taking their parents' places in government and business, the U.S. will move, I suspect, glacially—which means slowly but unstoppably—toward the Left, which I shall be frank to say means to me toward intellectual liberation, toward questioning instead of faith, and toward new political and economic ideas for which students are hungry and which are not being adequately supplied by their elders.

In a genuinely liberal society practicing a competition of ideas, dissident and subversive ideas would be honored. It has long been the practice in American society, however, to discredit them, as illustrated in the common use of the word *agitator* or the word *subversive* to bring moral opprobrium down on someone. Among educated young people today, I believe the agitator and subversive, on whom our futures depend, are rising in status, however slowly—unless I am, as is possible, simply taking a fling at wishful thinking.

That new political insights may someday flourish and that new political energies may be thrown into solving the nation's problems may also be foretold in the rise of many new political movements, perhaps including new political activity in labor unions, but in any case embracing black politics, women's liberation, gays, and grey panthers. I shall even include members of the National Rifle Association and of the Moral Majority. All of them are learning that politics is more important than Americans used to think it was; and all are consequently thinking, at least a little bit more, about a great variety of political issues beyond the single issue by which some are identified.

Rising political turbulence, as a long-term trend, carries some risks of serious political disorder with it. Although I look on the turbulence as healthy for the future, the members of the Tri-Lateral Commission and a scattering of social scientists fear it, and would like the restive American citizen to subside again into passivity. The ungovernability of the emerging democracy is their fear, rather than the inefficacy of the established democracy, which is mine.

Who is right? Is the turbulence to be feared or applauded? To answer, we are driven into a re-examination of long-standing

American political institutions. What happened in American politics in the '70s was not simply a product of shocks or other events in those years but instead a product of an interaction between those events and established institutions. The effects of Vietnam, Watergate, oil prices, and the other distresses of the '80s hit us as they did because ours is a particular kind of polity.

It is a polity, as already noted, of a high degree of homogeneity in political thought, higher still than the still fairly high homogeneity of Western Europe. Our political alternatives are formulated for us—or are reflected for us—by two political parties between which differences are small, especially in view of the role of Southerners in the Democratic Party. For almost all Americans, significantly dissident thought—even the only moderately dissident thought of non-Marxist American democratic socialists—is beyond the pale. Journals that see political alternatives as wider than those endorsed by the major parties enjoy only tiny readerships, and the crippling of political discourse is again nicely illustrated by the narrowness of debate on the much-admired McNeill/Lehrer television program on public issues. Hence at its foundations, the American polity is crippled. Its mind cannot range widely over its problems and alternative possible solutions.

Thus, for example, Vietnam became a national tragedy for both Vietnam and the U.S. Frustrated in its early attempts in Vietnam, the U.S. was incapable of rethinking not only means but ends. Communists are bad guys, Ho Chi Minh was a communist, Ho Chi Minh was a bad guy. So shoot! The analysis was almost that simple, and it was frozen into that form.

Why this homogeneity and resulting crippling of practical political thought in the U.S.? You can speculate as well as I. Its origins must lie well back in history. I suggest that one part of the story is to be found in the role of socio-economic class in American society. Scholars often comment on the relative absence of class conflict in America. What they often miss is that its absence may be attributable to the overwhelming success of upper strata in instilling their values in all strata. In that sense, the U.S. is the most, not the least, class-ridden society among the Western democracies, (compare, however, Japan on this dimension). We do not enjoy and profit from the competition of ideas that attends a more open expression of class conflict.

The new turbulence of American politics is, then, perhaps less to be feared as a democratic distemper and more to be applauded as the beginning of a wider and less rigid competition of ideas. But those who fear it sometimes point to one of its most disturbing (in their eyes) aspects: the escalation of demands on the political system, including the proliferation and then dogged defense of many forms of "entitlement," including all those of the welfare state, as well as new entitlements for Blacks, females, the handicapped, the elderly, and so on. Many of the critics of the new turbulence distinguish sharply, though more by their silence than by reasoned argument, between these widespread popular entitlements and new entitlements for business enterprises, as presaged by new forms of guarantee for Lockheed and Chrysler.

I do indeed believe that the aggregate of demands on government has become excessive, especially since some of the various demands are inconsistent with others. Government cannot both satisfy a demand for deregulation of pharmaceuticals testing and a demand for new testing programs. The excess of demands reflects new democratic agitation, one of the fountainheads of it being the welfare legislation of Franklin Roosevelt, on which base the demands have grown ever since.

But why excessive? Given the thinness of political debate, the customary answer is that the new demands of the last few decades, including those of the '70s, add up to more than can possibly be supplied. But clearly they do not. That the aggregate is too large is not because the new demands are too large but because the total of new and old demands is too large. But if you come to the table intending to eat and find that I arrived early and laid claim to a disproportionate share of the food, is the excess of claims on the food to be attributed to you, with your modest demands, or to me in my already advantageous position, or to the conflict between us?

The problem of excessive demand arises because the newcomers to the table at which income, political power, and the other values of social life are served find that long-established earlier claimants do not yield. Some observers of the alleged democratic distemper are distressed that the newcomers will not go away; they fear political disorder from the conflict that will increasingly exacerbate. I am inclined to applaud the new-comers, recognizing, however, that to avert political disorder the established claimants must yield.

The problem of excessive claims, present in the '70s and still to be with us for decades to come, was forestalled through much of the nineteenth century in three ways, two of which are declining in efficacy. First, an approach to the table by new-comers was fairly successfully aborted by ideology. Some ven-tures toward the table were tried, like the pre-Civil War labor union movement and the Populists later in the century; but they were turned back. On the whole, masses of people remained convinced that demands on the state for themselves were inap-propriate. That, they somehow learned and believed. Their docility left room for demands on the state from more politically aggressive minorities, as, for example, in the demands of canal and railroad builders for subsidies, or the demands of busi-nessmen for limited liability and other privileges which consti-tute the defining and enabling powers of the modern corpor-ation.

The ideological barrier to an excess of demands shows signs of substantial erosion, as indicated above in the gentle radicali-zation of college students and the proliferation of "liberation" movements. The next barrier still stands in great strength, how-ever. It is a constitutional law and tradition, implemented by many specific provisions of the law, that litters the political landscape with possibilities open to many participants in politics to veto the initiatives of others. In American politics, it is difficult to move, and few officials can even try. But it is easy to stop, and many officials do cry halt. Thus the President can veto Congress. Congress can refuse the President his programs. States can veto the Federal government, and vice versa. A congressional budgetary committee can veto enabling legis-lation by blocking funds. The House can veto the Senate, and the Senate, the House. And each of dozens of House and Senate Committees can stop action by the full house.

This great feature of American policy making is often defend-ed on the ground that it protects personal liberty from an overly powerful state. Whether it does or not, my point here is that it protects long-established claims on government and makes it realtively easy to veto new ones, thus exerting a powerful influence to block the claims of newcomers who have dared approach the table. I should also digress to point out that the proliferation of points of veto in American government helps explain its general incapacity, noted above, as a versatile problem solver. The distribution of power to veto is a designed crippling of the American government.

The third barrier to newcomers who reach the table is another kind of veto, one even more widely distributed in society than the veto authority resting in the hands of many kinds of government officials. It is the veto of government action, a veto that is invoked in the form of a claim to the rights of private property. The rights of private property—not your and my rights to own a bicycle but the rights of property to operate business enterprises—obstructed even early attempts at legislative protection of women and children in industry and today obstruct tax reform, public utility regulation, antitrust, labor legislation—in fact, there is no end to the list of problem areas in which the law of private property does not impose limits on government.

And that is fortunate for us all, most of you will say, because it guards us against too powerful a government and maintains an institutional system—the market system—through which the economy is better organized than if private property in production were greatly curbed. Those two allegations need not be debated at this point. Whatever the merits of private property in production, it is nevertheless a source of a crippling of the state—for good or bad—and, specifically, an enormously broad and strong wall of protection around the rights of those already at the table. Whatever its merits, private property in production does cripple the state as a problem solver and does militate against a reconciliation of new and old demands on the state. It is also the great entitlement that deprecates the newer and still emerging forms of political entitlement now under attack in Washington. It is an issue in almost every political conflict. One cannot otherwise understand the '70s (or any other period), including the popular attacks on business by environmental and other movements in the '70s and the active counterattack of business on them that soon followed.

Of these three barriers to new political demands, ideology seems to be in greatest decline, the vetoes of private property in some significant decline, the vetoes of government officials the most firmly maintained. And that raises another issue.

Because of the already noted thinness of political debate in the U.S., the possibility is not much investigated that a major cause of American inability to deal better with its problems is the fundamental structure of the Federal government. Not even academic political scientists bother much with such a question about fundamentals. Such an explanation deserves consideration, however.

To be sure, the decline of political parties has been noted with alarm. That the American government is too fragmented is another thesis about fundamental political structure that has also been given considerable airing. The debate on fragmentation has, on the whole, failed to make an elementary distinction: between fragmentation of responsibility to act, on the one hand, and fragmentation of authority to veto, on the other. The first, which is indiscriminately maligned in the attack on fragmentation, may be desirable both for efficiency and to protect freedom. It is the second that is more questionable.

Beyond these two issues, however, are many other questions about the structure of the Federal government. For one example, the incompetence of the process by which the president is chosen, as witnessed by a string of presidents since Franklin Roosevelt whose qualifications for office were in most cases dubious by any thoughtful appraisal. Or, for another example, the creation, through presidential selection of his closest advisors, of a private "cabinet" that need not consist of persons who have emerged as national leaders or who have not even had to pass serious congressional scrutiny. Or, for still another example, staffs for members of the House and Senate that permit members to undertake a variety of activities, such as doing favors for constituents, rather than attending to policy making. Members of both House and Senate have financed their own aggrandizement. They need not cooperate with their fellows, need not develop common policy ground, need not pool their fact-gathering and analyzing resources—in short, need not act in the role of members of a legislative assembly coping with the nation's problems. They have the budgets and staffs to make their reputations in many other ways.

All these examples point to at least a possibility that the present, largely unquestioned, design of American governed is itself a problem that helps account for our difficulties in the '70s, as well as those to be expected in the '80s and beyond. We are governed by presidents of dubious qualifications, often working with teams of cronies rather than experienced political leaders, and deferred to by congressmen and senators many of whom pursue interests more pressing to them than problem solving for the nation. That is the state of affairs to which the American constitutional tradition had brought us in the '70s.

Finally, to return to shocks of the 1970s, let me tell you of one I still feel, all the more so because my shock is that it shocks almost no one else. I hope only a few of you will dismiss my sense of shock as frivolous. Architecture, we are now being told by various students of society, tells us a great deal about the minds and sentiments of those who commission it. It is easy to believe that the American commitment to democracy is indeed symbolized architecturally in Washington: for example, in the design and placement of the Capitol building, in the Lincoln and Jefferson monuments, in the veneration shown George Washington by the central placement of his monument, and by the deeply respectful display of The Declaration of Independence and the Constitution. In the '70s the Federal government erected a splendid building, a monument in itself rather than no more than a practical office building as might have been devised, located among the great edifices and shrines of the nation, for the nation's police department, the Federal Bureau of Investigation. A symbolic error only? Or a significant statement? A trend?

Look further. Under its long-time chief, the Bureau, we came finally to realize, practiced a variety of forms of illegal surveillance and harassment of citizens such as, among many others, Martin Luther King, whose only offense to democracy was that he wished to extend its privileges. With this building, an enthusiastic Congress has chosen to honor an organization deeply troubling to friends of democracy and, beyond that, to honor the official who led it down antidemocratic paths, naming the edifice after him and engraving his name boldly on it, despite his hostility to civil liberties. It is a better symbol of a police state than of a democracy. Perhaps Congress was less malicious than careless in this venture. But if eternal vigilance is the price of liberty, our many congressmen have failed to meet a payment. And do not even know that they have failed.

6

Democracy and the Economy (1983)

Today's question is: What is the effect on democracy of our economic institutions? By "our institutions" I refer to those of North America and Western Europe.

One familiar answer is that no democratic nation state has ever developed except in a market-oriented economy. That is a deeply impressive historical fact.

A second familiar answer attempts to explain the historical relationship and predicts that it will continue: if no market system, then no democracy. The explanation is that in the Western democracies, vast and divisive tasks of economic organization are turned over to the market system. The peaceful processes of political democracy are possible only because potential disruptive strains are kept out of politics and settled in the market.

A third familiar answer to the question on effects of economy on democracy proceeds in two steps: (1) the core institutions of democracy are those that support personal freedom; and (2) only market systems provide consumer free choice, occupational free choice, and a wide range of other free choices in exchange relationships without which further political liberties are impossible.[1]

A fourth familiar answer is also in two steps. It is that (1) institutions of these countries are established and reshaped from time to time by democratic political processes; and (2) that fact is sufficient to qualify them as democratic.

Although each of these four reassuring answers is inconclusive—for example, the historical dependence of democracy on

---

1 These arguments run through many of the writings of Friedrich von Hayek: for example, *The Constitution of Liberty* (Chicago: University of Chicago, 1960). They can also be found in Frank Knight, "The Meaning of Democracy," in Knight, *Freedom and Reform* (New York: Harper and Brothers, 1947).

market system may change in the future—each answer is weighty; none can be simply dismissed. Nevertheless, I pass over them today and move on to other arguments. I do so because these familiar arguments have long been discussed. I want to consider new arguments and refinements of old arguments that point to possible adverse consequences for democracy of our economic institutions. That is, I want to look at the other side of the coin.

I shall approach the arguments about adverse effects on democracy by an indirect route, beginning with an examination of constitutional and democratic authority.

I. Constitutional and Democratic Authority

A fundamental phenomenon of political life is the distinction between rulers and ruled. With the exception of some very small political groups, politics requires leaders, hence also followers. It calls for proximate or immediate decision makers, hence also ordinary subjects or citizens. In some terminologies, it calls for elites, hence also mass. For our purposes, we treat as synonymous the terms *rulers, leaders, proximate decision makers,* and *elite*.

To identify a ruler or act of ruling, look for three conditions. First, a relatively small number of persons control a large number of persons. Second, their controls are highly asymmetric in that rulers exercise controls over subjects that are not matched by roughly equivalent reciprocal control of subject over ruler. Thirdly, the controls are exercised in purposive attempts of rulers to achieved tasks of organization and coordination, either for some public good or for exploitation.

Ruling is an asymmetric relationship, I have just said. But I did not say that the ruler has unilateral power over the ruled. For the ruled always have at least some small power over the ruler. Democracy is an institution that gives the ruler substantial powers over the ruled. Yet democratic rulers are still rulers. In any large political system, the most democratic ruler imaginable must exercise organizing and coordinating controls over ordinary subject/citizens in a relation of asymmetry. To speak with any precision at all, democracy is not self-rule. In the best of democracies, we ordinary citizens entrust rule to a group of officials, whom we hope to constrain and direct but whose function as our rulers we cannot eliminate.

We need rulers to organize and administer such tasks as the education of the young, the adjudication of disputes among citizens, the provision of pensions to the aged, national defense, the accumulation of capital for economic growth, and the deployment of the nation's mineral resources to various uses. In addition, in many circumstances in world history, rulers seize ruling functions not because we need their services but because they hope to subject us to their wills for their own advantage.

Consider now constitutionalism as a movement in political theory, ideology, and political practice to constrain rulers: specifically, to convert naked and arbitrary ruling power into less harsh, more predictable, and more controllable forms of control over us. Historically "we"—meaning various groups of people in different times and places—have tried to establish rule only by legally constituted authority. We have tried to arrange the political order so that we are ruled by persons authorized—given authority—to rule us rather than be ruled by persons who are simply stronger, more predatory, or better armed.

What are the specific conditions we seek to impose in order to constrain and direct rulers in suitable ways? The list is familiar and understandable.

1. That when authority is granted it be accompanied by responsibility of that authority to act. No power without responsibility.

2. That authority be granted to a role player not a named person. Thus we confer authority on a prime minister; the authority is granted to whoever qualifies for that role.

3. That one who holds authority use it for assigned public purposes but not for his private purposes.

4. That the holder of authority cannot transfer it to another, although he can delegate some of it to subordinates under his supervision. And it does not pass to his inheritors, as traditional royal power passes to offspring.

A fifth condition is difficult to enforce and is often violated. Nevertheless, we do try to provide

5. That the holder of the authority use it only for limited prescribed purposes.

In particular, with respect to this fifth condition, we try to prevent the holder of authority from employing his authority in an extended way to acquire more authority. One of many possible examples of what we try to prevent is the construction of a political machine. When, say, a mayor of Chicago uses his authority over jobs and municipal contracts to make people dependent on him so that they will vote as he tells them and make financial contributions to purposes he selects, he succeeds in developing an extra-legal organization over which he exercises authority beyond that originally conferred on him. Finally, a sixth condition:

6. That the exercise of authority be subject to a large body of procedural rules that assure "due process."

These six conditions specify the elementary or fundamental requirements of acceptable rulers or acceptable acts of rule over us. Let us look at the list again to see what unacceptable practices we have ruled out. Here I will, point by point, rewrite the list to specify not what is required but what we intend to prohibit.

1′ A grant of authority that imposes no responsibility to act.
2′ Authority that is granted to named persons rather than role players.
3′ Authority that is used for private purposes.
4′ Holders of authority who are free to transfer it to other persons as they wish by giving it away, selling it or passing it to offspring.
5′ Authority that is broadly granted so that it can be used to pursue a wide variety of purposes. Thus authority that can be used to gain authority, including authority to create a machine.
6′ Authority that is subject to relatively few procedural rules. The many restrictions of "due process" do not apply to it.

I believe that most of us would say that such a list as this one describes a thoroughly unacceptable set of rules for persons in authority. The list seems to characterize an earlier set of pre-constitutional rules no longer considered acceptable in constitutional or democratic systems. It seems to describe irresponsible power.

But consider. What is the contemporary significance of this second list? Where have we seen it? Is there something familiar about it, aside from its characterization of times past? Take note that each rule in the second list specifies a right—for example, a right to use authority for private purpose.

The second list is a set of rules or rights known as the law of private property. Private property in the means of production is a set of rules that confers authority over the society's resources. The rules impose no responsibility to act or to employ the resources in any public interest. Authority is granted to named persons, may be used for private purposes, can be given away, sold, bequeathed. And its exercise is subject to few procedural rules, unlike the due process rules that constrain governmental authorities.

The use of the authority of property to gain other authority—for example, to build a machine—is at the core of an understanding of property rights as rights to authority. Holders of authority over the society's resources create machines that are called business enterprises, which are wholly legal, while the machine of the political authority is either extra-legal or illegal. Like machine politicians, propertied holders of authority use their authority over property to make conditional offers of employment and conditional offers to buy other required inputs; hence, they become the ruling authorities in organizations, small and large, some of them vast.

Ruling powers based on property rights are not exercised only within the enterprise. Businessmen, who derive their powers over resources from property rights, make consequent decisions that rule all of us, whether employees or not, with respect to the technologies to be employed in economic life, industrial structure, air pollution, the health hazards of food additives, the safety of complex products like automobiles, the rate of capital accumulation, the allocation of resources to alternative possible uses, engagement in overseas commerce, and so on. Thus in the market-oriented systems, for the major organizing and coordinating tasks of society, there are two major groups of high authorities, leaders, or rulers: holders of governmental authorities and businessmen. Neither exercises conspicuously less ruling authority that the other, even if there are some functions that are entrusted to government officials exclusively.

For some decisions of persons who draw their authority from private property rules, we the public exert significant control through what we buy or refuse to buy. But that does not deny that these holders of authority are our rulers any more than elections of government officials deny that government officials are our rulers.

Some conventional "classical" interpretations of market relations overlook rulers and ruling through the rules of private property because they characterize market relations as simple buying and selling relations between two parties, each more or less equivalently controlling the other.[2] But that interpretation simply overlooks the ruling relation that develops between a selling corporation that must make many ruling decisions on product, technology, investment, and the like before it can even offer a product to millions of consumers. Such decisions, like governmental decisions on budget, foreign policy, or regional development, have to be made by a small group of proximate decision makers, that is, by a set of rulers.

Private property is not simply a set of rulers or rights with respect to personal assets: clothing, a watch or bicycle, perhaps a car or a house. The rules known by the name of private property do indeed apply to personal assets. But their larger significance is that they are a set of rules establishing authority over the society's productive resources and that, through the extended use of that authority, holders of it gain a wide authority over tasks of social organization and coordination, parallel to the authority of elected and appointed government officials.

You cannot have escaped noticing that I have presented the rules of private property in a way calculated to throw suspicion

2 For an interesting and sustained critique of these "classical" interpretations, see Samuel Bowles and Herbert Gintis, "The Power of Capital: On the Inadequacy of the Conception of the Capitalist Economy as 'Private,'" 14 *The Philosophical Forum* (Spring–Summer 1983).

on them, even to make them look indefensible. They are, however, defensible in that many informed and thoughtful people make a defense for them, despite the appearance I have given them here. This they do not by denying what I have said about them but by pleading in effect extenuating circumstances. Property rules, they will argue, work well despite those questionable features of them to which I am calling your attention. They organize production efficiently—that would be the most common claim for them. Or they do not, after all, permit irresponsible exercise of authority because competition between firms limits the discretionary authority of each holder of authority in the market.

Nevertheless, we have now seen the rules of property, as they operate in the market system, in such a light as to have to acknowledge the possibility that they are not at all satisfactory, that they are a set of rules that permits irresponsibility in the exercise of authority, and that they are not, consequently, consistent with democratic aspiration. That is the first important conclusion I come to today. I call into question the basic rules of private property as neither constitutional nor democratic.

Perhaps, however, the irresponsibility of propertied rule and its departures from constitutional and democratic practice will look different on a closer view. Fair enough. Let us look closer. Let us examine in more detail the possibilities that the authority of our market rulers is an obstacle to democracy. We begin with possibilities of undemocratic rule within the market system itself—that is, not in the state but in the market.

II. Undemocratic Rule within the Market System?

Perhaps most thoughtful and informed observers these days acknowledge that, with respect to employees, the corporation is authoritarian rather than democratic. Labor union influence softens that authoritarianism but by no means eliminates it. Some observers say it does not matter. They believe that democracy in the workplace is not required if citizens can enjoy the benefits of democracy outside the workplace. Or they argue that the undeniable values of democracy within the workplace have to be sacrificed for the sake of efficiency, despite growing claims, which clearly have not convinced them, that workplace democracy is efficient.[3] Other observers will simply claim that, if democratic political processes choose to perpetuate conventional authority in the workplace, then the authority of employer over employee is no more undemocratic than the authority of teacher over student, police over lawbreaker, or minister of industry over personnel in his ministry. Yet there remain many unanswered questions about workplace democracy. A later lecture in this series will attend to them.

As for rule by businessmen over all the rest of us, is it democratic or not? The most common claim is that consumers democratically control their business rulers by voting with their dollars, pounds, or lire. For many business decisions, consumers indeed do achieve popular control. Businessmen cannot long go on producing what no one will buy, nor will they fail ordinarily to produce what consumers stand ready to buy. But in this case, popular control is far from democratic control, for, as everyone knows, in the market some people have thousands, even millions of votes, and others have only a few or none. Here we come clearly face to face with a feature of authority in the market that does not nicely fit democratic aspiration. It is a feature—great inequality in popular control over authority—that is often defended on one ground or another—that it is necessary, for example, to provide incentives. Whatever the defense, control by voting with money is far removed from the egalitarian element in democratic thought.

Another familiar line of thought about undemocratic rule in the market is on externalities, earlier often referred to as *third-party* or *neighborhood effects of transactions*. If, at least under idealized circumstances, one can make an argument that the two parties to a transaction are free to exchange with each other or not as they please and that, consequently, neither is coerced, it has long been recognized that third parties are coerced. They are coerced, for example, to accept patterns of land use negotiated by buyers and sellers of land in transactions to which they were not a party. They may see pleasant rural land around their dwellings turned into ugly, noisy, and polluted industrial

3 These claims, as well as other aspects of workplace authority and workplace democratization, are examined in Carole Pateman, *Participation and Democratic Theory* (Cambridge: Cambridge University Press, 1970).

areas—all because of decisions of other people and over which they had no influence.

Again, these familiar observations I pass over simply because they are familiar. I would like to call your attention instead to a feature of market systems not yet sufficiently articulated despite its relevance to democracy in the market. In the market system, consumers, I have just said, can constrain and generally direct their rulers by buying or refusing to buy. In so far as that is true, they "vote" with money rather than ballots and vote perhaps even more effectively than with ballots. But the vote is curiously limited.

It is true that you and I can in that way vote for or against each of the enormous variety of products and services offered us. But you and I cannot vote in that way for our preferred technology, location of industry, organization and discipline of the workforce, or preferred method of executive recruitment and remuneration. Even more specifically, we cannot vote yes or no on the use of asbestos in products, or on the pollution of air and water. These decisions are, we might say, "delegated" to business managers, largely without constraint or direction through our purchases. Notice that the problem is not quite the same as the old problem of externalities or third-party injuries. The problem is an injury to me, a party to the exchange—a first or second but not a third party—and I cannot protect myself by "voting" with my dollars or lire. In the mechanism of the market, there is no procedure for popular or democratic or consumer control over these delegated decisions. The classical argument that consumers can control holders or propertied authority breaks down.

In conventional economic theory, it appears to have been assumed that consumers had no interest in the delegated decisions other than that they be made economically, and it was further assumed that competition among enterprises would force economical decisions on each businessman. Thus each manager would choose the lowest-cost technology for any given product and the lowest-cost location. Given the technological complexity of contemporary industry, there is no clear lowest-cost solution to production problems, and managers must exercise a broad discretion, over which consumers have almost no constraining control except for cost reduction. And, again given modern technology, consumers do now care—and care great-ly—about location, about chemicals used in industry, and about other delegated decisions that greatly affect their welfare. The older assumption that delegated decisions did not matter to consumers is therefore no longer valid. They care; and, within the rules of market authority, they can do nothing about it.

But perhaps this defect of democratic rule in the market system can be and is corrected by democratic politics. Govern-mental regulation of business—for example, governmental regu-lation of air pollution—can remedy through government those defects in market rule that consumers cannot remedy through voting with dollars and lire. With this possibility, many of us try to assure ourselves that authority based on property poses no obstacle to democracy. We must therefore now ask: Does the democratic state in fact give us democratic control of what we have called delegated decisions in the market system?

III. Influence of Propertied Authority on State Authority

In an oft-repeated principle of obscure origin, the authority of the highest officials in government—say, of chief executive and cabinet or legislature—is sufficient to design, restrict, or other-wise rewrite the authority that derives from the rights of prop-erty. And those whose authority derives from property rights have no authority to specify what authority is to reside with the government officials. Among others, however, Marxist thought has denied the clear domination of state over propertied authority. Often the relevant argument is that, although proper-tied authority is not itself sufficient to specify the authority of the state, propertied authority is employed in extended ways so that the state is reduced in its effective authority and cannot control the allocation of authority through property. In short, in Marxist language, the question is raised as to whether the state is autonomous; and the Marxian answers are either that its autonomy is at least significantly limited or that its autonomy is drastically curtailed by features of the economy.

If the state cannot control the authority of property and the powers of property built on the extended use of its authority, then we cannot count on the state to establish democratic control over what we have called delegated decisions in the market. The conclusion would be even broader than that. We cannot count on the state to correct any features of market rule that are undemocratic. The state may succeed in some efforts to correct them, but it will fail in others, and perhaps fail to a degree in all.

That the state is significantly limited by features of the economy is argued in many ways. Marxian doctrine that characterizes economy as foundation and state as no more than superstructure illustrates one way. Arguments based on class solidarity and bourgeois class domination of the state illustrate another. The two lines of argument often mesh.[4] Somewhat more modest arguments argue an intimacy of connection between market and state that limits the autonomy of both. These are intimacies, for example, through family connection or elite educational institutions, which both government and business leaders alike attend. Again I pass over familiar lines of analysis not because they are without merit but because they have already been much discussed. I go on instead to a particular line of argument about limitations on the autonomy of the state arising out of what I have elsewhere described as the privileged position of business in the politics of the state.[5]

This line of argument can be summarized as follows:

1. In market-oriented systems, there are, as we have already seen, two major groups of organizing and coordinating rulers: those who exercise state authority and those who exercise authority derived from the rules of private property: in short, government officials and business officials. Both are essential to us all.

2. The second group, business officials, cannot be commanded to discharge their essential functions, for they are not assigned responsibility with their authority. (And a general attempt generally to command them would constitute a termination of property rights in the means of production and an abandonment of the market system.)

4 They can be found throughout the Marxian literature: for example, in Nicos Poulantzas, *Political Power and Social Classes* (London: New Left Review Books, 1978); in Ralph Miliband, *The State in Capitalist Society* (New York: Basic Books, 1969); and in Miliband's reply in 59 *New Left Review* (January—February 1970); in Poulantzas's review of Miliband in "The Problem of the Capitalist State," 58 *New Left Review* (November–December 1969).
5 Lindblom, *Politics and Markets* (New York: Basic Books, 1977), Ch. 13.

3. They must be induced, gratified, indulged, or rewarded to give them incentive to perform necessary tasks of social organization or coordination.

4. Sufficient inducement does not arise spontaneously. Historically, and still today in underdeveloped economies, inducements have been provided or strengthened through governmental regulation and supply of credit, appropriate monetary policies; river, railroad, highway and airways development; tax concessions; subsidies; protected markets; development of overseas markets, sometimes through military force; curbing of labor union activity; research and development; occupational training; and the like. Precisely what is needed to stimulate business incentives varies somewhat from decade to decade and from country to country.

5. Weakness of incentives leads to economic stagnation, and specifically to unemployment.

6. Governmental rulers in the democracies are usually fearful of being turned out of office if the economy stagnates and unemployment rises.

7. Hence governments in these systems warp democracy to give high priority to devising such policies as businessmen want. This they are driven to do independently of any electoral pressure from businessmen. Indeed they will often identify needed changes in government policy to stimulate business incentive even before businessmen themselves explicitly ask for them.

8. Businessmen consequently achieve not a complete domination of the state but a degree of control over the state entirely disproportionate to their numbers, hence a degree of control over the state that does not satisfy the requirements of democracy.

It might be objected that many groups in society whose services are needed will not perform them without incentives to do so, hence they can, in effect, make disproportionate demands on government officials. Physicians who otherwise refuse to offer medical services have in some countries achieved a disproportionate control over government medical services. Unions can threaten to strike.

The point is valid. But there is a difference. Although many groups can here and there disproportionately influence public policy, no group is so situated as to achieve a constant, broad, and massive influence on policy. For businessmen as rulers in their market domain are the organizers of major social tasks, the more or less successful discharge of which is necessary to national survival and welfare. That is not true of any other group. A nationwide discontent of industrial workers has no necessary impact on public policy and may indeed not even be noticed unless it is made into an organized campaign. A nationwide discontent of businessmen leads immediately to slowed investment and unemployment, and that is true even if they do not articulate, discuss, or agree on such a reaction.

I want to stress that the privileged position of business in government arises because government officials understand that they must, at peril to themselves, meet business needs and not because businessmen enter into interest-group and party politics. But businessmen do in addition do so. It becomes apparent to businessmen that what they need in government policy may be contradicted by what voters ask for through their votes, their interest-group activity, and their other forms of political agitation and pressure—what I shall call *electoral activity*. Businessmen consequently try to turn popular electoral activity in a direction that supports or at least does not interfere with policies responsive to the privileged position of business. They enter into the interest-group activity of citizens, sponsoring some groups rather than others. They become the major source of financing for candidates and parties and thus undercut the dependence of candidates and parties on ordinary voters. In short, their privileged political position they reinforce with electoral activity.

Although research on finance of electoral activity is inadequate in all the Western democracies, limited as it is to counting the most obvious sources of campaign finance, it is probable that business sources provide the largest source of funds, exceeding by far labor union and all other sources. Businessmen enjoy an enormous advantage in financing political movements, interest-groups, parties, and candidates, for while ordinary citizens must tap their own incomes for such purposes, businessmen can divert corporate receipts into political activities of their own choosing. The grossly disproportionate influence of businessmen on electoral activity, and their ability to tap corporate funds for their own private political objectives, cannot be squared with democracy.

Both the privileged position of business and the advantages of businessmen in participation in electoral politics are often defended as necessary if market systems are to work successfully. Indeed, as I have said, they are necessary in order to provide for businessmen the incentives that they require as a condition of performing their essential functions. But that defense does not deny their adverse effect on democracy. At best that defense simply claims that the adverse effects are worth suffering for the sake of economic efficiency. That is to say, in our kind of system, efficiency is costly and is paid for by some surrender of democracy.

IV. Propertied Authority and the Control of Our Minds

We have now seen that democracy suffers both from direct market rule by holders of propertied authority and from the influence of those same holders of authority on the authority of the state. Thus we have established a two-fold set of adverse consequences of the economy on democracy. We now need to examine a third, which we identify in its own right although it might be seen alternatively as subsumed under the first two sets of adverse consequences.

Consider the possibility that conflicts between business requirements for public policy conflict with democratic electoral demands on policy and that business electoral participation fails to bend interest groups, candidates, and parties enough to eliminate the conflict. This might become the case because of some long-standing hostility to business needs. Those whose authority derives from private property constantly fear this possibility. Hence they undertake a steady propaganda designed to reduce any fundamental popular hostility to business needs. They do so both by teaching popular attitudes favorable to business and, more commonly perhaps, by teaching and in other ways inducing political acquiescence or docility.

Again, these phenomena are not well researched in any country. Whatever their frequency or magnitude, business communications designed to forestall electoral hostility to business take at least three forms the identification of which helps clarify the phenomenon. First, in all these systems, businessmen subject consumers to a barrage of messages urging them to find their satisfactions in purchases. It is reasonable to suppose, though systematic evidence has not been collected, that the barrage diverts citizens away from critical political judgment and toward acquiescing in existing political institutions and processes. They are turned toward spending as the major means of improving their lives.

Secondly, businessmen subject consumer citizens to a steady flow of commercial messages that, though not urging a purchase, attempt to teach confidence in business enterprises. An example is a flood of television broadcasting in the United States on energy exploration by petroleum corporations. These broadcasts contain no explicit political message. They leave an inference, however, that, since the oil companies are eagerly seeking new sources of energy, new governmental fuel conservation programs or new regulations of the industry are not necessary.

Third, businessmen subject citizens to a drumming of messages with explicit political content: Thus, explicit advocacy of free enterprise, or explicit identification of dissenters as disreputable agitators, or explicit denigration of radical thought as reprehensible rather than praiseworthy, or explicit defenses of inequality.

On none of these forms of political communication has research taken the trouble to measure the flow of communications from propertied origins in comparison with the flow from other origins. Again, however, such clues as we have, some of which I have identified in *Politics and Markets*,[6] point to a gross disproportion from business sources. The tracking of sources is complicated by a heritage of centuries of indoctrination from older sources now replaced by business. Hundreds of years ago lord and priest sought to indoctrinate the masses in unquestioning faith, loyalty, docility, and acceptance of inequality. So effectively have these messages been taught that parents and school teachers pass them on to offspring and students. Hence business messages that seek to teach acceptance of the authority

6 Lindblom, *Politics and Markets* (New York: Basic Books, 1977), Chs. 14 through 17.

of property, of its inequalities, of loyalty to the existing order, and a docile acceptance of leadership and distrust of dissenters need do little more than perpetuate old indoctrinations in language appropriate to the contemporary world.

To make these allegations is, of course, to take one side of a continuing argument. Does the ordinary citizen in a democracy actually enjoy the benefit of the competition of ideas which liberal thought prizes? Or, on the other hand, is he greatly curbed in the opinions he manages to entertain?

Not so many years ago, scholars often told us that propaganda, regardless of source, was not ineffective in changing minds. Their studies, however, were of messages over short time spans, such as an election campaign. We now know that propaganda can be powerful in curbing thought when, as does business propaganda, it persists for a lifetime, seeks to reinforce inherited opinions rather than stimulate new ones, and urges passivity rather than action.[7]

How much indoctrination is there? It is a crucial issue. For only if citizens possess significant capacity for critical political thought can we make a strong argument that elections are an important method for giving citizens democratic control over public policy. If their minds are crippled on political issues, then democracy is in some significant degree a sham, for they can use their popular control only to pursue policies they have been indoctrinated to prefer.

Can we today make any further headway in estimating the significance of propaganda from those who hold propertied authority? We shall try to make a contribution to the debate, not by citing examples of indoctrination but by looking at indirect or circumstantial evidence. Our analysis will not be conclusive but it will be illuminating and can advance the debate.

In all societies, even those called democratic, citizens reach a high degree of agreement on many highly complex political-economic issues. For example, a small minority of dissidents aside, continuing inequality in the distribution of wealth is almost everywhere accepted. Some people give positive prin-

7 Michael Mann, "The Social Cohesion of Liberal Democracy," 35 *American Sociological Review* (June, 1970).

cipled endorsement to inequality. Others simply uncritically accept the status quo. Or, for another example, despite disagreement on the merits of private enterprise, in all Western societies, only a few dissidents question the merit of the market system. Some evidence of that agreement is that in not a single market oriented democracy past or present has a government ever attempted to dispense with the market system, except in wartime emergency.

How does it happen that on complex social issues citizens come to share an overwhelming agreement? Agreement cannot be simply a multiple coincidence. It is a pattern somehow achieved for which an explanation is necessary. Given the complexity of many social issues, we would expect a variety of opinions to be in active competition and opinions to be diverse. Since on many we see that they are not diverse, we must ask why. Why does diversity give way to agreement?

The most common answer is tradition. The term *tradition* refers to the passing of a belief or practice from one generation to another. But tradition can account either for passing down a variety of diverse opinions or passing down an agreement. If tradition passes down agreement, we must ask how the agreement was formed. Tradition itself forms nothing, it only communicates it. Hence tradition does not explain why people agree.

Do people agree because their own life experiences are alike? The life experiences of our grandparents were not the same as ours; nor is the experience of the urban rich the same as that of the rural poor; nor is the experience of the highly educated the same as that of the unschooled. We must reject this explanation too as invalid.

Sometimes it is suggested that agreement spontaneously develops. Just what that means is not clear. If, however, it means that effective communications arise in many ways from many sources in response to many stimuli, then, again, we would expect spontaneous diversity rather than agreement. Again, the explanation has to be rejected.

Another kind of analysis sometimes offered as explanation runs in the following way: Democracy can exist only if conflicts are dampened by social agreement on fundamental rules and values. That is to say, agreement is a requirement for democracy. The proposition may be false. But even if it is true, it is no explanation of agreement at all. It is simply an allegation that only if agreement comes about is democracy possible. Whether it comes about, it does not say. How it might come about, it does not say.

A similar argument is anthropological. All societies, it is argued, are characterized by agreed beliefs. That is what makes them societies rather than mere collections of people. Again, we must reject this as an explanation of how the agreement is achieved. On that point it has nothing to offer—only the allegation that agreement occurs.

Next, however, we come to an explanation that is valid. People can—and often will—agree when they are brought to agreement by knowledge. People agree that the earth revolves around the sun because they know that it does. That is not a tautology. Agreeing and knowing are not the same. People can agree in ignorance or because they know something. When they all know something about a world that is the same world for all of them, then that knowledge brings them to agreement. If they all can observe the same reality, they can agree.

I do not mean that we agree that the earth revolves around the sun because we are all amateur astronomers. For our knowledge we often rely on observers other than ourselves. But if each observer on whom each of us relies knows the same reality, all observers will agree; and we who rely on them will then also agree.

Knowledge, then, explains many agreements. It still, however, leaves many politico-economic agreements unexplained. For we do not know that inequality in the distribution of wealth is a good thing, or that political docility is a good thing, or that market systems are desirable. The near universal agreement on these issues is to be distinguished sharply from knowledge. All these issues are beyond the range of actual knowledge. Indeed, it seems highly probable that disagreement on these issues is greatest among the most knowledgeable members of society. I do not deny that you or I may be quite convinced of our positions on each of such issues. But firmly as we hold to our opinions, we cannot point to knowledge as sufficient to explain such agreement as we find about us. Critics of market society, though few in number, make highly persuasive critical arguments and can draw on information no less successfully than advocates. We do not *know*, we can only believe, that market systems are desirable.

How then do we explain what continues to elude us—social agreement on complex issues for which knowledge is insufficient to be decisive. Why in ignorance, in the absence of conclusive argument, do we nevertheless agree so greatly? I suggest that the only remaining plausible answer is that we are indoctrinated. We have all been led uncritically to much the same opinion on a variety of complex issues on which, if we had been thinking carefully, we would have reached a diversity of opinion.

The hypothesis is consistent with—indeed it is largely perhaps simply another form of—the sociological and anthropological propositions that find sources of social agreement in dominant forms of communication: from parent to child, teacher to student, from priest and pastor to congregation, and, in an age of communications technology, from mass media to mass. What the sociological and anthropological propositions do not dwell on is the knowledge content of the communications—whether the communication is based on knowledge or, on the other hand, myth, superstition, dogma, and other forms of misinformation. Their propositions take for granted that a large part of the content of communication is dogma and other misinformation; but the propositions do not go on to draw my conclusion that, in the absence of knowledge sufficient to explain agreement, whatever agreement exists must be the consequence of indoctrination to bring us to agreement.

But indoctrination might have been of diverse sources and messages, with the result that we would have been indoctrinated in diversity. If instead indoctrination is the source of those social agreements that cannot be based on knowledge, then we can infer that the indoctrination was not diverse but relatively unified or homogeneous, without enough challenge from other doctrines to produce diversity. Hence we must infer that it is to be traced to overwhelmingly loud voices in society, past and present. In pre-democratic eras in the Western world, these dominant voices have been those of lord and priest, they are now those of business. As we have already noted, contemporary businessmen need for the most part only to reinforce older ideologies of inequality, political docility, and loyalty. They need add to older doctrines only newer forms of them appropriate to a contemporary corporate world, seeking, for example, to convert patriotism and loyalty to the nation state into an associated loyalty to the market and to the rights of property. In their current indoctrinations of each new generation, they are aided by parents, teachers, journalists, and intellectuals who, having already been indoctrinated, pass their indoctrinations on.

Take care to understand the character of my argument. I do not point to measurable flows of indoctrinating communications, messages, indoctrinations, and then claim to judge their effect from the observed magnitudes. Instead I infer from the existence of a pattern—a pattern of agreement—that a pattern of indoctrination must have established the agreement. How else could it have come about? I can find no other explanation.

My hypothesis thus is that the mere existence of agreement on complex issues on which knowledge is not available as a basis for agreement is itself evidence of patterned indoctrination. The hypothesis is probably unwelcome to some or many of you. It denies the existence of much of the freedom we think we enjoy. And it may seem like effrontery to offer so crucial a hypothesis on such indirect evidence.

For the skeptics, I repeat my qeustion. How else can you explain the agreement? Agreement of millions of people on highly complex issues on which there is ample room for a wide range of opinion is an extraordinary phenomenon. We take it for granted because we have all grown up in societies marked by such agreement. But it requires explanation. A random distribution of opinion would be marked by rich diversity. That the diversity on these issues is absent and is replaced by agreement is a social phenomonon of the first order of importance and represents a massive and persistent patterned influence on all of us. No thoughtful person can simply shrug it off as "natural," "spontaneous," "normal." It calls for explanation.

And when I challenge you to find another explanation than mine, I must caution you not to believe you have found one in functional theories that declare, for example, that all societies need common rules or values, just as they need a common language. If they do, we must still try to find an explanation for how the common rules or values are brought about, how the agreement, declared to be necessary, is actually achieved. My answer is that it cannot have been brought about without patterned indoctrination stemming from those groups in society that achieve a grossly disproportionate control over communications that shape political-economic attitudes. Earlier elites had such control; the elite of property exercises such disproportionate control over communications today, varying from country to country—perhaps declining in strength, I might also add—but nevertheless still disproportionately patterning our political beliefs.

The results of patterned indoctrination, as already noted, is that ordinary citizens cannot play their democratic roles effectively. And even the indoctrinators become indoctrinated by their own communications. Consequently democracy is much less effective as an instrument of popular control than much democratic theory describes it to be. In some large part, which we cannot measure, Western democracies are social mechanisms through which people demand of their governments what they have been taught by their elites to demand. Thus popular control is to a degree short circuited; democracy becomes circular.

V. Conclusion

To conclude, then. I have examined a few arguments that reflect concern that economic institutions obstruct democracy. But I have not examined all of them, for some are familiar and have been frequently discussed. Instead, I have chosen to examine a few which seem to be especially deserving of further analysis. They all refer to authority based on rights to private property in the means of production, and they all regard holders of propertied authority as persons who play a ruling role in society, along with government rulers.

I have identified three of their ruling roles. One is as rulers in the market system itself, as rulers not only of their own employees but as rulers of all of us as we are affected by what goes on in the market system. The second is their role in the state, business in politics. The third is their role in shaping our minds. In each of these three roles, we have found grounds for concern about their adverse effects on democracy. Private property, whether you approve of it or not, is, even at this late date in the development of the welfare state, not at home with democracy.

Part Two
Policy Making

7

Bargaining: The Hidden Hand in Government (1955)[1]

I. Introduction

At one time in the Western world almost all markets were black and those that were not were grey. In many quarters neither labor nor land was priced. Interest was usury, and usury was sin. Pursuit of worldly gain jeopardized one's soul, and the cash nexus was thought to be an intolerable kind of social bond. As time passed, it must (it seems to our times) have been plain for all who wished to look that markets were not so black as they had been painted; but it remained for Adam Smith to draw the kind of picture that enabled people to recognize the market for what it had come to be—a powerful coordinating institution whose obvious merits were unarguable, whatever its deficiencies.

It is not surprising that the constructive potential of the market remained obscured so long. The motives that bring men into the market are the ones called base rather than noble. Man in the market is often self-centered, petty, grasping, mean. How could any good come from such ugly behavior? Good, it was thought, could come only from these who intend good. Today we know that, just as the road to hell is paved with good intentions, so conversely, private vices can be public virtues. Good is one possible product of multiplying evil.

Although it was Smith who first saw the large picture clearly enough to devise a kind of model of it, the seminal idea is the one represented by Mandeville's "private vices, public virtues."

1 In developing the line of argument taken in this paper, the author has departed considerably from the position taken in *Politics, Economics, and Welfare* (Harpers, New York, 1953), which he co-authored with Robert A. Dahl. Certain brief passages from that book have, however, been adapted to this paper.

I choose Mandeville's idea for my text in this paper; I want to show that in what I call *bargaining in government* are to be found great and inadequately recognized possibilities of social coordination. There too, though we perceive it only obscurely, private vice may be public virtue.

By *bargaining* or *negotiation* I mean to refer to all the methods, stratagems, and tricks—to throwing one's weight around, forming alliances and coalitions, taking a partisan position, scheming for advantage, as well as horsetrading, back-scratching, log-rolling, jockeying, threatening, deceiving, lying, bluffing, but not excluding persuasion and courteous negotiation—through which controls over government officials by other government officials are made multilateral instead of unilateral, or multilateral in place of no controls at all.

Because this is an exploratory and imprecise paper, I cannot define bargaining very sharply. If we understand it as poorly as I argue to be the case in this paper, it can only be defined with satisfactory precision as we come to know it better. Perhaps, however, the major characterization of bargaining in government at an abstract level is this: Bargaining refers to a residual category of controls in government that are not accounted for in the sometimes explicit but commonly implicit hierarchical models of government to be found almost universally in political theory, especially administrative theory. Most political theory carries an implicit assumption that, if one strips away the less essential, government is revealed as a kind of pyramidal organization of unilateral authority and, if government is not this, it should be. I think these assumptions are false, both descriptively and normatively.

The techniques of bargaining, though they are to be found everywhere in and out of government, play a strategic role in creating a useful network of multilateral control in government. It is partly because some of this network is illegal and much (though not all) is extra-legal and is commonly condemned as the product of stupidity, partiality, and avarice, that it is no better understood than was the market in the days when almost all markets were black. For most people, bargaining has the status of a black government. Few people have seen the power of Mandeville's dictum beyond the market, which is not the only place where private vices are public virtues.

I want to pursue further the analogy between market and government. But I must first acknowledge the many objections to the analogy that spring to mind immediately. For example, part of Smith's genius was that he saw through the aphorism, "Your gain, my loss." In the market, trade offers benefits to both parties, hence public good. But in bargaining in government it often appears that one's victory is another's defeat. I shall show, however, that bargaining almost always (perhaps without exception) takes place because of the possibility of mutual gain to all the bargainers, although sometimes the only mutual gain is abating a pre-existing conflict by reaching a settlement.

More generally, it will be objected, the market provides curbs and offsets to private vices without which they would not become public virtues, but the same cannot be said for bargaining processes. This objection strikes to the heart of the issue, and I shall have to meet it in the course of this paper. But here and now let me say that the bargaining process is going to be, by ordinary standards of judgement, at best inferior to the market processes for the very reason given—that the curbs and counters, though effective to a significant degree in negotiation, are poorer than those of the market. I am going to make rather large claims for bargaining, but not unlimited claims. In the market, some private vices are public vices too; in bargaining in government some private vices are public catastrophes.

I also admit that on one score bargaining has been appreciated. In the form of constitutionally provided checks and balances it has long been accepted in political theory as a possible protection against excesses of government activity. But for the protection it offers we are often told by political scientists that we pay heavily in consequent failures of coordination in government. I am arguing that bargaining is a *method* of coordination, not a tolerable obstruction to coordination. And I would object to the ease with which, as the fear of government activity in the United States is justifiably played down by some political theorists, they dispose of checks and balances and other bargaining devices without regard to what was and still remains its contribution to rationality and coordination in public policy and without regard to the weaknesses of hierarchy.[2]

In their most ambitious form, my hypotheses would be that (1) bargaining is a universal method of decision making, hence of social coordination, to be found in all kinds of social structures, including government and the market among others, (2) the conditions most favorable to coordination through bargaining are to be found in market relations, where it is possible to devise such a system of curbs and counters as to minimize the control or power held by any one person, (3) the competitive market, or price system, therefore represents a limiting case of bargaining, (4) but the benefits of coordination through bargaining in government are, though very poorly understood, much larger than commonly realized and potentially even larger.

Notice the effect of putting the major thesis, which is the fourth hypothesis, into the context of the other three. I am claiming that bargaining or negotiation in government is a closer kin to Smith's "higgling of the market" than third-cousin-by-analogy. It is conceptually helpful to think of the price system as a special case (and highly differentiated form) of bargaining as a general process and to think of bargaining in government as another special (though not highly differentiated) case of the same general process.

2 See, as an example, Joseph P. Harris, "The Future of Administrative Management, in L. D. White, ed., *The Future Government in the United States,* p. 165 for the following:

"The fear of executive power and the doctrines of checks and balances and the separation of power are giving way before a rising demand for effective and able administration and recognition not only that executive leadership is essential but also that executives may be trusted with all the authority necessary to discharge the functions of government, as long as they are held to an effective responsibility.

"There will be great advances in administrative management in the future, but they will not come without opposition from timid souls or the privileged few who seek to maintain the status quo by keeping government weak and ineffective. Many will still look upon government as essentially corrupt and incompetent, but the voice of the mass of the people will demand with increasing insistence strong and effective government to cope with the problems of society. Outworn political theories, suited to an earlier, agricultural society when the functions of government were few and simple and the prime consideration was to control government and to prevent it from robbing individuals of their liberties, are disappearing under conditions demanding a positive state. The old shibboleths will still be heard, but they will have lost their weight. In their place will rise anew political theory based upon a positive, service state, guided and controlled by democratic processes but unfettered by crippling restrictions which bind it today."

II. Bargaining and Hierarchy

The potential role of the price system escaped our medieval forerunners because they had been brought up to see order in hierarchy and both chaos and evil in everything else. Lucifer was exiled from heaven because he dared try to bargain with the Lord, and the Devil threatened man by offering attractive bargains for man's soul. The only "right" authority was purely unilateral authority; religious ideology, church organization, and lay institutions confirmed this truth. And for all the Devil's proclivity for bargaining, even he required strict hierarchical organization of hell to make damnation eternal.

In the less distant past, hierarchy or central unilateral control continued its hold on men's minds partly by habit and partly, as we have seen, because it was very hard to believe that private vices could be public virtues. More generally, *men simply could not see the possibility of achieving any social goal except by making it some official's responsibility to pursue it.* This is the great appeal of hierarchy even today. If you want to accomplish something beyond the capacity of any one individual, you set up an organization whose leaders are made responsible for attempting it. If the job calls for a very large number of people, you divide up the responsibilities but maintain concentration on the objective by a chain of authority—of unilateral control—down through an organizational pyramid to make sure that each person pursues the objective or appropriate subobjective.

In extreme form, the notion that to accomplish a social objective someone must try to accomplish it degenerates into a proposition that most of us would reject at once—that only do-gooders do good. But in its less extreme form, it is almost everywhere today accepted as valid, despite its obvious inapplicability to the market, where social objectives are achieved without anyone's pursuing them. Aside from the price system, we are still wedded to the idea that, with relatively few exceptions, the way to reach social goals is to set them up as organizational objectives, which means then that the way to coordinate it to make it someone's job to coordinate, the way to serve the public is to motivate individuals to serve the public—in short, the way to get results is to organize power hierarchically.

We today still think largely in terms of one or the other of these two alternatives—hierarchy or price system. No one has done for a third alternative—bargaining—what Adam Smith did for the second alternative, the price system. Nevertheless, my hypothesis is that this third alternative is not to be viewed simply as a degeneration of hierarchy but as an alternative to it. Its usefulness in government is apparent to all of us where it is mixed with market bargaining, as in, say, a Wage Stabilization Board; but we require: (1) recognition of it as a more general process in government distinct from hierarchy, (2) painstaking study of it, and, eventually, (3) ways of distinguishing useful from disruptive bargaining.

III. Bargaining in American Government

A survey of bargaining in American government is useful as a preface to specific argument on the constructive potential of bargaining. If you ask a well-informed American to draw a chart representing the organization of American government, he might begin by drawing for you the picture to be found in many books on American government. At the top of the chart is the presidency and below it in the familiar pyramid are the many administrative agencies. Leaving aside in this instance the position of Congress on the chart, one test of his understanding would be whether he criss-crossed his diagram until it was black to indicate the lines of multilateral control through which agencies influence and control each other and through which subordinates control their superiors. If he did not, we would say that his picture was predominantly of the formally prescribed organization; if he did, his picture would represent more of the actual operating organization, of which prescribed organization is a part. But if you then asked your well-informed citizen to pick out those lines of control through which order or coordination are or could be achieved, as distinct from those lines of control through which private ends are pursued at public expense and which represent obstacles rather than aids to "good" government, he would erase most of the hatchwork.

Although I would erase much of the hatchwork, I would want to use a red pencil to distinguish the most useful lines of control from the less effective lines, the less effective often being prescribed rather than operating. A very large proportion of the red lines would follow bargaining rather than hierarchical relationships among the agencies.[3]

But I will go further. No one exercises unilateral power in American government. The ostensible unilateral powers are those *prescribed* through constitution, law, and custom; but the prescribed authority of any government official is only one arrow in his quiver. What he actually can and does do depends upon his control over other people through his prescribed authority, his budget, his alliances, and his strategic and tactical skill, and upon the similar control with similar weapons that others have over him. Consequently, the only way to understand the role of hierarchical authority in American government is to see it as an element in bargaining processes rather than as an alternative to bargaining. (In other governments, its role is not always so greatly reduced.) Even at the apex of the hierarchy it is the job of the President to bargain. Now, since hierarchy can only be understood in the context of bargaining and since hierarchy works its results only through bargaining, I am driven to the conclusion that one cannot attribute order to hierarchy and disorder to bargaining in American government.

And, incidentally, the higher one goes in American government the smaller the role of hierarcal control as distinguished from bargaining controls. Only the very petty bureaucrat is far enough removed from the decision-making process to go his unilateral way. Yet even his control over his subordinates is compromised by gentle bargaining with his secretary, which is as inevitable as death and taxes.

Now, some examples of bargaining in American government: First are the structures specialized for it—formal agencies whose function is largely to reconcile conflict and reach decisions where we prefer not to settle such responsibility on any one hierarchical shoulder: among others, the Cabinet, conference committees in the Congress, the Republican Policy Committee, the Joint Chiefs of Staff, the National Security Council, Con-

---

3 A distinction is often drawn between the formal and informal organization, or the prescribed and operating organization, or the presumed and the effective organization. The argument of this paper is not designed to make this distinction again but to employ it to point out that the informal, the operating, the effective organization (the terms are roughly identical) is a bargaining organization.

gressional party caucuses, and, in large part, the political parties themselves. To take one of these examples, the Joint Chiefs of Staff is an arena for hard-fought negotiations; and its tradition of unanimity in decision making discloses how greatly whatever hierarchical authority it possesses depends upon finding a settlement on which all negotiators can agree. Meeting together as the JCS, the individual Chiefs concede to one another a high degree of autonomy, which again means that, unless they strike a happy bargain, each goes his own way.

The head of a Department is one of a second set of illustrations of the role of bargaining: high-placed officials in agencies not specialized for bargaining but whose individual role is that of a bargainer. Because titles conform to position in the prescribed hiearchy, not to position in the bargaining process, the role of these officials is often obscured. But commonly the head of an agency is not so much called upon to give orders to his subordinates as to serve as chief bargainer for them. The civilian secretaries of the military services are excellent examples. Almost without exception they view their responsibility as that of protecting the service that they are presumed to, but do not, govern. They fight their own service's battles by bargaining with the other services, with other branches of government and with the President. Similarly, the Secretary of Labor, Secretary of the Interior and Secretary of Commerce view their jobs largely as that of protecting the special interests under their juridsdiction and for which they bargain furiously with other Cabinet secretaries, with Congressional leaders, with the Bureau of the Budget, and with the President himself. The evidence of this is clear from the daily newspaper, but the secretaries themselves give us the most convincing testimony, as in the Ickes diaries.

But bargaining is not monopolized by heads of organizations. A third set of illustrations embraces those organizations in which negotiations with other organizations go on at many levels of both organizations; for example, the Army Engineers and the Bureau of Reclamation, the Department of Agriculture and the Department of the Interior, and the Budget Bureau and almost any other government agency.

The Corps of Engineers from 1940 to 1944 refused to abide by the President's explicit order that the King's River project in California be carried out by the Reclamation Bureau: Confident of support from the House Committee on Flood Control, the Corps violated the President's instructions and lobbied for its own jurisdiction over the project. Yet these two agencies can form an alliance to bargain with a common enemy, as when in 1944 the President advocated a Missouri Valley Authority to unify the work carried on by a half-dozen different federal agencies. The Corps of Engineers and the Reclamation Bureau promptly produced the Pick–Sloan Plan, which allocated spheres of influence in the Missouri Valley and guaranteed the continued dominance of both agencies in the area.

The Budget Bureau was established to provide a more central hierarchical overview and control of the budget, and this has been accomplished to a degree. But significantly, it has inevitably become a powerful bargainer. It is looked upon as the bargaining arm of the President in dealing with Congress on the one hand and the administrative agencies on the other; the Director of the Budget is everywhere conceded to be the President's man. Even more revealing, the Bureau has succeeded in marking off an area of autonomy for itself that permits it to bargain with the President over the terms on which it will subsequently be the presidential bargainer.

Beyond a certain point it is pointless to cite further examples of bargaining in government organized largely through bargaining. Once you begin to look for it, it is easy to find thread in cloth. Still, to advance closer to the proposition that bargaining is useful, which says more than that it merely exists, it will be helpful to have a look again at the key bargainer in American politics, the politician. Considering the confusing mixture of bargaining controls in American government, I should be excused for introducing him as the Hamlet in this omelette.

Despite an unwillingness of Americans to respect the politican—a reluctance that arises from the very role that is thrust upon him—the politician is indeed a key figure in American life, as he must be in any democracy. Now the politician is, above all, the man whose career depends upon successful negotiation of bargains. To win office he must negotiate electoral alliances. To satisfy his electoral alliance he must negotiate alliances with other legislators and administrators, for his control depends upon negotiation. Most of his time is consumed in bargaining. This is the skill he cultivates; it is the skill that distinguishes the master politician from the political failure. And though the politician frequently neglects the substantive issues of policy in order to maintain, restore, or strengthen his alliances for bargaining, this is where, as we propose, his private vices may become public virtues.

The politician is as much the human embodiment of a bargaining society as any single role-player can be. Because he is a bargainer, a negotiator, he does not often give orders. He can rarely employ unilateral controls. Even as a chief executive or cabinet officer, we have seen, he soon discovers that his control depends upon his skill in bargaining. The role calls for actions such as compromise, renunciation, face-saving of oneself, which are morally ambiguous or even downright immoral to people with rigorous standards. Yet clearly without the work of the politician a society such as ours would fly into its myriad separate warring parts.

Given the role of the politician as bargainer (and I shall have more to say below on why this is a useful role), there is no dominant group of politicians unified enough to control all the bureaucratic agencies. Even the most casual study of the relations between government bureaucracies and their prescribed political superiors shows this to be the case. Each bureaucratic agency is a part of a special network of control relations consisting of its clients, who often can be stimulated to lobby in behalf of the agency when its control, status, or security is threatened; its bureaucratic allies; its bureaucratic rivals; its links with Congressional politicians, usually in the legislative committee with jurisdiction over its activities, or in the appropriations subcommittee handling its budget; its links with Presidential politicians and their subordinates—Cabinet officers, White House aides, Budget Bureau officials. Some agencies like the Budget Bureau are "Presidential agencies" in the sense that they are responsive mostly to Presidential politicians; others are clearly "Congressional agencies"; others are partly captured by individuals or organizations outside the government; still others lean one way or another but manage to retain considerable autonomy with respect to all outside controls.

This is why bureaucratic leaders come to be participants in a bargaining process. If their status, power, or security is threatened by Presidential politicians, they stimulate an alliance with Congressional politicians. Conversely, if menaced by Congressional politicians, they look to the Presidential politicians for allies. In either case they may also induce their clients to use their influence to "save" the agency from the threats of one group of politicians or another. Naturally allies cannot be had for nothing; bureaucratic leaders bargain with suitable rewards: loyalty, information, remission of penalties, projects, or a host of other alternatives.

IV. The Virtues of Bargaining

For those not yet tired of the chase, we have come finally within distance of the quarry. It is a puzzling animal. Though its grunts and cries from the underbrush had often disturbed our peace of mind, hardly anyone had thought such an ugly and awkward animal worth domesticating. Still, we see that it bears certain family resemblances to the now highly bred work-horse whose ancestor Adam Smith found wandering in the forest (because he stopped looking at the trees). We have therefore pursued it to where we have it cornered and can now observe its appearance better than we had before and hence form some judgement of its strength and temper. In the case of an animal as downright nasty as this one, is the only good one a dead one? Or is it worth domesticating? For that matter, is it really as wild as it looks?

I propose several different lines of argument to support my hypothesis that bargaining is not wholly wild and is well worth domesticating in spite of its atavistic tendencies.

1. What can be made of the distinction between the inevitability and the usefulness of bargaining which is used to affirm the former while denying the latter? Bargaining is not only inevitable; it is inevitable in many places. Its ubiquity should give one pause. If every government official above a certain petty level spends a large amount of his time bargaining, as I believe is the case, one ought to be sympathetically disposed to finding hidden virtues in it. Of course, I would not argue that crime was desirable because ubiquitous. But few people are criminals. On the other hand, everyone sins; and here the "everybody's doing it" argument carries some weight, since we

all are quick to recognize that sin would not be universal if it did not have its points. We have found industriousness hidden in avarice, enthusiasm in immoderation, courtesy in dishonesty, ambition in envy, self-expression in profanity, serenity in intemperance, even business acumen in theft.

This argument is anything but conclusive, but the fact that every important government official finds bargaining necessary in order to carry on his work, and the fact that the recource to bargaining is not obviously correlated with any defects of intelligence or character suggests that for bargaining, as for sin, it *may* be true that inevitability means desirability.

Inevitability means desirability in still another more meaningful sense. Because the world can never be anything like the utopias we can imagine, we are often caught between what is desirable in utopia and what is the most desirable of realizable alternatives. One can easily imagine, for example, a world peopled by persons of such intelligence and nobility of character as would find a price system unnecessary and involvement in it demeaning. Significantly even today, when we better understand the limits on man's rationality and character than ever before, much (though by no means all or even most) of the criticism of the price system is justified only if the validity of utopian standards of conduct is assumed. But most of us would insist that in its place the price system is a highly desirable institution because we have formed a judgement of the realizable alternatives, among which the price system displays much merit. Having made a virtue out of a necessity in this case, we might do the same for bargaining. However disorderly it appears, compared to any realizable alternatives it is superior in many circumstances.

2. This brings us to consider what the realizable alternatives are. In many circumstances, the price system is superior to bargaining; but, because the price system is a highly differentiated social structure, its usefulness is limited to one large area of social organization. Frequently, therefore, the choice appears to come down, as we know, to hierarchy or bargaining. Clearly then, if hierarchy can be shown to be impossible or clearly inferior in any important circumstances, bargaining becomes the best of all *possible* worlds. I think this can be shown.

First, hierarchy is impossible in American government except as one of several bargaining controls. We have already shown that high-placed officials in our "hierarchies" are negotiators with other high-placed officials and with their own subordinates and that their hierarchical role is largely reduced to umpiring bargains among subordinates, where necessary. As bargainers, they use their prescribed hierarchical authority merely as one weapon among many.

But why is this so? Only to a degree is it a characteristic of governments generally that hierarchy is only an element in bargaining. The answer is that American government is built upon a constitutional separation of powers that makes the bargaining process the very heart of government. In the United States, the structure of government prescribed by the Constitution, court decisions, and traditions makes bargaining essential to policy determination. Consider: (1) federalism; (2) the composition and procedures of the Senate; (3) the bicameral legislature; (4) the separation of President and Congress, and the checks and balances between them; (5) differences in the constituencies of officials; (6) fixed and overlapping terms of Representatives, Senators, and the President; (7) constitutional restraints on legislative authority; (8) judicial review; (9) the amending process; (10) a decentralized party system; and (11) the devolution of power to committee chairmen in Congress whose position derives from seniority. All these make hierarchy impossible except as an appendage to bargaining. And the price of reducing bargaining in American government in any significant degree is an impossible restructuring of the whole government edifice; short of that, whatever order or disorder to be found in government policies is largely the product of bargaining. The only way to claim that bargaining is not useful is to claim that government is not useful, for in the United States, governing is bargaining.

Secondly, hierarchy as an alternative to bargaining is impossible in certain circumstances in any government. To take an extreme, dictators can exercise power only through employing large elements of bargaining in their hierarchies. It has been persuasively argued that the domination of the Politburo depended upon its skill in maintaining a bargaining relation among the three main hierarchies in the Soviet Union—the party, the secret police, and the non-party "technicians." By throwing its support to any two of these hierarchies, the Polit-buro could always control the third. In Germany during the Second World War, policy toward the Soviet Union was subject to a constant bargaining among four main groups, one including Himmler, Borman, and Hitler himself; another around Alfred Rosenberg, a third around Goebbels, and a fourth of professional soldiers and diplomats.

No dictator is mighty enough to stay in power standing alone. He needs the consent of army leaders, of the leaders of the secret police, of other important leadership groups, or of a sufficiently large alliance of some of them as to control the others. He can only expect his orders to be obeyed by the leaders around him because they find it in their interests to obey. Hence he cannot rule without offering advantages to them; and, knowing it, they indicate at what price their loyalty can be won. These subsidiary leaders are in turn in the same relation to their subordinates as is the dictator to them. Hence up and down the hierarchical ladder, unilateral controls are compromised by a network of the multilateral controls of a bargaining process. Hierarchy is not enough.

In any democracy the subordination of hierarchy is always more marked than in dictatorship even if it is less marked than in American government. In a democracy, hierarchy is inevitably limited by the fact and consequences of social plural-ism. Democracy requires a considerable degree of plura-lism—that is, a diversity of social organizations with a large measure of autonomy with respect to one another. Pluralism is required for a number of reasons: (1) In large-scale democracy, a diversity of social organizations is necessary so that different individuals, powerless by themselves, can each find allies and leaders with which to pursue their different social objectives. (2) Pluralism facilitates the rise of competing political leaders with different loyalties and support. It places a premium on the leader skilled in settlement of conflict rather than on the Messi-anic type. (3) It increases the probability that one is simul-taneously a member of more than one organization (hence action by a leader against an enemy organization is inhibited by the fact that he may strike at his own people). (4) The plurality of organizations provides a means of competing com-munication and information. In all these ways, pluralism develops the complex distribution of control necessary to democracy rather than the monolith of control useful to the dictator.

But with pluralism comes bargaining. For, if groups working through a common government retain some degree of autonomy with respect to one another—and this is what social pluralism means—they can arrive at governmental decisions only through bargaining. Moreover, groups engaged in national bargaining—political parties, government bureaucracies, pressure groups, legislative chambers—are themselves composed of groups, and these in turn break down still further. Hence bargaining is desirable at all levels in democracy, not merely among top leaders, but between top leaders and subordinates up and down a lengthy chain of reciprocal control.

It is worth dwelling on this subsidiary point a moment. Most of the leaders in the categories just mentioned are leaders by sufferance. Although the hierarchical component is great in parties, government agencies, nongovernmental hierarchies, pressure groups, and communications, these organizations are also in varying degrees marked by internal bargaining. The fact that most of these organizations are voluntary, or partly voluntary, means that leaders cannot push their unilateral control too far; if they do, they will lose their following. Hence the governmental process is not merely a matter of having these top leaders strike a bargain. They must bargain in turn with subleaders, who have their subleaders to bargain with, and so on down to the last echelon of activity. Hierarchy is no substitute for bargaining in these circumstances.

3. The third line of support for the hypothesis that bargaining is not wholly wild and is worth domesticating rests on a proposition that I want to introduce explicitly as an hypothesis because, although I think it is correct, it offers remarkable opportunities for research and verification. First, however, let me propose that one reason that bargaining is useful in government is that bargaining power is not at all equally distributed among the bargainers. Equality of bargaining power is so plausible an ideal that one is tempted to miss its ridiculousness. I know of no way to define it even roughly, except for bipartisan bargaining where the logical test of equality is a deadlock. But apply this test of equality, say, in collective bargaining in labor markets; and it becomes clear that equality is to be avoided. Very, very crudely,

equality in bargaining power could be held to mean that every party to the bargain comes away feeling that no one did substantially better than he. Certainly, however, this is not to be desired either, for the test of the settlement ought to be its coincidence with the public interest, somehow defined, not the satisfaction of the partisans, though the latter is relevant. Between tax collector and tax dodger, parent and child, President and individual Congressmen, civilian secretary and general, most of us quickly see the merit of inequality, even if the desirable pattern of inequality in more complicated bargaining is difficult to recognize.

Now the hypothesis. *An official's bargaining power depends in large part upon the coincidence of the goals he pursues in bargaining and the public interest, here defined as the achievement of widely shared goals.* If this is true, bargaining is clearly not so wild as it looks. What is the evidence? What are the determinants of bargaining power? Characteristics of personalities, appearance, and speech are only minor factors. What are the *major* determinants?

Again the analogy with the market is illuminating. There, bargaining power depends mainly upon one's position in the market, not one's personality characteristics, although the latter are not inconsequential. In labor markets, for example, the union's bargaining power depends upon the success with which it can conduct a strike, if it must fall back on one, and upon the employer's position in the market *vis-a-vis* his competitors, customers, and sources of supply. Generally in the market, a bargainer is powerful to the extent that he has alternative customers or sources of supply while his adversary does not. Similarly the bargaining power of a government official depends upon his position in the bargaining arena.

Now, in part, the official's position in the bargaining arena depends upon his hierarchical position—the higher the position in the hierarchy, the more the bargaining power. To the extent that this is true, it does not strike at our hypothesis about bargaining power and in fact lends weight to it. The higher the position in the hierarchy, the more probable that the bargaining official speaks for widely shared goals rather than for the narrower goals pursued by lower-level officials with specified and limited responsibilities. The principal determinant of a man's bargaining power, however, is revealed in the strategy of the politician. As we have shown, he is the key bargainer. Bargaining is his skill, or his *modus operandi*. How does he nurture his bargaining power? How does he make it grow?

The answer has already been given in the earlier discussion of the role of the politician. He pursues *power through alliances*. Bargaining in government is not two-sided. And when more than two interests appear, the only way to win is to find common cause with a majority of the bargainers.

The participants in a bargaining process are many, it is often plain to see. Only rarely are there no more than two. To be sure, only two bargainers may face each other at some particular time and place, but they may speak for still other interests not represented at the moment, and they will ordinarily consider their settlement no more than tentative until it has been bargained out with others not present. Bargaining is often quite informal and commonly incredibly complex; hence the bargainers are not to be identified simply as those present on any one particular occasion.

I need not dwell on the alliance as the major source of bargaining power, because it is obvious that no man stands alone in politics. What he can do depends upon his finding a group with which he can travel. It may be one alliance today, another tomorrow; or the same yesterday, today, and tomorrow; but always his strength depends upon finding other political leaders who want to pursue with him some common objectives. Even the President needs allies; he dare not use even his formally prescribed powers without their consent.

The glue—better call it flour-and-water paste—that binds the alliance together is a common objective. Now since different political leaders, whether in Congress or the bureaucracy, represent different electorates and special interests, the search for a common objective as a basis for a coalition becomes a search for values shared by different electorates and special interests. This is why an official's bargaining power depends upon his pursuing widely shared values. He finds allies by proposing objectives that he believes will appeal to a wide group of interests, including his own. And this is how bargaining can serve the public interest.

Politics is not an art or science pursued by philosopher-kings who find the public interest in the sky, but is a craft practiced by negotiators who know that the public interest can never be anything else but the common goals of different people. Every important interest has its representatives in Washington. If the public interest is to be served, this is as it should be. Every interest must have its representatives and these representatives must exhaustively explore potential areas of agreement to find one common cause out of may diverse ones. Not "In God We Trust," but the other side of the coin, *"E Pluribus Unum."*

Several other determinants of bargaining power are worth mentioning because, again, they award power more to those who pursue common values than to those who do not. They operate directly on bargaining power to some degree; but their powerful effect is through influencing an official's attractiveness as an ally. One is his power over a budget, another is the number of nonofficials for whom he can "speak," still another is his prescribed hierarchical authority, already mentioned. Large budget, constituency and authority increase bargaining power; but they probably also mean that the official has been given large means to accomplish large objectives for a large number of people. Correspondence between his bargaining power and his interest in widely shared values is surely more than accidental.[4]

4. Have I not begged the whole of the foregoing argument by assuming that the objective on which the bargainers could agree to form a coalition was something better than agreement to line their own pockets or pursue other gains for government officials as a group? I have two replies for this: the first more conclusive, the second more interesting. The first is that in a democracy it is always possible that political leadership in any branch of the government will feather its own nest or otherwise fail the electorate; and I would add, it is inevitable that it will

---

4 The fact that prescribed hierarchical authority is one determinant of bargaining power is a boon. For rewriting the prescription is a means of redressing inequalities in bargaining power that do not serve the public interest. Hence, I would say, with only slight apology for having said it before, that the skillful use of hierarchical prescription can make negotiation serve the public interest much better than it ever has. The prerequisite, of course, is that we distribute hierarchical authority to regulate bargaining power, because this is what it actually does in any case, instead of pretending that the hierarchical powers are more or less complete in themselves.

do so more than we wish. But the political leader is in fact under great pressures to spend a large amount of his time pursuing objectives desired by his Congressional or bureaucratic constituents. Whatever his private motives, he has to do a minimum to keep his job. Now insofar as his performance disappoints us—and here we come to the point—it spoils the results of hierarchy (viewed as an alternative to bargaining) as well as the results of bargaining. That is to say, this objection to bargaining is also an objection to hierarchical form of democracy or to any other imaginable form of democracy; and it therefore does not undercut my general hypothesis that in a real world, bargaining is often the most useful method of government.

My second reply raises the elusive question of what the public interest is that officials are to serve. Which makes the best sense—the concept of public interest implicit in the hierarchical model of government, or the concept implicit in the idea of bargaining? Superficially the answer is as clear as it is wrong—that the concept implicit in the hierarchical model, because it postulates a kind of dispassionate central responsibility for social welfare, is superior to the alternative concept, which postulates a fragmented, partial view of welfare. It is wrong because there is no one public interest, as we all know. Until what is sauce for the goose is also sauce for the gander, no social goal can be anything more than a compromise of conflicting individual goals.

What does this hierarchical overview of society's welfare amount to anyway? At worst, it postulates a society apart from its members, enjoying gains and suffering losses as though "society" were some giant engaged in eating, playing, loving, hating. At best, it assumes a capacity somewhere in the hierarchy to find standards by which all conflicts of interest can be resolved so that it can be said that some one program best pursues the public interest. But there are no such standards; the standards themselves are included in the values on which people differ. This is why, even in would-be hierarchical decision-making processes, decisions at the very top are always negotiated. There are simply too many valid interpretations of "the public interest."

Earlier I spoke of the public interest as the achievement of widely shared values. Without entering too deeply into the meaning of the term (I would prefer to avoid it if it were not current in the field), I suggest that frequently the only way we have of knowing whether values are widely shared is that they are or are not achieved as the result of a bargain. We often declare that the public interest is, for some kinds of issues, synonymous with what the majority prefers. But on many issues the majority is silent—that is, majority preferences cannot be put to a vote. Under these circumstances, we can think of a decision's being made either hierarchically or through bargaining. As a practical test of what values are widely shared, the settlement of the issue by bargaining will often be superior to an hierarchical determination.

Hence, within a certain range *the public interest is represented by an agreement among partisan interests, which is the way bargainers see it, not a goal or state of affairs having some validity other than as a practical bargained compromise.* Much of hierarchy's appeal is attributable to our carrying around in our minds unsophisticated notions of what we mean by the public interest; contrariwise, much of our suspicion of bargaining and of our inability to see any order in its superficial disorderliness is attributable to our refusal to confess that the public interest is often nothing more than any one of a group of many possible agreements among conflicting individual and group interests.[5]

5. If bargainers see the public interest for what it is and are not confused by a mystique, this is not the only way in which bargaining contributes to rationality in the weighing of alternative policies. Let me suggest some others, as additional ground for valuing the bargaining processes. In doing so, I draw a distinction between the all-inclusive problem of achieving efficient social or governmental organization and the more specific problem of achieving rational calculation on suitable objec-

5 Although many political theorists are extremely sophisticated on the pitfalls in the concept of the public interest or general welfare, confusion on this concept is sometimes at the root of their inability to give the devil of bargaining his due. See, for example, how Herring's view that "groups must be willing to recognize that the state has a purpose which transcends their own immediate ends" leads him to neglect the constructive role of bargaining in his *Public Administration and Public Interest,* especially pp. 8, 380, and 383. See also V. O. Key, Jr. in L. D. White ed., *The Future of Government in the United States,* Chicago, Ill.: Univ. of Chicago, 1942, pp. 145–163.

tives and means. How does bargaining assist rational calculation (aside from its contribution to dispelling the myth of the public interest)?

Its second contribution on this score is that it solves a problem that would drive a philosopher-king to the end of his wits—the problem of insuring that the common values of no significant group will be neglected in the final reconciliation of values necessary for policy decisions. The most perfect of realizable hierarchical authorities will neglect some important values; while a bargaining government, on the other hand, provides powerful motivation for each group to speak for what it wants—and not meekly in the tradition of "we respectfully call your attention to . . ." We may even fear that, without the motivation of the opportunity to bargain, no one will dredge up all the available and relevant facts.

The hierarchical authority, it might be argued, can take account of all the relevant variables, whether fact or value, if assisted by a research team. Think for a moment, however. Why, when it is thought that a man may have violated the law or infringed upon another's rights, do we turn to litigation instead of research? Why the court room, the partisan attorney, and the pursuit of victory instead of the study, the scholar, and the pursuit of truth? Because, for all the miscarriages of justice in courts of law, we do not believe the researcher can give every man his due or bring out every fact and value favorable to him. We want a social mechanism in which every man can speak for himself or find someone to speak for him. Litigation is one such mechanism, specialized to a particular category of problems in rational calculation. Bargaining, I suggest, is another much more generally useful one. In their places, both are effective methods (as compared to any practicable alternatives) for the rational calculation of correct means and ends. Despite the fact that both are powered by motives quite removed from the pursuit of truth or knowledge, they will in their places be superior to any other methods for rational calculation.

I think a clue is to be found here as to why academic minds are biased toward hierarchy and against bargaining. The role of the academic expert on the staff of the hierarchical decision maker is fairly clear and need not put the expert in any morally ambigous position. The model academic man does not want to serve special interests, neither does the model hierarchical decision maker. They are both sophisticated do-gooders, much as the academic man hates to admit it. And both of them see the problem of reconciling conflicting interests in the same way, as a matter of judgement in weighing values. For these reasons, research is a handmaiden of hierarchy as it can never be to bargaining. The bargainer wants to use research to pursue special interests and immediately runs afoul of the expert's "morality." (Unhappily it may be no less foolish and disruptive a morality than that of the attorney who refuses to defend anyone except the innocent.) Moreover, the bargainer believes that a defensible reconciliation of conflicting values and facts *for policy-making purposes* cannot be undertaken in any one person's mind but must be bargained out; and this is apparently a very subtle point for academic minds to grasp. Whether the bargainer goes too far, I shall not judge; but certainly his position is correct for a large category of decisions. In other words, in many circumstances, because the most rational policy will follow from the pursuit of special interests, research will either aid the pursuit or be irrelevant. This is more than the academic mind can stand.

A third aid to rational calculation to be found in bargaining is its feedback. Model hierarchy postulates that big decisions are made at the top and the details adjusted to fit at the bottom. At a high level, we decide what kind of a war we wish to be prepared to fight, and the choice of this or that electronic gear for a class of bombers is a detail. Everyone knows this is not so, even if he misses the significance of his insight. A new piece of electronic equipment may make it possible to redesign the bomber, redesign the Air Force, redesign the war. Sometimes, then, the big decisions become obvious and are more safely delegated to subordinates than the little decisions that have become big. Bargaining provides some insurance that the decisions made at low levels will have more of an impact on the decisions at the top than is permitted in the model of hierarchy, which is weak on this kind of feedback. (I also suspect that bargaining arrangements permit policy makers to move quickly to any point at which decisions are critical, while hierarchical arrangements, because they establish more rigid lines of authority, confine policy makers to certain categories of "important" decisions whether they are at any time important or not.)

Fourthly, bargaining makes no demands, as hierarchy does, for an enormous span of attention and competence in contemplating a decision. This is really a more generalized form of some of the claims I have already made for bargaining as an aid to rational calculation, but the generalization is useful in suggesting again the analogy with the price system. Viewed as a method of rational calculation, the price system has the great merit of eliminating the need for grand calculations for the whole economy and substituting for them the relatively petty calculations of how to make a fast buck or whether to have hamburger again for dinner tonight. Similarly bargaining breaks down cosmic decisions into manageable ones. What is good for my group? is an easier question than, What is good for the nation? If bargaining provides, as I have been arguing it does, a method of reconciling the diverse answers, the gain in rationality, for some kinds of decisions, can be large.

But finally the unique and telling contribution of bargaining to rational calculation is that it motivates men to search exhaustively and ceaselessly for common goals. Hierarchical authority compromises conflicting interests—*this is the result of the judicious weighing of conflicting values that is characteristic of model hierarchy.* Bargaining endlessly explores areas of *agreement* instead of taking the short cut of *compromise.*

Why does a bargainer rack his brains in the search for a common basis for agreement? Because that is how he wins allies—hence bargaining power. Since this is the test of his success, he does nothing with more diligence, more patience, more skill and more imagination than that with which he explores the jungle of conflict ferreting out values on which people agree. His hope is to make the largest possible number of people better off, and no one worse off; and he often succeeds.

I would like to make this point emphatically. Earlier I tried to show that the bargainer gained power by forming alliances and that, because the alliances were based upon common interests, his power was related to his desire to pursue widely shared goals. What I want to stress here is that, although there are countless common goals, conflict of other goals obscures them and they are consequently dificult to find. While hierarchical leaders take the easy way of compromise, bargainers are highly motivated to look and keep on looking, to develop skill in looking, and to become resourceful in finding hidden common goals. And, of course, the search for common values, even where none are found, clarifies goals and reduces pointless conflict stemming from mistaken self-interests. Most of what the public knows about its social goals represents this educational by-product of bargaining.

6. On a ship in a storm, we do not trouble to keep a good course; we worry about remaining afloat. In a democracy, skeptics will say, rational calculation is a luxury; the problem of democracy is survival. Why do some democracies survive and others not? The answer is not wholly understood, but one part of it is that in the United States and the other successful democracies some of the common values (including democracy itself) on which citizens unite are more important to them than the values on which they disagree. Were this otherwise, a large minority would rather abandon democracy than be outvoted. Where it is true, to be outvoted is to lose values less essential than the common values pursued in the democracy.

That we have common values to unite us is in part the good fortune of our history. But it is also explained by the fact that bargaining makes it the business of our governmental leaders, as we have just explained, to uncover every possible area of agreement. Hence, for those who worry more about democracy's health than its intelligence, the search for agreement is no less important, and the virtue of bargaining no less apparent. We owe the health of democracy to the schemer, the man with a deal, the lowly politician, and the administrator, who instead of running his department is out winning friends and influencing people. Without their contriving, only extraordinary luck would make democracy possible.

7. Bargaining is desirable in policy making but not, one may object, in administration. If such an objection did not exist, I would want to invent it, because in answering it I am pushed on to a further main line of argument in support of bargaining in government. Let us begin, however, with the objection itself.

That bargaining is desirable in policy making but not in administration is in very large part correct, I not only concede but insist. But this is not an objection to what I have claimed for bargaining. Only to the extent that one can separate administration from policy making is the proposition useful, which means that it is hardly useful at all. For, as every political scientist knows, the distinction between policy making and administration does not follow the distinction between the legislative and the administrative branches of government. Policy is made everywhere in government—by the President, in the Congress, and at every level in the bureaucracies. If it is countered that only very small issues of policy are decided at the lower administrative levels, the answer is that only small bargains need to be struck, not that bargaining becomes useless. Once we agree that bargaining is desirable largely as an aid to policy making, we have agreed on its universal merit in government.

Whether or not some administrative functions can be distinguished from policy making need not detain us. I am not sure that they can; but, if I assume so for the sake of argument, it will still be true that some policy making is to be found at every level in government. Actually, I am more interested in what we could all agree to be major decisions rather than details, and these are decisions in which the policy-making function is obvious. They are clearly not restricted to the nonadministrative branches of government. Hence, if bargaining is not suitable for administrative tasks, it is nevertheless desirable for the administrative branch of government.

This is not all, however. In developing this line of thought further, it becomes an important argument independent of the objection to bargaining from which it sprang. To begin with, consider the policy-making functions in the hands of administrative agencies and officials in American government: for example, the Atomic Energy Commission, Joint Chiefs of Staff, Secretary of State, Federal Trade Commission, Federal Communications Commission, Interstate Commerce Commission, Railway Labor Board, Commission of Public Roads, Harold Stassen, Curtis LeMay, Sherman Adams, Alfred Gruenther, Gabriel Hauge, Randolph Burgess, Arthur Burns. Many hundres of members of the Executive Branch of government have policy-making functions not to be dismissed as of small significance.

Within what range of discretion do these administrative officers decide policy? Blueprints aside, one of the outstanding developments in democratic government everywhere is the decline of legislative control over such administrators as these.

Almost everywhere legislative politicians appear to have passed the zenith of their power: They are everywhere being displaced by executive politicians. The growth of government action has required decisions that in sheer number, detail, prerequisite knowledge, and dispatch cannot be made in legislatures; thus great discretion passes to executive politicians. Congress has more than it can do; further extension of government functions can only mean a diminution of Congressional control.

We face therefore a problem in what I shall call democracy at the second level. Popular control over government policy operates at several levels. Of these, two are well known. At one, voters control a legislature; and it can persuasively be argued that public control of the legislature is secularly improving. At the second level, the legislature controls the officials immediately responsible for governmental functions. At this second level, it can persuasively be argued that democracy is weak and is perhaps actually breaking down.

Hypothetically, two courses of action are open to make public officials more responsible. The first is a drastic reorganization of American government along the lines of the British model, in which the legislature largely abandons its traditional role. It adds a third level to democratic government. Voters to some extent control the legislature; the legislature to some extent controls the Cabinet; and the Cabinet to some extent controls those immediately responsible for governmental functions, although this is admittedly too simple a picture. The control of the legislature is largely that of exercising a general control over the Cabinet through threat of removal, and each member of the legislature surrenders hope of exercising any particular control over the policy of the Cabinet during its term of office. The effective legislature, in the sense in which Americans understand legislative functions, becomes the Cabinet.

In Britain, the legislature serves as a kind of continuing embodiment of the election returns; it guarantees that executive politicians will roughly adhere to their campaign programs or, in dealing with emergencies and new demands, will not stray excessively from basic public attitudes as reflected by legislative politicians. But the role of legislative politicians in deliberately shaping the great bulk of the decisions made by executive politicians is exceedingly attenuated. They are umpires, who sometimes rule the ball out of bounds; but they do not carry the ball themselves or, except by enforcing the basic rules, determine the strategy.

The second course of action may be inferior to the first, but it is consistent with the American commitment to separation of powers and hence may be the only practicable alternative for this country. If the legislature cannot control the executive politicians who increasingly displace the Congressional politicians as policy makers, and if the legislature will not surrender its power to a cabinet, *the executive politicians must control each other.* This is what bargaining comes down to. Inadequate as it appears a method of maintaining democracy at the second level, bargaining is the only remaining alternative. Had we not been practicing it for these many decades during which Congressional control has declined, we would find government even less responsible to the electorate than it is. Again, it is the bargainer who has kept the ship afloat. He could do better if he were not so often compelled to keep out of sight.

8. Finally, those who believe that bargaining is at best only a small service to American government have to put up with their inability to find a superior alternative in many concrete situations that can be identified. Would they really prefer a single hierarchical head of the military instead of the Joint Chiefs as a bargaining group? Would they prefer that President Eisenhower refuse to bargain out top policy with Congressional leaders, as well as with his own close staff of "advisers," that Dulles be freed from the power exercised over him by the military and the Department of Defense, that the TVA ride rough-shod over the Department of Agriculture in its soil conservation (or vice versa), that the Budget Bureau either command or obey but never negotiate with every other government agency? When it comes down to actual situations, everyone will find some use for bargaining. And as a *minimum minimorum* bargaining is often useful if only to counter someone who is already bargaining.

IV. The Deficiencies of Bargaining

I do not think the deficiencies of bargaining undermine any of the arguments I have employed to demonstrate its usefulness.

They do, however, indicate its costs. The major deficiency is that appropriate counters to any individual's bargaining power are not always present. This does not mean that negotiation is not to be desired under the circumstance, for no better alternative may be available. But it does mean that the price of bargaining is sometimes irresponsible authority, which, though it is often also the price of using hierarchy, is not to be dismissed lightly. To be sure, we do not want a counter to every power. As was explained, equality of bargaining power is no defensible objective. What is desirable, however, is that bargaining power rise from alliances rather than, say, from verbal skills, certain undesirable kinds of tactical stubborness, or mere lack of scruples. One of our hypotheses was that this is the case, but exceptions are obviously many and important.

As explained earlier, the bargaining made necessary and desirable by social pluralism is supplemented by that made necessary by the additional constitutional factors in American government. What is added is not wholly to be desired. Carried to decision-making processes in which a stronger hierarchical element is desirable, bargaining in the wrong place at the wrong time accounts for some of the worst aspects of American government: (1) It explains why conflicting interests often result not in agreement but in the paralysis of public policy, as is illustrated most dramatically by the filibuster; (2) it also gives disproportionate power to the leaders of strategic minorities; (3) it sometimes leads to the substitution of irrational agreement through log-rolling for agreement upon some common goal; and (4) it favors the most highly organized groups. Each of these results is widely viewed as deplorable.

No doubt the extravagance of bargaining in American government party accounts for the common unwillingness to concede that it has much merit at all. But to believe that it is overdone in American government is quite different from believing that it has no great and useful role to play or that it cannot play its role much better than it does.

V. Some Further Suggestions

I believe that the argument of this paper is sufficiently strong to undermine the confidence with which many political theorists have identified coordination with hierarchy to the neglect of bargaining, but that the argument is by no means strong enough to demonstrate the truth of the positive propositions I have developed. These remain only hypotheses and they call for verification.

The need for more sympathetic study of bargaining processes I need not therefore labor. I should like to throw out, however, a few suggestions on further study not already implicit in the foregoing argument.

1. Neither democracy nor bargaining within a democracy is possible without social agreement on both certain fundamental ends and certain political means. The agreement is generally achieved through social indoctrination, as well as through at least rough strategic calculations that individuals make regarding their fellows; and once achieved it acts as a constraint upon everyone, including bargainers. In addition, additional restraints are imposed upon particular groups through role requirements representing values likewise indoctrinated into the particular group and strategically calculated by the group members. Like the special restraints upon a physician, judge or scientist, role restraints probably operate upon bargainers in government, even if weakly. Although the extent to which bargaining is controlled by the general and role restraints taken together is significant, potential control through these means runs far beyond what is presently realized. The existence, strength, and sensitivity to bargaining's low repute of these role restraints based on shared values should presumably be taken account of in further study. It seems doubtful that bargaining could ever take place without some common values from which to proceed and without hope of potential agreement larger than that with which bargaining commences. This hypothesis is itself worth verifying, but it is only the beginning of a study of the social framework of agreement in which bargaining takes place.

2. Beyond a theory of bargaining in government lies the possibility of more generalized theories of bargaining, in which bargaining in government and in the market are special cases. One can do little more than speculate about what might be possible, but a few possibilities can be imagined.

Suppose we think of a continuum along which different kinds of bargaining are ranked according to the degree to which the bargainer possesses discretionary power. The extreme or pole at which discretion disappears corresponds very roughly to situations in which the decision is somehow determined by the structure of wants of the population rather than by anyone's authority; and, of course, we do not ask that any real-world situation correspond to the extreme. We have a model tailor-made for this extreme (though in fact I purpose such an extreme in order to accomodate just this model), the model of pure competition. We can easily rewrite the theory of competition and monopoly in terms of bargaining, since much of it is already so couched. If we do, the enterpreneur who in pure competition is without discretionary control over price becomes the bargainer with zero bargaining power, whose prices and outputs are determined by the pattern of wants in the community.

Now move toward the right from the extreme of zero bargaining power. Even imperfect competition provides counters on bargaining power probably superior in reducing discretion to any to be found outside the market. Let us therefore place on the left half of the continuum a model of real-world market bargaining. Better still, we might specify real-world market bargaining in which bargaining power of buyer and seller depends upon alternatives open to buyer and seller respectively. To the right of this competitive bargaining model we would then place a model of what I shall call *noncompetitive market bargaining,* distinguished from competitive bargaining by the fact that power will depend upon techniques for restricting the alternatives to which the other bargainer can turn.

The distinction here is that in the first case a seller, for example, has power over a buyer because he, the seller, can easily turn to an alternative buyer if he wishes; but in the second case his power is based upon techniques for restricting the buyer's alternatives. I think the distinction is important, although it may be a matter of taste. One way to see why it might be significant is to observe that, to the extent that counters reduce bargaining power in competitive bargaining toward zero, the model turns into the model of pure competition. In the second case, however, that of noncompetitive market bargaining, reduction of bargaining power moves toward offsetting monopoly powers, which is a horse of quite different color from pure competition. I suggest, therefore, that noncompetitive bargaining, which begins to look a little like bargaining in government, be placed to the right of competitive bargaining on the continuum.

Now comes a long gap in the continuum. Somewhere to the right of center, let us say arbitrarily, we place bargaining by alliance in government and still further to the right other largely unspecified forms of bargaining in government in which alliances are relatively less important and other determinants of power—say negotiating skills or personal loyalties—are more dominant. Without adequate models of bargaining in government, it is impossible to say much more than that a variety of bargaining situations in government could probably be ranged across the continuum toward the pole at the right, representing some kind of extreme of discretionary power.

What to put at the extreme becomes an intriguing question. If I had the answer, I would be a long way toward understanding bargaining. But let me suggest a not impossible answer, derived from analogy between the competition-monopoly continuum. Perhaps the extreme is hierarchy, even if at first sight it appears to belong on an entirely different continuum. It may be that the most fruitful way to develop a generalized theory of bargaining is to treat pure competition and strict hierarchy as the two limiting cases, for in the one case counters reduce power to zero and in the other case there is no counter at all. Still another possibility that enlarges one's vision is to think of the right-hand pole as representing anarchy in the derogatory sense of the term. In that case, pure competition can be viewed at one extreme as the only existing model of anarchistic harmony; and the opposite extreme can be viewed as anarchistic disorder in which every man is king save that he has no subjects.

3. Somehow, however, a general understanding of bargaining must do even better than embrace the phenomena so far mentioned. For bargaining takes place within the family and in all kinds of informal social relationships, which call for attention no less than the formal arenas. And it is to be found everywhere within voluntary organizations and among them, just as it is found both within government agencies and among them. It also plays a critical role in American politics beyond that discussed in this paper because of the great organized pressure groups whose leaders negotiate with one another and with

government officials. Moreover, because of the variety of circumstances in which it occurs, a general theory must embrace bargaining among leaders with attached constituencies as well as bargaining among individuals in which no leader-follower relation is present. A clarification of this difference will also require accounting for bargaining both with and without the strong hierarchical component to be found in bargaining in government. In the construction of the general theory or in any feeble steps toward understanding the process, I would suggest the obvious usefulness of game theory, even if it is written at a level of generality that abstracts from most of the variables that must eventually be incorporated into the theory. And presumably there are possibilities of employing some of the older tools of economic theory in generalizing beyond the market.

4. If there is one aspect of bargaining that deserves more attention than I have given it, it would be bargaining's capacity for revealing frustrations and wants otherwise missed and for making adjustments of policy in the light of them. We dislike pain even more than we dislike squeaky wheels, which only offend our ears. We would not, however, survive without the pain that signals us to take our hands from hot stoves and teaches us to dodge heavy falling objects, nor—to speak more generally—without the nervous system that makes it possible for us to coordinate and adjust to the warnings received. The bargaining network is the nervous system of the body politic. We put up with much discomfort because of it, and American government suffers from a chronic case of nerves. But who wants to be numb, let alone spastic?

8

The Science of "Muddling Through" (1959)

Suppose an administrator is given responsibility for formulating policy with respect to inflation. He might start by trying to list all related values in order of importance, e.g., full employment, reasonable business profit, protection of small savings, prevention of a stock market crash. Then all possible policy outcomes could be rated as more or less efficient in attaining a maximum of these values. This would of course require a prodigious inquiry into values held by members of society and an equally prodigious set of calculations on how much of each value is equal to how much of each other value. He could then proceed to outline all possible policy alternatives. In a third step, he would undertake systematic comparison of his multitude of alternatives to determine which attains the greatest amount of values.

In comparing policies, he would take advantage of any theory available that generalized about classes of policies. In considering inflation, for example, he would compare all policies in the light of the theory of prices. Since no alternatives are beyond his investigation, he would consider strict central control and the abolition of all prices and markets on the one hand and elimination of all public controls with reliance completely on the free market on the other, both in the light of whatever theoretical generalizations he could find on such hypothetical economies.

Finally, he would try to make the choice that would in fact maximize his values.

An alternative line of attack would be to set as his principal objective, either explicitly or without conscious thought, the relatively simple goal of keeping prices level. This objective might be compromised or complicated by only a few other goals, such as full employment. He would in fact disregard most other social values as beyond his present interest, and he would for the moment not even attempt to rank the few values that he regarded as immediately relevant. Were he pressed, he would quickly admit that he was ignoring many related values and many possible important consequences of his policies.

As a second step, he would outline those relatively few policy alternatives that occurred to him. He would then compare them. In comparing his limited number of alternatives, most of them familiar from past controversies, he would not ordinarily find a body of theory precise enough to carry him through a comparison of their respective consequences. Instead he would rely heavily on the record of past experience with small policy steps to predict the consequences of similar steps extended into the future.

Moreover, he would find that the policy alternatives combined objectives or values in different ways. For example, one policy might offer price level stability at the cost of some risk of unemployment; another might offer less price stability but also less risk of unemployment. Hence, the next step in his approach—the final selection—would combine into one the choice among values and the choice among instruments for reaching values. It would not, as in the first method of policy making, approximate a more mechanical process of choosing the means that best satisfied goals that were previously clarified and ranked. Because practitioners of the second approach expect to achieve their goals only partially, they would expect to repeat endlessly the sequence just described, as conditions and aspirations changed and as accuracy of prediction improved.

I. By Root or by Branch

For complex problems, the first of these two approaches is of course impossible. Although such an approach can be described, it cannot be practiced except for relatively simple problems and even then only in a somewhat modified form. It assumes intellectual capacities and sources of information that men simply do not possess, and it is even more absurd as an approach to policy when the time and money that can be allocated to a policy problem is limited, as is always the case. Of particular importance to public administrators is the fact that public agencies are in effect usually instructed not to practice the first method. That is to say, their prescribed functions and constraints—the politically or legally possible—restrict their attention to relatively few values and relatively few alternative policies among the countless alternatives that might be imagined. It is the second method that is practiced.

Curiously, however, the literatures of decision making, policy formulation, planning, and public administration formalize the first approach rather than the second, leaving public administrators who handle complex decisions in the position of practicing what few preach. For emphasis I run some risk of overstatement. True enough, the literature is well aware of limits on man's capacities and of the inevitability that policies will be approached in some such style as the second. But attempts to formalize rational policy formulation—to lay out explicitly the necessary steps in the process—usually describe the first approach and not the second.[1]

The common tendency to describe policy formulation even for complex problems as though it followed the first approach has been strengthened by the attention given to, and successes enjoyed by, operations research, statistical decision theory, and systems analysis. The hallmarks of these procedures, typical of the first approach, are clarity of objective, explicitness of evaluation, a high degree of comprehensiveness of overview, and, wherever possible, quantification of values for mathematical analysis. But these advanced procedures remain largely the appropriate techniques of relatively small-scale problem solving where the total number of variables to be considered is small and value problems restricted. Charles Hitch, head of the Economics Division of RAND Corporation, one of the leading centers for application of these techniques, has written: "I would make the empirical generalization from my experience at RAND and elsewhere that operations research is the art of sub-optimizing, i.e., of solving some lower-level problems, and that difficulties increase and our special competence diminishes by an order of magnitude with every level of decision making

1 James G. March and Herbert A. Simon similarly characterize the literature. They also take some important steps, as have Simon's recent articles, to describe a less heroic model of policy making. See *Organizations* (John Wiley and Sons, 1958), p. 137.

we attempt to ascend. The sort of simple explicit model which operations researchers are so proficient in using can certainly reflect most of the significant factors influencing traffic control on the George Washington Bridge, but the proportion of the relevant reality which we can represent by any such model or models in studying, say, a major foreign-policy decision, appears to be almost trivial."[2]

Accordingly, I propose in this paper to clarify and formalize the second method, much neglected in the literature. This might be described as the method of *successive limited comparisons*. I will contrast it with the first approach, which might be called the *rational-comprehensive* method.[3] More impressionistically and briefly—and therefore generally used in this article—they could be characterized as the branch method and root method, the former continually bulding out from the current situation, step by step and by small degrees; the latter starting from fundamentals anew each time, building on the past only as experience is embodied in a theory, and always prepared to start completely from the ground up.

Let us put the characteristics of the two methods side by side in simplest terms.

Rational-Comprehensive (Root)	Successive Limited Comparisons (Branch)
1a. Clarification of values or objectives distinct from and usually prerequisite to empirical analysis of alternative policies.	1b. Selection of values, goals and empirical analysis of the needed action are not distinct from one another but are closely intertwined.

2 "Operations Research and National Planning—A Dissent," 5 *Operations Research* (October, 1957), p. 718. Hitch's dissent is from particular points made in the article to which his paper is a reply; his claim that operations research is for low-level problems is widely accepted.

For examples of the kind of problems to which operations research is applied, see C. W. Churchman, R. L. Ackoff and E. L. Arnoff, *Introduction to Operations Research* (John Wiley and Sons, 1958); and J. F. McCloskey and J. M. Coppinger eds., *Operations Research for Management*, Vol. II (The Johns Hopkins Press, 1956).

3 I am assuming that administrators often make policy and advise in the making of policy and am treating decision making and policy making as synonymous for purposes of this paper.

2a. Policy-formulation is therefore approached through means-end analysis: First the ends are isolated; then the means to achieve them are sought.

2b. Since means and ends are not distinct, means-end analysis is often inappropriate or limited.

3a. The test of a "good" policy is that it can be shown to be the most appropriate means to desired ends.

3b. The test of a "good" policy is typically that various analysts find themselves directly agreeing on a policy (without their agreeing that it is the most appropriate means to an agreed objective).

4a. Analysis is comprehensive; every important relevant factor is taken into account.

4b. Analysis is drastically limited:
  i) Important possible outcomes are neglected;
  ii) Important alternative potential policies are neglected;
  iii) Important affected values are neglected.

5a. Theory is often heavily relied upon.

5b. A succession of comparisons greatly reduces or eliminates reliance on theory.

Assuming that the root method is familiar and understandable, we proceed directly to clarification of its alternative by contrast. In explaining the second, we shall be describing how most administrators do in fact approach complex questions, for the root method, the "best" way as a blueprint or model, is in fact not workable for complex policy questions, and administrators are forced to use the method of successive limited comparisons.

A. *Intertwining Evaluation and Empirical Analysis (1b)*

The quickest way to understand how values are handled in the method of successive limited comparisons is to see how the root method often breaks down in *its* handling of values or objectives. The idea that values should be clarified, and in advance of the examination of alternative policies, is appealing. But what happens when we attempt it for complex social problems? The first difficulty is that on many critical values or objectives, citizens disagree, congressmen disagree, and public administrators disagree. Even where a fairly specific objective is prescribed for the administrator, there remains considerable room for disagreement on subobjectives. Consider, for example, the conflict with respect to locating public housing, described in Meyerson and Banfield's study of the Chicago Housing Authority[4]—disagreement which occurred despite the clear objective of providing a certain number of public housing units in the city. Similarly conflicting are objectives in highway location, traffic control, minimum wage administration, development of tourist facilities in national parks, or insect control.

Administrators cannot escape these conflicts by ascertaining the majority's preference, for preferences have not been registered on most issues; indeed, there often *are* no preferences in the absence of public discussion sufficient to bring an issue to the attention of the electorate. Furthermore, there is a question of whether intensity of feeling should be considered as well as the number of persons preferring each alternative. By the impossibility of doing otherwise, administrators often are reduced to deciding policy without clarifying objectives first.

Even when an administrator resolves to follow his own values as a criterion for decisions, he often will not know how to rank them when they conflict with one another, as they usually do. Suppose, for example, that an administrator must relocate tenants living in tenements scheduled for destruction. One objective is to empty the buildings fairly promptly, another is to find suitable accommodation for persons displaced, another is to avoid friction with residents in other areas in which a large influx would be unwelcome, another is to deal with all concerned through persuasion if possible, and so on.

4 Martin Meyerson and Edward C. Banfield, *Politics, Planning and the Public Interest* (The Free Press, 1955).

How does one state even to himself the relative importance of these partially conflicting values? A simple ranking of them is not enough; one needs ideally to know how much of one value is worth sacrificing for some of another value. The answer is that typically the administrator chooses—and must choose—directly among policies in which these values are combined in different ways. He cannot first clarify his values and then choose among policies.

A more subtle third point underlies both the first two. Social objectives do not always have the same relative values. One objective may be highly prized in one circumstance, another in another circumstance. If, for example, an administrator values highly both the dispatch with which his agency can carry through its projects *and* good public relations, it matters little which of the two possibly conflicting values he favors in some abstract or general sense. Policy questions arise in forms which put to administrators such a question as: Given the degree to which we are or are not already achieving the values of dispatch and the values of good public relations, it is worth sacrificing a little speed for a happier clientele, or is it better to risk offending the clientele so that we can get on with our work? The answer to such a question varies with circumstances.

The value problem is, as the example shows, always a problem of adjustments at a margin. But there is no practicable way to state marginal objectives or values except in terms of particular policies. That one value is preferred to another in one decision situation does not mean that it will be preferred in another decision situation in which it can be had only at great sacrifice of another value. Attempts to rank or order values in general and abstract terms so that they do not shift from decision to decision end up by ignoring the relevant marginal preferences. The significance of this third point thus goes very far. Even if all administrators had at hand an agreed set of values, objectives, and constraints, and an agreed ranking of these values, objectives, and constraints, their marginal values in actual choice situations would be impossible to formulate.

Unable consequently to formulate the relevant values first and then choose among policies to achieve them, administrators must choose directly among alternative policies that offer different marginal combinations of values. Somewhat paradoxically, the only practicable way to disclose one's relevant marginal values even to oneself is to describe the policy one chooses to achieve them. Except roughly and vaguely, I know of no way to describe—or even to understand—what my relative evaluations are for say, freedom and security, speed and accuracy in governmental decisions, or low taxes and better schools than to describe my preferences among specific policy choices that might be made between the alternatives in each of the pairs.

In summary, two aspects of the process by which values are actually handled can be distinguished. The first is clear: Evaluation and empirical analysis are intertwined; that is, one chooses among values and among policies at one and the same time. Put a little more elaborately, one simultaneously chooses a policy to attain certain objectives and chooses the objectives themselves. The second aspect is related but distinct: The administrator focuses his attention on marginal or incremental values. Whether he is aware of it or not, he does not find general formulations of objectives very helpful and in fact makes specific marginal or incremental comparisons. Two policies, X and Y, confront him. Both promise the same degree of attainment of objectives a, b, c, d and e. But X promises him somewhat more of f than does Y, while Y promises him somewhat more of g than does X. In choosing between them, he is in fact offered the alternative of a marginal or incremental amount of f at the expense of a marginal or incremental amount of g. The only values that are relevant to his choice are these increments by which the two policies differ; and, when he finally chooses between the two marginal values, he does so by making a choice between policies.[5]

As to whether the attempt to clarify objectives in advance of policy selection is more or less rational than the close intertwining of marginal evaluation and empirical analysis, the principal difference established is that for complex problems the first is impossible and irrelevant, and the second is both possible and relevant. The second is possible because the administrator need not try to analyze any values except the values by which alternative policies differ and need not be concerned with them except

5 The line of argument is, of course, an extension of the theory of market choice, especially the theory of consumer choice, to public policy choices.

as they differ marginally. His need for information on values or objectives is drastically reduced as compared with the root method; and his capacity for grasping, comprehending, and relating values to one another is not strained beyond the breaking point.

B. *Relations between Means and Ends (2b)*

Decision making is ordinarily formalized as a means-ends relationship: Means are conceived to be evaluated and chosen in the light of ends finally selected independently of and prior to the choice of means. This is the means-ends relationship of the root method. But it follows from all that has just been said that such a means-ends relationship is possible only to the extent that values are agreed upon, are reconcilable, and are stable at the margin. Typically, therefore, such a means-ends relationship is absent from the branch method, where means and ends are simultaneously chosen.

Yet any departure from the means-ends relationship of the root method will strike some readers as inconceivable. For it will appear to them that only in such a relationship is it possible to determine whether one policy choice is better or worse than another. How can an administrator know whether he has made a wise or foolish decision if he is without prior values or objectives by which to judge his decisions? The answer to this question calls up the third distinctive difference between root and branch methods: How to decide the best policy.

C. *The Test of "Good" Policy (3b)*

In the root method, a decision is "correct," "good," or "rational" if it can be shown to attain some specified objective, where the objective can be specified without simply describing the decision itself. Where objectives are defined only through the marginal or incremental approach to values described above, it is still sometimes possible to test whether a policy does in fact attain the desired objectives; but a precise statement of the objectives takes the form of a description of the policy chosen or some alternative to it. To show that a policy is mistaken one cannot offer an abstract argument that important objectives are not achieved; one must instead argue that another policy is more to be preferred.

So far, the departure from customary ways of looking at problem solving is not troublesome, for many administrators will be quick to agree that the most effective discussion of the correctness of policy does take the form of comparison with other policies that might have been chosen. But what of the situation in which administrators cannot agree on values or objectives, either abstractly or in marginal terms? What then is the test of "good" policy? For the root method, there is no test. Agreement on objectives failing, there is no standard of "correctness." For the method of successive limited comparisons, the test is agreement on policy itself, which remains possible even when agreement on values is not.

It has been suggested that continuing agreement in Congress on the desirability of extending old age insurance stems from liberal desires to strengthen the welfare programs of the federal government and from conservative desires to reduce union demands for private pension plans. If so, this is an excellent demonstration of the ease with which individuals of different ideologies often can agree on concrete policy. Labor mediators report a similar phenomenon: The contestants cannot agree on criteria for settling their disputes but can agree on specific proposals. Similarly, when one administrator's objective turns out to be another's means, they often can agree on policy.

Agreement on policy thus becomes the only practicable test of the policy's correctness. And for one administrator to seek to win the other over to agreement on ends as well would accomplish nothing and create quite unnecessary controversy.

If agreement directly on policy as a test for "best" policy seems a poor substitute for testing the policy against its objectives, it ought to be remembered that objectives themselves have no ultimate validity other than that they are agreed upon. Hence agreement is the test of "best" policy in both methods. But where the root method requires agreement on what elements in the decision constitute objectives and on which of these objectives should be sought, the branch method falls back on agreement wherever it can be found.

In an important sense, therefore, it is not irrational for an administrator to defend a policy as good without being able to specify what it is good for.

D. *Noncomprehensive Analysis (4b)*

Ideally, rational-comprehensive analysis leaves out nothing important. But it is impossible to take everything important into consideration unless "important" is so narrowly defined that analysis is in fact quite limited. Limits on human intellectual capacities and on available information set definite limits to man's capacity to be comprehensive. In actual fact, therefore, no one can practice the rational-comprehensive method for very complex problems, and every administrator faced with a sufficiently complex problem must find ways drastically to simplify.

An administrator assisting in the formulation of agricultural economic policy cannot in the first place be competent on all possible policies. He cannot even comprehend one policy entirely. In planning a soil bank program, he cannot successfully anticipate the impact of higher or lower farm income on, say, urbanization—the possible consequent loosening of family ties, possible consequent eventual need for revisions in social security and further implications for tax problems arising out of new federal responsibilities for social security and municipal responsibilities for urban services. Nor, to follow another line of repercussions, can he work through the soil bank program's effects on prices for agricultural products in foreign markets and consequent implications for foreign relations, including those arising out of economic rivalry between the United States and the U.S.S.R.

In the method of successive limited comparisons, simplification is systematically achieved in two principal ways. First, it is achieved through limitation of policy comparisons to those policies that differ in relatively small degree from policies presently in effect. Such a limitation immediately reduces the number of alternatives to be investigated and also drastically simplifies the character of the investigation of each. For it is not necessary to undertake fundamental inquiry into an alternative and its consequences; it is necessary only to study those respects in which the proposed alternative and its consequences differ from the status quo. The empirical comparison of marginal differences among alternative policies that differ only marginally is, of course, a counterpart to the incremental or marginal comparison of values discussed above.[6]

1. *Relevance as Well as Realism*

It is a matter of common observation that in Western democracies public administrators and policy analysts in general do largely limit their analyses to incremental or marginal differences in policies that are chosen to differ only incrementally. They do not do so, however, solely because they desperately need some way to simplify their problems; they also do so in order to be relevant. Democracies change their policies almost entirely through incremental adjustments. Policy does not move in leaps and bounds.

The incremental character of political change in the United States has often been remarked. The two major political parties agree on fundamentals; they offer alternative policies to the voters only on relatively small points of difference. Both parties favor full employment, but they define it somewhat differently; both favor the development of water power resources, but in slightly different ways; and both favor unemployment compensation, but not the same level of benefits. Similarly, shifts of policy within a party take place largely through a series of relatively small changes, as can be seen in their only gradual acceptance of the idea of governmental responsibility for support of the unemployed, a change in party positions beginning in the early 30s and culminating in a sense in the Employment Act of 1946.

Party behavior is in turn rooted in public attitudes, and political theorists cannot conceive of democracy's surviving in the United States in the absence of fundamental agreement on potentially disruptive issues, with consequent limitation of policy debates to relatively small differences in policy.

Since the policies ignored by the administrator are politically

6 A more precise definition of incremental policies and a discussion of whether a change that appears "small" to one observer might be seen differently by another is to be found in my "Policy Analysis," 48 *American Economic Review* (June, 1958), p. 298.

impossible and so irrelevant, the simplification of analysis achieved by concentrating on policies that differ only incrementally is not a capricious kind of simplification. In addition, it can be argued that, given the limits on knowledge within which policy makers are confined, simplifying by limiting the focus to small variations from present policy makes the most of available knowledge. Because policies being considered are like present and past policies, the administrator can obtain information and claim some insight. Nonincremental policy proposals are therefore typically not only politically irrelevant but also unpredictable in their consequences.

The second method of simplification of analysis is the practice of ignoring important possible consequences of possible policies, as well as the values attached to the neglected consequences. If this appears to disclose a shocking shortcoming of successive limited comparisons, it can be replied that, even if the exclusions are random, policies may nevertheless be more intelligently formulated than through futile attempts to achieve a comprehensiveness beyond human capacity. Actually, however, the exclusions, seeming arbitrary or random from one point of view, need be neither.

2. *Achieving a Degree of Comprehensiveness*

Suppose that each value neglected by one policy-making agency were a major concern of at least one other agency. In that case, a helpful division of labor would be achieved, and no agency need find its task beyond its capacities. The shortcomings of such a system would be that one agency might destroy a value either before another agency could be activated to safeguard it or in spite of another agency's efforts. But the possibility that important values may be lost is present in any form of organization, even where agencies attempt to comprehend in planning more than is humanly possible.

The virtue of such a hypothetical division of labor is that every important interest or value has its watchdog. And these watchdogs can protect the interests in their jurisdiction in two quite different ways: First, by redressing damages done by other agencies; and, second, by anticipating and heading off injury before it occurs.

In a society like that of the United States in which individuals are free to combine or pursue almost any possible common interest they might have and in which government agencies are sensitive to the pressures of these groups, the system described is approximated. Almost every interest has its watchdog. Without claiming that every interest has a sufficiently powerful watchdog, it can be argued that our system often can assure a more comprehensive regard for the values of the whole society than any attempt at intellectual comprehensiveness.

In the United States, for example, no part of government attempts a comprehensive overview of policy on income distribution. A policy nevertheless evolves, and one responding to a wide variety of interests. A process of mutual adjustment among farm groups, labor unions, municipalities and school boards, tax authorities, and government agencies with responsibilities in the fields of housing, health, highways, national parks, fire, and police accomplishes a distribution of income in which particular income problems neglected at one point in the decision processes become central at another point.

Mutual adjustment is more pervasive than the explicit forms it takes in negotiation between groups; it persists through the mutual impacts of groups upon each other even where they are not in communication. For all the imperfections and latent dangers in this ubiquitous process of mutual adjustment, it will often accomplish an adaptation of policies to a wider range of interests than could be done by one group centrally.

Note, too, how the incremental pattern of policy making fits with the multiple pressure pattern. For when decisions are only incremental—closely related to known policies, it is easier for one group to anticipate the kind of moves another might make and easier too for it to make correction for injury already accomplished.[7]

Even partisanship and narrowness, to use pejorative terms, will sometimes be assets to rational decision making, for they can doubly insure that what one agency neglects, another will not; they specialize personnel to distinct points of view. The claim is valid that effective rational coordination of the federal

7 The link between the practice of the method of successive limited comparisons and mutual adjustment of interests in a highly fragmented decision-making process adds a new facet to pluralist theories of government and administration.

administration, if possible to achieve at all, would require an agreed set of values[8]—if *rational* is defined as the practice of the root method of decision making. But a high degree of administrative coordination occurs as each agency adjusts its policies to the concerns of the other agencies in the process of fragmented decision making I have just described.

For all the apparent shortcomings of the incremental approach to policy alternatives with its arbitrary exclusion coupled with fragmentation, when compared to the root method, the branch method often looks far superior. In the root method, the inevitable exclusion of factors is accidental, unsystematic, and not defensible by any argument so far developed, while in the branch method the exclusions are deliberate, systematic, and defensible. Ideally, of course, the root method does not exclude; in practice it must.

Nor does the branch method necessarily neglect long-run considerations and objectives. It is clear that important values must be omitted in considering policy, and sometimes the only way long-run objectives can be given adequate attention is through the neglect of short-run considerations. But the values omitted can be either long-run or short-run.

E. Succession of Comparisons (5b)
The final distinctive element in the branch method is that the comparisons, together with the policy choice, proceed in a chronological series. Policy is not made once and for all; it is made and re-made endlessly. Policy making is a process of successive approximation to some desired objectives in which what is desired itself continues to change under reconsideration.

Making policy is at best a very rough process. Neither social scientists, nor politicians, nor public administrators yet know enough about the social world to avoid repeated error in predicting the consequences of policy moves. A wise policy maker consequently expects that his policies will achieve only part of what he hopes and at the same time will produce unanticipated consequences he would have preferred to avoid. If he proceeds

8 Herbert Simon, Donald W. Smithburg, and Victor A. Thompson, *Public Administration* (Alfred A. Knopf, 1950), p. 434.

through a *succession* of incremental changes, he avoids serious lasting mistakes in several ways.

In the first place, past sequences of policy steps have given him knowledge about the probable consequences of further similar steps. Second, he need not attempt big jumps toward his goals that would require predictions beyond his or anyone else's knowledge, because he never expects his policy to be a final resolution of a problem. His decision is only one step, one that if successful can quickly be followed by another. Third, he is in effect able to test his previous predictions as he moves on to each further step. Lastly, he often can remedy a past error fairly quickly—more quickly than if policy proceeded through more distinct steps widely spaced in time.

Compare this comparative analysis of incremental changes with the aspiration to employ theory in the root method. Man cannot think without classifying, without subsuming one experience under a more general category of experiences. The attempt to push categorization as far as possible and to find general propositions which can be applied to specific situations is what I refer to with the word *theory*. Where root analysis often leans heavily on theory is the most systematic and economical way to bring relevant knowledge to bear on a specific problem. Granting the assumption, an unhappy fact is that we do not have adequate theory to apply to problems in any policy area, although theory is more adequate in some areas—monetary policy, for example—than in others. Comparative analysis, as in the branch method, is sometimes a systematic alternative to theory.

Suppose an administrator must choose among a small group of policies that differ only incrementally from each other and from present policy. He might aspire to "understand" each of the alternatives—for example, to know all the consequences of each aspect of each policy. If so, he would indeed require theory. In fact, however, he would usually decide that, *for policy making purposes*, he need know, as explained above, only the consequences of each of those aspects of the policies in which they differed from one another. For this much more modest aspiration, he requires no theory (although it might be helpful, if available), for he can proceed to isolate probable differences by examining the differences in consequences associated with past differences in policies, a feasible program because he can take his observations from a long sequence of incremental changes.

For example, without a more comprehensive social theory about juvenile delinquency than scholars have yet produced, one cannot possibly understand the ways in which a variety of public policies—say on education, housing, and policing—might encourage or discourage delinquency. And one needs such an understanding if he undertakes the comprehensive overview of the problem prescribed in the models of the root method. If, however, one merely wants to mobilize knowledge sufficient to assist in a choice among a small group of similar policies—alternative policies on juvenile court procedures, for example—he can do so by comparative analysis of the results of similar past policy moves.

II. Theorists and Practitioners

This difference explains—in some cases at least—why the administrator often feels that the outside expert or academic problem solver is sometimes not helpful and why they in turn often urge more theory on him. And it explains why an administrator often feels more confident when "flying by the seat of his pants" than when following the advice of theorists. Theorists often ask the administrator to go the long way round to the solution of his problems, in effect ask him to follow the best canons of the scientific method, when the administrator knows that the best available theory will work less well than more modest incremental comparisons. Theorists do not realize that the administrator is often in fact practicing a systematic method. It would be foolish to push this explanation too far, for sometimes practical decision makers are pursuing neither a theoretical approach nor successive comparisons, nor any other systematic method.

It may be worth emphasizing that theory is sometimes of extremely limited helpfulness in policy making for at least two rather different reasons. It is greedy for facts; it can be constructed only through a great collection of observations. And it is typically insufficiently precise for application to a policy process that moves through small changes. In contrast, the comparative method both economizes on the need for facts and directs the analyst's attention to just those facts that are relevant to the fine choices faced by the decision maker.

With respect to precision of theory, economic theory serves as an example. It predicts that an economy without money or prices would in certain specified ways misallocate resources, but this finding pertains to an alternative far removed from the kind of policies on which administrators need help. On the other hand, it is not precise enough to predict the consequences of policies restricting business mergers, and this is the kind of issue on which the administrators need help. Only in relatively restricted areas does economic theory achieve sufficient precision to go far in resolving policy questions; its helpfulness in policy making is always so limited that it requires supplementation through comparative analysis.

III. Successive Comparison as a System

Successive limited comparisons is, then, indeed a method or system; it is not a failure of method for which administrators ought to apologize. Nonetheless, its imperfections, which have not been explored in this paper, are many. For example, the method is without a built-in safeguard for all relevant values, and it also may lead the decision maker to overlook excellent policies for no other reason than that they are not suggested by the chain of successive policy steps leading up to the present. Hence, it ought to be said that under this method, as well as under some of the most sophisticated variants of the root method—operations research, for example—policies will continue to be as foolish as they are wise.

Why then bother to describe the method in all the above detail? Because it is in fact a common method of policy formulation, and is, for complex problems, the principal reliance of administrators as well as of other policy analysts.[9] And because it will be superior to any other decision-making method available for complex problems in many circumstances, certainly superior to a futile attempt at superhuman comprehensiveness. The reaction of the public administrator to the exposition of method doubtless will be less a discovery of a new method than a better acquaintance with an old. But by becoming more conscious of their practice of this method, administrators might practice it with more skill and know when to extend or constrict its use. (That they sometimes practice it effectively and sometimes not may explain the extremes of opinion on "muddling through," which is both praised as a highly sophisticated form of problem solving and denounced as no method at all. For I suspect that in so far as there is a system in what is known as "muddling through," this method is it.)

One of the noteworthy incidental consequences of clarification of the method is the light it throws on the suspicion an administrator sometimes entertains that a consultant or adviser is not speaking relevantly and responsibly when in fact by all ordinary objective evidence he is. The trouble lies in the fact that most of us approach policy problems within a framework given by our view of a chain of successive policy choices made up to the present. One's thinking about appropriate policies with respect, say, to urban traffic control is greatly influenced by one's knowledge of the incremental steps taken up to the present. An administrator enjoys an intimate knowledge of his past sequences that "outsiders" do not share, and his thinking and that of the "outsider" will consequently be different in ways that may puzzle both. Both may appear to be talking intelligently, yet each may find the other unsatisfactory. The relevance of the policy chain of succession is even more clear when an American tries to discuss, say, antitrust policy with a Swiss, for the chains of policy in the two countries are strikingly different and the two individuals consequently have organized their knowledge in quite different ways.

In this phenomenon is a barrier to communication, an under-

9 Elsewhere I have explored this same method of policy formulation as practiced by academic analysts of policy ("Policy Analysis," 48 *American Economic Review* [June, 1958], p. 298). Although it has been here presented as a method for public administrators, it is no less necessary to analysts more removed from immediate policy questions, despite their tendencies to describe their own analytical efforts as though they were the rational-comprehensive method with an especially heavy use of theory. Similarly, this same method is inevitably resorted to in personal problem solving, where means and ends are sometimes impossible to separate, where aspirations or objectives undergo constant development, and where drastic simplification of the complexity of the real world is urgent if problems are to be solved in the time that can be given to them. To an economist accustomed to dealing with the marginal or incremental concept in market processes, the central idea in the method is that both evaluation and empirical analysis are incremental. Accordingly I have referred to the method elsewhere as *the incremental method*.

standing of it promises an enrichment of intellectual interaction in policy formulation. Once the source of difference is understood, it will sometimes be stimulating for an administrator to seek out a policy analyst whose recent experience is with a policy chain different from his own.

This raises again a question only briefly discussed above on the merits of like-mindedness among government administrators. While much of organization theory argues the virtues of common values and agreed organizational objectives, for complex problems in which the root method is inapplicable, agencies will want among their own personnel two types of diversification: administrators whose thinking is organized by reference to policy chains other than those familiar to most members of the organization and, even more commonly, administrators whose professional or personal values or interests create diversity of view (perhaps coming from different specialties, social classes, geographical areas) so that, even within a single agency, decision making can be fragmented and parts of the agency can serve as watchdogs for other parts.

9

Economic Development, Research and Development, Policy Making: Some Converging Views (1962)[1]

CHARLES E. LINDBLOM AND
ALBERT O. HIRSCHMAN

When, in their pursuit of quite different subject matters, a group of social scientists independently of each other appear to converge in a somewhat unorthodox view of certain social phenomena, investigation is in order. The convergence to be examined in this paper is that of the views of Hirschman on economic development, Burton Klein and William Meckling on technological research and development, and Lindblom on policy making in general. These three independent lines of work appear to challenge in remarkably similar ways some widely accepted generalizations about what is variously described in the literature as the process of problem solving or decision making. Before discussing the interrelations of these views, we will give a brief description of each.[2]

I. Hirschman on Economic Development

A major argument of Hirschman's *Strategy of Economic Development* (1958) is his attack on "balanced growth" as either a

---

1 This article is a revised version of Paper No. P–1982, The RAND Corporation, Santa Monica, California, May 4, 1960.
2 Another line of related work is represented in Andrew Gunder Frank's "conflicting standards" organization theory. It is sufficiently different to fall outside the scope of the present article but sufficiently similar to be of interest to anyone who wishes to explore further the areas of unorthodoxy described here. (See Andrew Gunder Frank, "Goal Ambiguity and Conflicting Standards: An Approach to the Study of Organization," 17 *Human Organization* (1959), pp. 8–13; Andrew Gunder Frank and R. Cohen, "Conflicting Standards and Selective Enforcement in Social Organization and Social Change: A Cross-Cultural Test," in paper read at American Anthropological Association Meeting [December, 1959].)

sine qua non of development or as a meaningful proximate objective of development policy. His basic defense of *unbalanced growth* is that, at any one point of time, an economy's resources are not to be considered as rigidly fixed in amount, and that more resources or factors of production will actually come into play if development is marked by sectoral imbalances that galvanize private entrepreneurs or public authorities into action. Even if we know exactly what the economy of a country would look like at a higher plateau, he argues, we can reach this plateau more expeditiously through the path of unbalanced growth because of the additional thrusts received by the economy as it gets into positions of imbalance.

Take an economy with two sectors that are interdependent in the sense that each sector provides some inputs to the other and that the income receivers of each sector consume part of the other sector's final output. With *given* rates of capital formation and increase in the labor supply, it is possible to specify at any one time a certain pair of growth rates for both sectors that is optimally efficient from the points of view of resource utilization and consumer satisfaction. This is balanced growth in its widest sense. Unbalanced growth will manifest its comparative initial inefficiency through a variety of symptoms: losses here, excess profits there, and concomitant relative price movements; or, in the absence of the latter, through shortages, bottlenecks, spoilage, and waste. In an open economy, a possible direct repercussion is a balance-of-payment deficit. In other words, sectoral imbalances will induce a variety of sensations—presence of pain or expectation of pleasure—in the economic operators and policy makers, whose reactions should all converge toward increasing output in the lagging sector.

To the extent that the imbalance is thus self-correcting through a variety of market and nonmarket mechanisms, the economy may be propelled forward jerkily, but also more quickly than under conditions of balanced expansion. Admittedly, the process is likely to be more costly in terms of resource utilization, but the imbalances at the same time *call forth* more resources and investment than would otherwise become available. The crucial, but plausible, assumption here is that there is some "slack" in the economy; and that additional investment, hours of work, productivity, and decision making can be

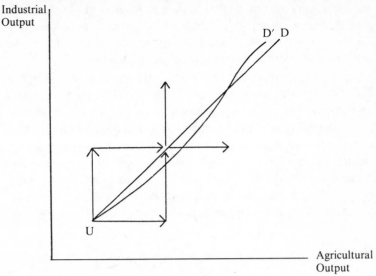

Fig. 1. Balanced vs. Unbalanced Growth

squeezed out of it by the pressure mechanisms set up by imbalances. On the assumption of a given volume of resources and investment, it may be highly irrational not to attempt to come as close as possible to balanced growth; but without these assumptions there is likely to exist such a thing as an "optimal degree of imbalance." In other words, within a certain range, the increased economy in the use of given resources that might come with balanced growth is more than offset by *increased resource mobilization* afforded by unbalanced growth.

A simplified geometrical representation of balanced versus unbalanced growth is as follows: Let there be two sectors of the economy, such as agriculture and industry, whose outputs are measured along the horizontal and vertical axes, respectively. Let point U be the point at which the underdeveloped economy finds itself and D or D' the goal at which it aims. At this stage, assume certainty and unanimous agreement about this goal. Balanced growth then aspires to a movement along such a line as UD or UD'. At the end of each investment period the economy would find itself producing outputs corresponding to successive points on such lines[3] (see Figure 1). Unbalanced growth means to strike out first in one direction (see arrows) and then, impelled by resulting shortages, balance-of-payments pressures, and other assorted troubles, in the other. Hirschman argues that by traveling along this circuitous route, which is likely to be more costly because of the accompanying shortages and excess capacities, the economy may get faster to its goal. Note that there are several varieties of unbalanced growth with varying degrees of pressure. For instance, to start by developing industry is likely to introduce more compelling pressures (because of the resulting food shortages, or, if food is imported, because of the balance-of-payments difficulties) than if the sequence is started by an expansion in agricultural output.

II. Klein and Meckling on Research and Development

Another apparently converging line is represented in the work of Klein and Meckling, who have for several years been studying military experience with alternative research and development policies for weapons systems.[4] They allege that development is both less costly and more speedy when marked by duplication, "confusion," and lack of communication among people working along parallel lines. Perhaps more fundamentally, they argue against too strenuous attempts at integrating various subsystems into a well-articulated, harmonious, general system; they rather advocate the full exploitation of fruitful ideas regardless of their "fit" to some preconceived pattern of specifications.

Suppose a new airplane engine is to be developed and we know that it ought to have certain minimal performance characteristics with respect to, say, range and speed. A curve such as *SS* in Figure 2 may represent this requirement. Is anything to be said here in favor of approaching the goal through an unbalanced path, rather than through shooting straight at the target?

3 We introduced line *UD'* to suggest that balanced growth is not necessarily linear. "Balance" implies that one knows what the appropriate proportions are at each stage of development, but not necessarily that a constant proportion between two or more absolute rates of growth must be preserved.
4 See B. Klein and W. Meckling, "Application of Operations Research to Development Decisions," 6 *Operations Research* (1958), pp. 352–363; and B. Klein, "A Radical Proposal for R and D," *Fortune* (May, 1958), p. 112.

The first and perhaps most important point made here by Klein and Meckling is that there is no single point to shoot at, but a great number of acceptable combinations of the two performance characteristics (shown in Figure 2 by the set of all points lying to the northeast of the curve SS). It is perfectly arbitrary for anyone to pick out a point such as S' as *the* target to shoot at even though this point may be in some sense the expected value of the desired technological advances. The argument then proceeds to show that because of this range of acceptable outcomes, and because of the uncertainty as to what is achievable, *any* advance in the northeasterly direction (such as PP') should be pushed and capitalized on, rather than bent at great effort in the direction of any arbitrarily predetermined target.

The assumption here is that inventions and technical progress follow a "path of their own" to which we should defer: In other words, instead of getting upset at an early stage of development with the "lack of balance" between the two performance specifications (the engine that is being developed is all speed and very little range), we should go on developing it as best we can without reference to point S'. The simplest reason for this is that we may land anyway with a combination of the two characteristics that is acceptable for the purpose at hand: At P'' we have much more speed than we originally bargained for and enough range.

But then there may be other, more interesting reasons why "a wise and salutary neglect" of the balance between the two performance requirements may be desirable in the earlier stages of research and development. A second possibility is that, as an invention or technological advance matures and is fully articulated, possibilities of adjustment may appear that are not present earlier. In Figure 2 we represent this phenomenon by two boundaries PB and PB' that limit the range within which trade-offs between the two characteristics (along the dotted curves) are possible. If these boundaries diverge as shown in our figure, then we would postpone our attempt at trade-offs until we reach the range of greater flexibility (point C).

Third, sometimes the new product that is being developed and which at one stage seemed to be so top-heavy with one of our two requirements will veer around along the path PD and,

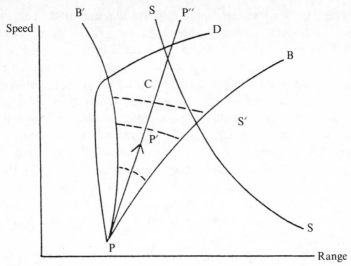

Fig. 2. Alternative Paths of Development of Two Performance Characteristics

in the course of its "natural" development, will acquire the required amount of the second characteristic. To be sure, to assume that this will inevitably happen would require that one places his faith in some basic harmonies, similar to the Greek belief that the truly beautiful will possess moral excellence as well.[5]

Most of what has been said for products with several characteristics applies also to systems with several complementary components. But some of the problems in which we are interested come into sharper focus when we deal with systems where individual components can be independently worked at and perfected. Here also Klein and Meckling advocate full articulation of the components, even though this may mean uneven advances in their development and disregard for their over-all integration into the system at an early stage.

Once again, a principal reason is uncertainty. The final configuration of the system is unknown, and knowledge increases as some of the subsystems become articulated. In the first place, knowledge about the nature of one subsystem increases the

5 To assume the existence of such basic harmonies may be foolish, but it certainly helps us in making crucial decisions such as choosing a wife or a profession.

number of clues about the desirable features of another, just as it is easier to fit in a piece of a jigsaw puzzle when some of the surrounding pieces are already in place. Second, if two pieces (subsystems) have been worked at independently, it is usually possible to join them together by small adjustments: What is important is to develop the pieces, even though they may not be perfectly adjusted to each other to start with.

Obviously if the subsystems are being perfected fairly independently from one another it is likely that one of them will be fully developed ahead of the others, a situation quite similar to that where one sector of the economy races ahead of another. Also it is likely that even if they reach the point of serviceability together, some of them will be "out of phase" with the others, as in the case of a hi-fi system with an amplifier that is far too good for the loudspeaker.[6]

III. Lindblom on Policy Making

A third converging line is represented in Lindblom's papers on policy-making processes.[7] These papers aspire to fairly large-scale generalizations or to what, in some usages, would be called theory construction; while the points of departure of Hirschman and Klein and Meckling are two widely different, but still fairly specific, problem-solving contexts. The differences among the

6 B. Klein, "The Decision-Making Problem in Development," Paper No. P-1916, The RAND Corporation (February, 1960) gives a straightforward exposition of the logical and empirical differences between development decisions and decisions to maximize the use of existing resources. He again advocates looseness in goal-setting and gradual, oblique, or multiple approaches to the goal. In doing so, Klein now emphasizes the contrast between the decision maker in established production processes who accepts the relatively small uncertainties he faces as a datum, and the development decision maker whose chief purpose is to reduce the huge variance of the inital estimates so that successive investment and production decisions can be made with increasing degrees of confidence. In addition, he argues that it is of rather secondary interest to the developer to achieve an efficient combination of inputs. His main interest is achieving a breakthrough to a new product or to radically improved performance characteristics.

7 "Policy Analysis" in 48 American Economics Review (1958), pp. 298–312; "Tinbergen on Policy Making" in 66 Journal of Political Economics (1958), pp. 531–538; "The Handling of Norms in Policy Analysis" in M. Abramovitz, ed., Allocation of Economic Resources (1958), pp. 160–179; and "Decision Making in Taxation and Expenditure" in Universities—National Bureau of Economic Research, Public Finances; Needs, Sources, and Utilization (1961).

studies in this respect make the convergences all the more note-worthy.

Lindblom's point of departure is a denial of the general validity of two assumptions implicit in most of the literature on policy making. The first is that public policy problems can best be solved by attempting to understand them; the second is that there exists sufficient agreement to provide adequate criteria for choosing among possible alternative policies. Although the first is widely accepted—in many circles almost treated as a self-evident truth—it is often false. The second is more often questioned in contemporary social science; yet many of the most common prescriptions for rational problem solving follow only if it is true.

Conventional descriptions of rational decision making iden-tify the following aspects: (1) clarification of objectives or values, (2) survey of alternative means of reaching objectives, (3) identification of consequences, including side effects or by-products, of each alternative means, and (4) evaluation of each set of consequences in light of the objectives. However, Lind-blom notes, for a number of reasons such a *synoptic* or compre-hensive attempt at problem solving is not possible to the degree that clarification of objectives founders on social conflict, that required information is either not available or available only at prohibitive cost, or that the problem is simply too complex for man's finite intellectual capacities. Its complexity may stem from an impossibly large number of alternative policies and their possible repercussions from imponderables in the delin-eation of objectives even in the absence of social disagreement on them, from a supply of information too large to process in the mind, or from still other causes.

It does not logically follow, Lindblom argues, that when synoptic decision making is extremely difficult it should never-theless be pursued as far as possible. And he consequently suggests that in many circumstances substantial departures from comprehensive understanding are both inevitable and, on specific grounds, desirable. For the most part, these departures are familiar; and his exposition of them serves therefore to formalize our perceptions of certain useful problem-solving strategies often mistakenly dismissed as aberrations in rational problem solving.

These strategies, which we shall call *disjointed incrementalism*, are the following:

A. Attempt at understanding is limited to policies that differ only incrementally from existing policy.
B. Instead of simply adjusting means to ends, ends are chosen that are appropriate to available or nearly available means.
C. A relatively small number of means (alternative possible policies) is considered, as follows from A.
D. Instead of comparing alternative means or policies in the light of postulated ends or objectives, alternative ends or objectives are also compared in the light of postulated means or policies and their consequences.
E. Ends and means are chosen simultaneously; the choice of means does not follow the choice of ends.
F. Ends are indefinitely explored, reconsidered, discovered, rather than relatively fixed.
G. At any given analytical point (*point* refers to any one individual, group, agency, or institution), analysis and policy making are serial or successive; that is, problems are not "solved" but are repeatedly attacked.
H. Analysis and policy making are remedial; they move *away* from ills rather than *toward* known objectives.
I. At any one analytical point, the analysis of consequences is quite incomplete.
J. Analysis and policy making are socially fragmented; they go on at a very large number of separate points simultaneously.

The most striking characteristic of disjointed incrementalism is (as indicated in I) that no attempt at comprehensiveness is made; on the contrary, unquestionably important consequences of alternative policies are simply ignored at any given analytical or policy-making point. But Lindblom goes on to argue that through various specific types of partisan mutual adjustment among the large number of individuals and groups among which analysis and policy making is fragmented (see J), what is ignored at one point in policy making becomes central at another point. Hence, it will often be possible to find a tolerable level of rationality in decision making when the process is viewed as a whole in its social or political context, even if at each individual policy-making point or center analysis remains incomplete. Similarly, errors that would attend overly ambitious attempts at comprehensive understanding are often avoided by the remedial and incremental character of problem solving. And those not avoided can be mopped up or attended to as they appear, because analysis and policy making are serial or successive (as in G).

While we cannot here review the entire argument, Lindblom tries to show how the specific characteristics of disjointed, incrementalism, taken in conjunction with mechanisms for partisan mutual adjustment, meet each of the characteristic difficulties that beset synoptic policy making: value conflicts, information inadequacies, and general complexity beyond man's intellectual capacities. His line of argument shows the influence of pluralist thinkers on political theory, but he departs from their interest in the control of power and rather focuses on the level of rationality required or appropriate for decision making.

IV. Points of Convergence

If they are not already obvious, specific parallels in the works reviewed are easy to illustrate. Compare, for example, an economy that is in a state of imbalance as the result of a sharp but isolated advance of one sector and a weapons system that is out of balance because a subsystem is "too good" in relation to the capacity of another system. Just as for a sector of the economy, it is possible that a completed subsystem is "too advanced" only in comparison with some preconceived notion, and that actually its unexpectedly high performance level is quite welcome, either because it improves upon over-all system performance or because it happily compensates for the lag of some other component behind the norms originally set. On the other hand, a component can be "too advanced" in a real sense; as in a hi-fi set, where the performance of a component depends not only on its capacity but also on inputs from other components. This situation corresponds exactly to that of an economy in structural imbalance. The laggard components turn into bottlenecks for the full utilization of the *avant-garde* component's capacity. Yet even though such a system or economy represents in itself an inefficient utilization of inputs, it may nevertheless be a highly useful configuration, if it is conceived as a stage in the development process. For it may be expected that attempts will be made to improve the weaker subsystems or sectors so that the capability of the stronger ones may be fully utilized. In the process, the weaker systems or sectors may be so improved that they become the stronger ones, and the stage thus set for a series of seesaw advances which may carry the over-all "goodness" of our system or economy beyond what might have been achieved by maintaining balance.

For both economy and weapons system we are talking in terms of probabilities. There can be no certainty that with one *avant-garde* subsystem readied the others will dutifully be put in place or improved. The existence of the Maginot Line along the French-German border failed to call forth a corresponding effort along the Belgian frontier to guard against the possibility of a German strategy aimed at circumventing the Line.

This example illustrates an important point: A "system" or economy is never quite finished. Today's system or economy-inbalance is likely to turn into tomorrow's subsystem or economy-out-of-balance, because of unforeseeable repercussions, newly emerging difficulties, unanticipated counterstrategies, changing tastes or techniques, or whatever other forces with which the system or economy has to deal.[8] But these repercussions, difficulties, and counterstrategies could not possibly be fully visualized in advance. The transportation system consisting of highways, gasoline and repair stations, and automotive vehicles is found incomplete; first because of inadequate accident prevention, and later also because of smog. The new system of defense against infections through antibiotics is suddenly "out of balance" because of the development of new varieties of drug-resistant microorganisms. In these cases, it would have been impossible to foresee the imbalance and incompleteness that emerged clearly only after the new system had been in operation for some time.

Once it is understood that a system is never complete or will never stay complete, the case against spending considerable effort on early integration and simultaneous development of

---

8 It is hardly necessary to mention the similarity, in this respect, between the Maginot Line and some of our present defense systems such as the DEW Line.

subsystems is further strengthened. For if we do achieve early integration and simultaneity, we are much more likely to succumb to the illusion that our system is actually complete in itself and needs no further complements and watchfulness than if we had built it up as a result of seesaw advances and adjustments which do not provide for a natural resting place.[9]

As another specific illustration of convergence, consider the sequence of moves in problem solving as described, on the one hand, in developmental terms by Hirschman, Klein and Meckling and, on the other hand, in political terms by Lindblom. Recall the picture of desired progress where we wished to move from one fixed point (the present) to another fixed point in a two-dimensional diagram. From existing levels of output in industry and agriculture (or range and speed in aircraft) we wished to move to higher levels for both. Imagine a situation in which two parties with different preferences want to go off in two different directions. Lindblom argues that in this situation the best way to make progress is through "mutual adjustment," i.e., by a series of moves and countermoves in the

9 The examples of the Maginot Line, of automobile traffic, and of antibiotics bring up an additional problem. In the latter two cases, the incompleteness of the system is forcefully brought to our attention through accidents and eye irritation, and through new types of infection. The trouble with some other systems that turn into subsystems is that the mutation may not be so easily detected, or that it may be detected only when it is too late, as was precisely the case with the Maginot Line.

There is real difficulty about the meaning of "too late." The imperfections of automobile traffic and antibiotics were discovered too late for the victims of accidents and new-type infections, but not too late, we hope, for the rest of us. The defects of the Maginot Line were discovered too late to save France in 1940, although not too late to win the war against Hitler. This suggests that there may be cases where we cannot afford to do our learning about the imperfections and imbalances of a system through the failures, irritations, and discomforts that are the natural concomitants and signals of the imbalance. Such situations present us with a well-nigh insoluble task, similar to the one which would face a child who had to learn to walk without being permitted to fall. Here the temptation is particularly strong to prepare in advance a perfect theoretical solution. Yet we know from all that has been said that reliance on such a solution would be most likely to bring about the failure one is seeking to avoid. One way of dealing with situations in which we feel we cannot afford to learn the "hard way" is to develop institutions whose special mission it is to be alert to and to detect existing and developing system imbalances: In a democracy, some institutions of this kind are a free press and an opposition party. For national defense a certain amount of interservice rivalry may serve the same purpose, as each service has a vested interest in pointing out the "holes" in the other services' systems.

course of which a higher plateau can be reached even without prior agreement about the eventual goal. "Individuals often agree on policies when they cannot agree on ends. Moreover, attempts to agree on ends or values often get in the way of agreements on specific policies."[10] Furthermore, it is possible, and even likely, that the value systems of the two parties will move more closely together once an advance that is tolerable to both has been achieved. "The decision-maker expects to learn about his values from his experiences and he is inclined to think that in the long run policy choices have as great an influence on objectives as objectives have on policy choices."[11]

Lindblom's reasoning reinforces the others. It parallels Klein and Meckling's emphasis on the inevitability of moving forward through move and countermove, in what appears an arbitrary, somewhat aimless fashion, rather than Hirschman's stress on the efficiency of such a sequence in squeezing out additional resources. Nevertheless, the idea that unbalanced or seesaw advances of this kind are efficient in some sense is also present. Instead of focusing on the limited supply of decision makers and on the desirablity of placing some extra pressures behind investment decisions, Lindblom emphasizes the limited supply of knowledge and the limited area of agreement that exists among the various powerholders, and visualizes a series of sequential adjustments as a way to maximize positive action in a society where ignorance, uncertainty, and conflict preclude not only the identification, but even the existence, of any "best" move.

But we can do better than illustrate parallels. We can explicitly identify the principal points of convergence.

1. The most obvious similarity is that all insist on the rationality and usefulness of certain processes and modes of behavior which are ordinarily considered to be irrational, wasteful, and generally abominable.

2. The three approaches thus have in common an attack on such well-established values as orderliness (cf. Hirschman's "model of optimum disorderliness"[12] balance, and detailed pro-

---

10 "Tinbergen on Policy Making," *op. cit.*, p. 534.
11 "Decision Making in Taxation and Expenditure," *op. cit.*, p. 309.
12 In *The Strategy of Economic Development* (New York, 1958), p. 80.

gramming; they all agree with Burke that some matters ought to be left to a "wise and salutary neglect."

3. They agree that one step ought often to be left to lead to another, and that it is unwise to specify objectives in much detail when the means of attaining them are virtually unknown.

4. All agree further that in rational problem solving, goals will change not only in detail but in a more fundamental sense through experience with a succession of means-ends and ends-means adjustments.

5. All agree that in an important sense a rational problem solver wants what he can get and does not try to get what he wants except after identifying what he wants by examining what he can get.

6. There is also agreement that the exploration of alternative uses of resources can be overdone, and that attempts at introducing explicitly certain maximizing techniques (trade-offs among inputs or among outputs, cost-benefit calculations) and coordinating techniques will be ineffective and quite possibly harmful in some situations. In a sense more fundamental than is implied by theories stressing the cost of information, the pursuit of certain activities that are usually held to be the very essence of "economizing" can at times be decidedly uneconomical.

7. One reason for this is the following: For successful problem solving, all agree it is most important that arrangements exist through which decision makers are sensitized and react promptly to newly emerging problems, imbalances, and difficulties; this essential ability to react and to improvise readily and imaginatively can be stultified by an undue preoccupation with, and consequent pretense at, advance elimination of these problems and difficulties through "integrated planning."

8. Similarly, attempts at foresight can be misplaced; they will often result in complicating the problem through mistaken diagnoses and ideologies. Since man has quite limited capacities to solve problems and particularly to foresee the shape of future problems, the much maligned "hard way" of learning by experiencing the problems at close range may often be the most expeditious and least expensive way to a solution.

9. Thus we have here theories of successive decision making; denying the possibility of determining the sequence *ex ante*,

relying on the clues that appear in the course of the sequence, and concentrating on identification of these clues.

10. All count on the usefulness for problem solving of subtle social processes not necessarily consciously directed at an identified social problem. Processes of mutual adjustment of participants are capable of achieving a kind of coordination not necessarily centrally envisaged prior to its achievement, or centrally managed.

11. At least Hirschman and Lindblom see in political adjustment and strife analogues to self-interested yet socially useful adjustment in the market.

12. All question such values as "foresight," "central direction," "integrated overview," but not in order to advocate *laissez-faire* or to inveigh against expanded activities of the state in economic or other fields. They are in fact typically concerned with decision-making and problem-solving activities carried on by the state. In their positive aspects they describe how these activities are "really" taking place as compared to commonly held images; and insofar as they are normative they advocate a modification of these images, in the belief that a clearer appreciation and perception of institutions and attitudes helpful to problem-solving activities will result.

Although many of these propositions are familiar, they are often denied in explicit accounts of rational decision making; and at least some of them challenge familiar contrary beliefs. Either the convergences are an unfortunate accident, or decision-making theory has underplayed the degree to which "common sense" rational problem-solving procedures have to be modified or abandoned. Account must be taken of man's inertia, limited capacities, costs of decision making, and other obstacles to problem solving, including uncertainty, which is the only one of the complicating elements that has been given sustained attention. And most investigations of uncertainty have been within the narrow competence of statistical theory.

---

13 An even higher authority might be invoked, namely the Sermon on the Mount: "Take therefore no thought for the morrow, for the morrow will take care of the things of itself."

V. Points of Difference

These similarities in approach, with their widely different origins, structures, and fields of application, are even better understood if their remaining points of difference are identified.

The basic justification for rejecting traditional precepts of rationality, planning, and balance is somewhat different for the three approaches here examined. For Lindblom it is *complexity*, i.e., man's inability to *comprehend* the present interrelatedness and future repercussions of certain social processes and decisions, as well as imperfect knowledge and *value conflicts*. For Klein and Meckling it is almost entirely *future uncertainty*, i.e., man's inability to *foresee* the shape of technological breakthroughs, or the desirability of letting oneself be guided by these breakthroughs if and when they occur, instead of following a predetermined sequence. For Hirschman it is the difficulty of mobilizing potentially available resources and decision-making activity itself; the *inadequacy of incentives* to problem solving, or, conversely, the need for *inducements* to decision making.

Although Klein's and Meckling's concern with future uncertainty could formally be viewed as a special case of Lindblom's problem of inadequate information, their treatment of the research and development problem is different enough from Lindblom's treatment of information inadequacies to argue, against its being so viewed. Hirschman's concern with inducements to problem-solving activity is quite different from either Lindblom's or Klein's and Meckling's concern with limits on cognitive faculties. He argues not that men lack knowledge and capacity to solve problems in an absolute sense, but that there is always some unutilized problem-solving capacity that can be called forth through a variety of inducement mechanisms and pacing devices. These different reasons for supporting the same conclusions make the conclusions more rather than less persuasive, for the reasons supplement rather than invalidate each other.

That they are complementary reasons is, of course, indicated by the overlap of the Lindblom and the Klein–Meckling approaches on the problem of imperfect information, and by some Hirschmanlike concern for research and development *incentives* in the Klein–Meckling study. It is also true that Hirschman develops as a secondary theme the difficulties of ignorance and uncertainty in economic development. For instance, his partiality toward "development via social overhead capital shortage" is based in part on the position that shortages and bottlenecks remove uncertainty about the direction of needed overhead investments. Similarly, he emphasizes the importance of unforeseen or loose complementary repercussions, such as "entrained wants" that arise in the course of development, and asserts that imports are helpful in inducing domestic production because they remove previous doubts about the existence of a market.

From the differences in the main thrust of the respective arguments, certain other major differences emerge, differences which do not deny the convergences, but which, on the other hand, ought not be submerged by them. For example. Hirschman's argument that a very heavy reliance on central planning will often be inappropriate for underdeveloped countries looks superficially parallel to Lindblom's argument that *partisan* mutual adjustment can sometimes achieve efficiencies that could not be achieved through overambitious attempts at central omniscience and control. Yet on closer scrutiny, Hirschman's cautions about centralism only secondarily refer to the *general* difficulties of managing complex affairs that strain man's incentives and intellectual capacities. Instead he argues that a conventional, centrally planned attempt to define and achieve a balance among many varied lines of development will be less helpful than a similarly central attempt to estimate and manage the critical linkages through which economic growth is forced or induced.[14]

Hirschman's explicitly declared view of decision making for economic development is almost entirely one of central planning, or at least problem solving by persons—such as planning board managers or officials of international agencies—who assume some general responsibility toward the economy as a whole, and whose point of view is therefore that of a central planner. Hirschman's policy maker or operator is, with only a few exceptions, such a person or official; and Hirschman's

14 This argument against the attempt at balanced growth is quite different from Hirschman's other argument that balance in growth is not desirable even if achieved.

prescriptions are always addressed to such a person. By contrast, Lindblom's policy maker is typically a partisan, often acknowledging no responsibility to his society as a whole, frankly pursuing his own segmental interests; and this is a kind of policy maker for whom Hirschman, despite his between-the-lines endorsement of him, makes no explicit place in his formulation of the development process.

A further important point of difference between Hirschman and Lindblom appears to lie in Hirschman's emphasis on discovering and utilizing the side-effects and repercussions of development decisions, as compared to Lindblom's readiness to recommend at any given "point" neglect of such repercussions. It is indeed a major thesis of Hirschman that analysis of a prospective investment project should above all try to evaluate its effect on further development decisions instead of conventionally concentrating on its own prospective output and productivity. Specifically, every decision should be analyzed to discover its possible "linkages" with other decisions that might follow it. For example, a prospective decision to encourage the importation of some consumer goods, such as radios, should consider not simply the economy's need for these goods but the probability that their importation will in time lead to a decision by domestic investors to assemble them locally, as well as the "linkage effects" of such assembly operations on further domestic production decisions.

Hirschman's book *The Strategy of Economic Development* (1958) is both an attempt to uncover such linkages and a prescription that developers seek to uncover them in every possible case. Lindblom suggests that this kind of by-product, the indirect consequences of a decision that flow from the decision's effect on still other decision makers, will often escape the analyst in any case; hence, he should not try to always anticipate and understand it, but instead should deal with it through subsequent steps in policy making, if and when it emerges as a problem. Since, as Lindblom sees it, policy-making is not only *remedial* and *serial* but also *fragmented*, both intentionally and accidentally neglected consequences of chosen policies will often be attended to either as a remedial next step of the original policy makers or by some other policy-making group whose interests are affected. Hence policy as a complex social or political process rises to a higher level of comprehensiveness and rationality than is achieved by any one policy maker at any one move in the process.

The contrast between Hirschman and Lindblom on this point can be overdrawn, however. For one thing, Hirschman feels that calculations which purport to give greater rationality to investment planning may often interfere with development, because they typically do not and cannot take the "linkages" into account; whereas more rough-and-ready methods may be at least based on hunches about such linkages. Second, Hirschman's practical advice to policy makers is similar to Lindblom's when he tells them to go ahead with unintegrated and unbalanced projects on the ground that, in an interdependent economy, progress in some sectors will serve to unmask the others as laggards and will thereby bring new pressures toward improvement. In his general prescription, more implicit than explicit, that development planners try to move the economy wherever it can be moved, that is, seize on readiness to act whereever it can be found, Hirschman is endorsing Lindblom's suggestion that many consequences can best be dealt with only as they actually show themselves.

As a further point of difference, it is implicit in what has been said in the preceding paragraphs that Hirschman's thinking about secondary effects is preoccupied with possible bonuses to be exploited, Lindblom's with possible losses to be minimized. Again, the difference is easy to overstate: Hirschman too is at times concerned with possible losses, even if Lindblom has not explored at all the possibility of bonuses. Hirschman, however, relies on correct diagnosis of linkages for protection from damaging side effects; and his position is therefore parallel to his position on exploiting bonus effects. Only secondarily[15] does he count on Lindblom's remedial, serial, and fragmented kind of process for minimizing losses.

VI. Concluding Remarks

As Hirschman would now give uncertainty, complexity, and value conflict a more central place in justifying his conclusions

---

15 *The Strategy of Economic Development, op. cit.*, p. 208ff.

on economic development policy, so also Lindblom's and Klein's and Meckling's analyses could be strengthened by taking into account the fact that the policies they defend could also be justified because they permit mobilization of resources and energies that could not be activated otherwise. Perhaps these latter analyses could go beyond the statement that the processes of research and development and of policy making are of necessity piecemeal, successive, fragmented, and disjointed; they could try to define typical sequences and their characteristics, similar to Hirschman's "permissive" and "compulsive" sequences. Once the intellectual taboo and wholesale condemnation are lifted from some of the policies Klein, Mecklin, and Lindblom defend, it becomes desirable to have a closer look at the heretofore incriminated processes and to rank them from various points of view. It is useful to ask questions such as the following: As long as we know that a system is going to be out of balance anyway when the subsystems develop, what type of imbalance is most likely to be self-correcting? An answer to this question could affect the desirable distribution and emphasis of the research and development effort. Detailed descriptions of types of incremental meandering would also be interesting; perhaps this would more clearly differentiate between a sequence that leads to reform and another that leads to revolution.

One problem deserves to be mentioned again. The processes of economic development, research and development, and policy making must all rely on successive decision making because they all break new, uncertain ground. Therefore these processes must let themselves be guided by the clues that appear en route. Snags, difficulties, and tensions cannot be avoided, but must on the contrary be utilized to propel the process further. The trouble is that the difficulties are not only "little helpers," but may also start processes of disintegration and demoralization. An intersectoral imbalance sets up a race between the catching-up, forward movement of the lagging sector and the retrogression of the advanced one. The greater the pressure toward remedial positive action, the greater is the risk if this action does not take place. There is a corresponding situation in systems development. The more a system is out of balance, the greater will presumably be the pressure to do something about it, but also the more useless is the system should no action be forthcoming.

All three approaches therefore have one further characteristic in common: They can be overdone. There are limits to "imbalance" in economic development, to "lack of integration" in research and development, to "fragmentation" in policy making which would be dangerous to pass. And it is clearly impossible to specify in advance the optimal doses of these various policies under different circumstances. The art of promoting economic development, research and development, and constructive policy making in general consists, then, in acquiring a feeling for these doses.

This art, it is submitted by the theories here reviewed, will be mastered far better once the false ideals of "balance," "coordination," and "comprehensive overview" have lost our total and unquestioning intellectual allegiance.

10

New Decision-Making Procedures Governing Research on and Treatment of Catastrophic Diseases (1970)*

In 69 *Columbia Law Review* (1969) a Note, "Scarce Medical Resources," summarizes the law bearing on providing or failing to provide ordinary and unusual medical services and goes on to analyze decision problems arising in dialysis and organ transplantation on which the law is yet to be made. The Note accomplishes an excellent overview of theoretical and practical considerations bearing on the design of necessary decision-making procedures and includes a catalogue of their principal major alternative features.

Where do we go from there? I am going to try to advance the discussion, not by trying to pursue further the issues raised in the Note, but by indicating the character of the further analysis needed.

For the design of improved decision-making processes to govern research and therapy for catastrophic diseases, there are no available formulae, no established guidelines, no standard blueprints, no decision-making procedures in comparable problem areas that can simply be copied. We know a good deal about organizations, collective problem solving, decision-making processes, public administration, public policy making and politics; but all our information taken together is far from giving us specific design and guideline for complex decision making. What is required, therefore, is the art of practical judgement, at best only supported but never displaced by our social scientific knowledge.

Unable to derive from theory or social science a set of specifi-

* Published with the permission of J. Katz and A. M. Capron.

cations for good decision-making procedures, the best an analyst of decision-making can do is, as an act of practical judgement, to offer the tentative opinion that this or that improvement in decision-making procedures is probably desirable. But
practical judgement of that kind is subjective, tentative and
fallible. If it leads to action, we would expect it often to be
misguided, in which case new judgements have to be made and
new reforms attempted. Or if the judgement and action are not
in fact actually mistaken, the reforms are often inadequate. If
so, new judgements are needed to devise ways of strengthening
them. And at the same time it seems inevitable that we upgrade
our ambitions with each new success in reform, so that even
the best of practical judgements of one year seem disappointing
by the standards of a new year or decade.

Hence practical judgements have to be sequentially reconsidered as we read the ever revolving record of successes and
failures. In addition, we learn from closely related success and
failure: Any one of us who is designing improved decision-
making procedures, say, for allocating heart transplants, will
learn something from the record of those who are engaged in
a sequence of improvements on decision making, say, for dialysis and kidney transplants.

Moreover, even if our knowledge of decision making were
almost perfect and we could indeed specify a near ideal decision-
making procedure for any problem needing one, what would
be good today would not necessarily be good tomorrow. And
this not only because medical technology constantly changes
and throws up new problems to us, and not only because our
aspiration—our sense of what we will tolerate—changes from
time to time. An additional complication is that decision-making procedures, like all forms of social organization, are unstable. Some organizations go soft, some turn hard. Some get
flabby, some rigidify. But all social organizations, like persons,
have a kind of life of their own and cannot be designed to stay
put. So even if one could conceive of an ideal decision-making
apparatus, maintaining its ideal qualities would require constant
restructuring.

My purpose in identifying at least these three major complications in the design of good decision making—the inadequacy
of our scientific knowledge about decision making; changing

problems, opportunities, and aspirations; and the instability of social organizations—is not to sabotage the task of design but to direct it. Designers should aspire not to nearly ideal decision-making procedures, but to acceptable imperfect ones, to procedures whose imperfections will be informative, and to those that do not resist further reform.[1]

Beyond that general conclusion, the three general difficulties of decision-making design just referred to point to a host of specific major difficulties in design, only a few of which I am going to single out here for their special importance.

I. The Difficulties of Defining "Good" Decision Making

A fundamental specific difficulty, the mere statement of which ramifies in several directions, is that, though we are designing decision-making procedures to get "good" decisions, we do not know what "good" decisions are. That is, we cannot define the qualities we want in the decisions to come out of the designed procedures. For analysts of decision-making procedures whose intellectual habits require that the solution to a problem be well defined *before* it is sought—specifically, in this case, that "good" decisons be well defined before we search for procedures to make good decisions—our inability to define in any systematic way the qualities we want in the decisions to be made is a baffling, sometimes paralyzing complexity in the design of decision-making procedures. And even for those of us who are willing to work on poorly defined problems, our inability to specify systematically what qualities we want in the output, in the decisions to be reached in a designed decision-making system, is distressing. The problem would indeed be much simpler if we knew what kind of decisions we wanted.

Why can we not specify the kinds of decisions we want?

---

1 This line of argument can be fashioned into a double-edged recommendation. On the one hand, the design of decision-making processes should be a sequential, self-corrective, never-ending exploratory process. And on the other hand, decision-making procedures should be designed so that, faced with their problems, the decision makers themselves can approach their problems in a sequence of tentative, self-correcting, exploratory steps. Designer of decision-making machinery and actual decision maker both need to see their problems in this way.

A. *Correct Decisions?*

Clearly we cannot seriously propose that we want correct decisions, where *correct*, its synonyms and its antonyms carry such meanings as they do in sentences like: "The judge was correct in overruling the attorney's objection," or "Am I right in believing we have met before?" or "The Reserve Board made a mistake in reducing interest rates at that particular time." In examples like these, whether a decision is correct or incorrect, right or mistaken, is settled by an appeal to an accepted, though often only implicit, criteria. There is at least in principle a clear empirical test, in short, for whether the decision falls within a class of decisions that are defined as the solution to the decision problem.

When society, or you or I, contemplates some decision such as an allocation of research funds to competing worthy projects or problem areas or the allocation of an organ to only one of competing would-be recipients, we will, as a practical matter, have no difficulty in throwing out some possible decisions as preposterous—for example, awarding the organ to someone already near death for causes other than his need for the organ—but we will always be faced with a remaining vast array of possible decisions no one of which can be demonstrated to be more correct than any other. Under these circumstances, informed and thoughtful people will, to be sure, reach a decision with which they might thereafter feel comfortable, that they would be willing to defend, and that they could demonstrate had emerged from a thoughtful interchange of facts and judgements. But they will not be able to show that it was tested successfully against some generally agreed "solution" to the problem and was found to conform, as other possible decisions did not.

There are of course some people, in the tradition of Plato, who believe that there is at any one time a one best state of affairs for man, hence one best set of institutions, one best allocation of resources, one best allocation of public funds. But even these people acknowledge that mankind has not yet discovered these optima nor is it on the point of doing so. Hence, even for them, as a practical matter they have no criteria by which the kinds of decisions for which we want to design procedures can be tested for correctness. Moreover, even if these optima could in fact be discovered, finding them and then deriving from them criteria of correctness for specific policy decisions would take vastly more time than decision makers have at their disposal when, day by day and month by month, they must reach decisions.

All of this everyone pretty well knows, and I give it the attention I do only to emphasize its implication for our task. Most of us have the habit—the intellectual habit—of believing that we can only solve a problem when we have a criteria for its solution. What I am arguing is that we are here faced with a task of designing good decision-making procedures without having adequate criteria for distinguishing between good and bad decisions. Specifically, we have no criteria for distinguishing correct from incorrect decisions.

B. *Decisions That Adjust Interests?*

Nor, to continue the argument, do we have any other adequate criteria for distinguishing between good and bad decisions and hence guiding our design of decision-making procedures in the direction of good decisions. Most people would say that, since we cannot determine whether decisions are correct or incorrect, the best we can do is consider decisions as ways of resolving or aggregating interests. That is to say, two decisions on such problems as concern us here do not differ in their degrees of correctness but differ in the interests they serve. A decision will favor the interests, for example, of diabetics as against heart cases, or a decision may favor the interests of researchers over the interests of therapists. Or the interests of the poor as against the well-off, or vice versa.

Leaving aside criminal interests and certain other predatory or exploitative interests, by this view of the decision process all interests are said to be deserving. Moreover, in a democratic society, we say that in some sense the interests of any one man are neither more nor less deserving than the interests of any one other.

The analysis of interests gives us much less help in defining good and bad decisions than we might think. It is disappointing on many counts.

1. Who knows whose interests?

First, it leaves quite up in the air the question of whether good decisions are those that experts believe will serve the interests of various groups in the society or whether good decisions are those that serve the interests of these groups as they themselves perceive them. We may be easily satisfied that decisions ought to respond to your interests and mine as we ourselves perceive them for decisions, say, on who should be president, mayor, or senator or on how much taxes we should pay. For we see no possible expert group in the society likely to perceive our interests more accurately than we perceive them ourselves. But for decisions on the allocation of health research funds to competing claimants or decisions on the allocation of dialysis units, it is not at all clear that you and I can ascertain our own interests as well as can a physician, or an economist, or a trained public administrator, among other experts who might be more competent than we.

2. Unknowable and nonformed interests

What is even worse for the interests approach is that in an important sense many of our supposedly relevant interests are unknowable. To be sure, the manufacturers of dialysis equipment may have an identifiable interest in promoting its use, but it probably makes very little sense to say that the great mass of citizens in a nation have either more or less of an interest in one kind of research or therapy than in another. To be sure, the statistical incidence of some diseases is greater than that of others, but on the other hand some diseases are more dangerous than others for those persons whom they hit, and then again some diseases are expected to respond more promisingly to research and therapy than others. So that, weighing all these factors together, it is impossible to correlate different allocations of funds, say, to different patterns of interests, justifying one pattern over another on the ground that it better corresponds to the pattern of interests.

Paradoxically, for many decisions on research and treatment of catastrophic diseases, it is probably easier to find a citizen interest in good decision making, however undefined, than to find a citizen interest in any particular decision outcome.

3. Whose and what interests should weigh how much?

A further complication. Where interests can be ascertained—that is, when they indeed actually exist and when there is some competent way of determining what they are—we have no adequate criteria for specifying what kind of interests or whose interests should prevail over others and to what degree. Suppose, for example, that we know beyond doubt that one decision will give larger health benefits to migrant workers, another to school children, and another to central-city Blacks. These interests are in competition. Do we have any way of knowing which of the three decisions is best?

4. The inapplicability of democratic ideas

Here our only recourse seems to fall back on certain egalitarian and democratic ideas. But—perhaps surprisingly—they are of very limited help. The egalitarian or democratic commitment to treat the interests of any one man as neither more nor less worthy than the interests of any other man is a highly qualified commitment. Taken in a mechanical and literal sense, it would prescribe that we give no more medical care to a man who breaks his leg than to a man who is in perfect health, no more education to a highly talented young scientist than to the most ordinary grade-school scholar. Strictly speaking, it would also prescribe that in a conflict between police officer and reckless driver, the preference of the police officer for apprehending the driver should be considered no more important than the interest of the driver in driving as he pleases.

In actual fact, the democratic commitment to equality is not literal; it is really a highly discriminating commitment to equal treatment for a very narrow band of interests—interests in form of government, in selection of major political officials, in "equal protection under the law," and occasionally in choice of general over-arching policies, as exemplified in the relatively infrequent use of referenda on public issues. But as between the disabled and the healthy, the young and the old, the urban and the rural, the poor and the wealthy, the resourceful and the dependent, the venturesome and the timid and so on, we know their needs are different and unequal; and we have long practiced and can think of many good reasons for practicing many specific forms of inequality in weighing their interests against each other. Obviously we recognize special needs, unusually deserving interests, and special roles.

And so we come out, not only with a conclusion that there are no satisfactory criteria for weighing interests for the kinds of decisions we have in mind but that in addition we have to reject specifically the criteria that decisions be democratic in their weighing of interests. We reject that criteria not because it is incorrect—clearly we do not wish decisions to be undemocratic—but because it is wholly inadequate as a guide for good decisions except for the narrow band of major political decisions for which the democratic criterion serves. It simply does not apply in any very useful way to decisions on research and treatment for catastrophic diseases.

My main point, it ought to be remembered again, to which all these particulars are subordinated, is that we cannot guide our efforts in designing the decision-making procedures by first specifying what we mean by good decisions. For we have no adequate criteria for good decisions. In the first place, we cannot say that certain decisions are correct or incorrect. Secondly, for several reasons we cannot find in the interest approach to decision making any adequate criteria. And thirdly, in particular, in pursuit of the interest approach, we find that democratic or egalitarian formulas for aggregating interests are quite inadequate for our kind of decision problem.

II. Appraising Decision Process Directly Rather Than by Reference to Result

If we cannot work toward good decision making by first specifying what we mean by a good decision, the other route is to try to specify criteria for good decision processes directly and without respect to the decision outputs. That is to say, if we cannot say that a decision-making procedure is a good one because it produces decisions that we agree are good, we might be able to say it is a good one because we know it is at least an informed and thoughtful process. Or that the procedure is marked by certain other desirable features.

A. *Some Helpful Platitudes*

In this example we have perhaps already put our finger on about the only general a priori criteria for good decision making *process* that we can find. We would probably all agree that decision procedures should be informed, thoughtful and deliberate, marked by relatively full and candid exchange of opinion; and we would add that participants in the deliberation should not be obviously self-serving, nor incapable of being influenced by what they hear, nor marked by any other identifiable traits that reasonable men would almost unanimously hold to be a disqualification.

For the reasons already given above, we cannot go further and specify that the procedures be democratic or by any other formula formally egalitarian. Nor do we want any direct kind of electoral control, even one that works through the Congress or state legislature, to regulate at all closely the decisions of officers, boards, and committees who administer dialysis programs. Nor is there any sense in a kind of misconceived democratic control in which representatives of various participating or interested groups—hospital administrators, physicians, fund administrators, public health officials, and economists—are each granted one vote as though equal votes for each of various specialized role players—or for each of the groups they represent—was comparable to equal votes among citizens.

But then we seem to be left with a discouragingly inadequate and imprecise set of criteria for decision processes. To offer information, thoughtfulness, fairmindedness, tolerance, and so forth seems to offer not criteria but platitudes.

Our situation is, however, not quite so bad as it looks. In the first place, even if these seem to be platitudinous suggestions for decision making, they are still good suggestions. In fact, almost all thoughtful people would agree that these virtues are indispensable to good decision making, and they are platitudinous only because they are so universally agreed to be indispensable. Secondly, they are not always found in existing decision-making procedures, some of which are badly informed, and self-serving for the participants in them. Hence they do, for all their generality and looseness, point to improvements. Thirdly, they direct us away from will-o'-the-wisp pursuits of formulas, gimmicks, easy blueprints for good decision making; and they remind us that we should not, after all, be looking for any half-magical solutions to the problem of design of good decision-making procedures. Fourth, in doing so they hint to us—and this is a matter to be explored further below—that there may be a very wide array of possible "good" decision-making procedures—specifically, any that are marked by these general characteristics—and that we therefore do not have to torment ourselves with the suspicion that there is some very small number of good ones that we must desperately try to find.

But can we not find, any thoughtful reader ought to be asking at about this point, some maxims from organization theory, the study of public administration, or decision theory that specify practical criteria for good decision processes? Indeed we can. But I am going to indicate why we cannot use them by discussing a number of them under a heading—"Treacherous Maxims"—that characterizes them correctly, not as categorically wrong, but as unreliable.

B. *Treacherous Maxims*

Maxim 1. Decision making should be structured so that the problem calling for a decision can be seen comprehensively in its entirety. The obvious objection to this highly appealing maxim is that the attempt to understand and digest a whole problem often overloads the decision-making procedure. Men, even in committees, possess only limited, finite cognitive capacities; and problems are often complex beyond man's capacity to grasp them. Feasible decision making therefore sometimes requires that man act half blindly, and it almost always requires that they not wait for all relevant information but act only on a limited view permitted by the partial information they possess. One cannot defend this maximum by interpreting it to prescribe that missing information be provided, for missing information is often too costly to obtain, or could not be obtained in the time available to the decision makers, or would overload the decision makers if they had it. How much of an overview decision makers should have, how much information they have, how much they should try to get, and how much they should try to digest we cannot generalize about. Clearly it will depend on circumstances. But in any case the maxim is not helpful.

Maxim 2. The decision making should be designed so that the criteria or guidelines for reaching decisions are available to the decision makers. On this superficially plausible maxim, I need say no more than that the first major section of this paper was given over to showing that criteria or guidelines for good decisions are not available for the category of decisions with which we are concerned.

An alternative form of this maxim specifies that good decision making is principled decison making, and bad decision making is by contrast decision making over-influenced by the circumstances of a particular case and in which principles are compromised. In actual fact, however, for all complex decision making, the relevant principles are in conflict. They have to be compromised—inescapably so; and the compromise has to reflect the demands of the particular circumstances.

Maxim 3. Decision making should be designed for consistency of decisions, both over time and as between related decisions at any one time. Consistency is a virtue indeed, but only in its place. Where decision making is established for a new problem area, as in the circumstances we are examining, the decisions have to be exploratory, tentative. It is to be expected that many mistakes will be made. Intelligent and thoughtful decision makers, capable of learning, will therefore not be consistent, nor should they be urged to be. Moreover, where decisions always reflect a compromise of principles, depending on particular circumstances, an appropriate compromise will give a dominant position in one decison to the same principle that is pushed down into a very subordinate position in another decision. So that even decisions reached almost simultaneously will appear to reflect an inconsistent treatment of principles. For both these reasons, the consistency maximum is treacherous.

Maxim 4. Decision making should be designed so that for any single category of decisions which are alike in issues posed, in variables under consideration, and in persons affected, there is a single central decision-making group or supervising authority. The rationale behind this maxim is consistency. The maxim in fact simply states the institutional or organizational requirement for achieving consistency. If, for the reasons just given, the consistency maxim is not acceptable, then neither is this maxim.

In actual fact, decentralized and independent decision-making units may, because of constraints common to them all or because of attitudes, values or procedures common to them all, not necessarily act inconsistently with each other; and because they are not overburdened as one central agency would be, will often act both more intelligently and expeditiously than a centralized unit. But even if they are inconsistent with one another, their inconsistencies may be of the defensible form identified in the discussion of Maxim 3.

Maxim 5. Decision making should be designed to bring a maximum of intelligence to decisions. Or, alternatively, decision-making should be as rational as possible, as little arbitrary as possible. Having said above that decision making should be informed and thoughtful, it would seem that I am driven to accept this fifth maxim. But the maxim goes too far. In the first place, it is subject to the same objections as the first maxim—a maximum of fact-finding and analysis is prohibitively costly, too time consuming, and will sometimes break down the decision-making system through overload.

In addition, the maxim seems to deny the serviceability of arbitrary methods. Yet for some complex decisions, rules of thumb and other arbitrariness is, at least on a priori grounds, no less desirable than attempts at rational analysis that cannot possibly be conclusive or even approach conclusiveness. The literature on dialysis and transplants already recognizes that allocation of equipment and organs by lot and by a first-come first-served system are respectable competitors to more deliberative methods of allocation. A maxim that has the effect of ruling these arbitrary methods out of consideration is unacceptable.

I would further question the usefulness of this maxim on a ground that strikes deeply and fundamentally against common superficially plausible views of decision-making processes. We must always remember that some human problems are probably best kept outside the scope of deliberate decision making. Some outcomes should be less "decided upon" than merely "happen." It may be, for example, that we are better off for not being able to decide on the sex of our children. The most conspicuous major example of social organization through non-decision is, of course, economic organization through the market system in which we get systematic "decisions" on how resources should be allocated and how income should be distributed without any decision maker's ever facing these questions as items on his own decision-making agenda. These results "happen" as by-products of much simpler decisions of individuals and organizations to buy or sell.

Maxim 6. Insofar as it is possible to lay down criteria for correct or good decisions, decision-making procedures should be designed to maximize the possibility that each decision reached satisfies the criteria. A maxim like this seems compelling, but it is unacceptable because it blinds us to a choice we must make between two decision-making strategies. By the first strategy, decision makers invest their energies and time in hitting on target, in getting the best possible decision. By the second strategy, they foreswear that ambition and instead embark on a sequence of tolerable decisions, each one designed so that its effects can be read as feedback for the next decision in the series. For a complex enough problem where hitting the target is improbable, the second strategy is superior. The second strategy, to which the maxim is blind, calls for a design of decision making marked by error, speed, tentativeness, careful monitoring of feedback and incorporation of feedback into subsequent decisions.

Maxim 7. Decision-making should be designed so that those responsible for a decision are identifiable and can be held responsible. Again, a highly persuasive maxim is not reliable, for there will be circumstances in which anonymity is required for courageous decisions, as well as other circumstances in which a diffused responsibility, not specifically locatable anywhere, is a protection against the divisiveness in the groups affected by the decision.

Maxim 8. Decision-making procedures should require that those who make decisions be able to justify them with supporting reasons if called upon to do so. The rationale for such a maxim harks back to the view that good decision making is a matter of finding positions that accord with adequate criteria. But decision-making bodies do not in fact usually work backward from agreed criteria to decisions. Half a dozen men may agree on a decision without agreeing on the criteria for the decision at all; and one man, speaking for himself, may explain his decision by reference to no more than *his* criteria. Or he may see himself as having reached his decision as an act of practical judgement without being able to articulate any ruling criteria. Or another may see his decision as a product of conflicting criteria aggregated in some act of judgement that he cannot articulate in order to defend what he did. These apparently untidy ways of reaching decisions are necessarily and thoroughly acceptable.

One can go on with such a list. All kinds of maxims of decision making have been suggested in the literature; and all of them turn out to be treacherous in application.

It is about time again to repeat that I am not making these discouraging points in order to argue the impossibility of designing good decision-making procedures but only to specify better the character of the design problem, the intellectual resources we have to bring to the problem, and the most fruitful approaches to design.

The line of argument about the maxims tells us again that there are no magic roads to good decision-making procedures, no easy solutions to design problems. So far, then, we have not much more to build on than the virtues of information, thoughtfulness, candor, tolerance and the other platitudinous virtues of good decision making. Can we go any further?

III. Backing into Good Decision Making

I think we have to build the further examination of good decision for catastrophic diseases on the assumption that *any procedure marked by our platitudinous virtues is as good as any other so marked unless it is marred by specific defects for which specific evidence and argument as to their existence can be marshalled.*

At first blush, the statement looks like an evasion—and a silly one at that. It appears to say that good decision-making procedures are those that are not bad.

On more careful consideration, the effect of the statement or proposal can be seen to be something quite different. It proposes that instead of looking for positive features of good decision making (beyond the platitudinous virtues), a search in which we are defeated at every turn, we look for specific, identifiable, observable defects of known or hypothetical decision-making processes that otherwise possess as a minimum the merit of the platitudinous virtues. In other words, it suggests that if we cannot find objective grounds or even overwhelming agreement among decision-making designers on what kinds of decision-making procedures they endorse, we can find conclusive or overwhelmingly persuasive evidence of evil to be rooted out. We cannot make a frontal attack on good design, but we can back into good design by backing away from bad design.

It follows that the pathway to the design of good decision-making is not so much through the literature on decision-making and policy-making processes as through a meticulous examination of what might be objected to in existing or proposed procedures. And as for proposed procedures, so long as they possess the platitudinous virtues, there should be no burden of proof on the proponent of one of them to show that his system is the best. Instead we should ask whether we can find any specific defects in it—not failures of its features to meet some ideal, but specific, concrete shortcomings.

For an example, a compelling objection to a decision-making system might be that in any conflict between medical and lay participants, the medical people *always* won, or that they *always* lost. We do not need to know positively what good decision making is to be almost certain that either would be a poor system. So also could we judge a system poor if every time its decisions were insensitive to changing problems and opportunities. Or if it resulted in seriously adverse morale problems for physicians and researchers.

If there were only a few possible defects, we could specify their absence as criteria for good systems. There are, however, countless possibilities.

Following this strategy of design, we will find—and it will be a disconcerting finding to people who want tidier solutions—that a large number of decision-making procedures, each differing significantly from the other, will have to be pronounced equally good. I see no reason to refuse to accept that conclusion. Long habits of thought fight against it, to be sure. But it seems to be correct. To say that they have to be pronounced equally good is not to deny that they will differ in the decisions they give rise to. Nor is it to deny that the difference in their decision outputs will be consequential. We will simply have to say about different decision-making procedures that they produce different outcomes, that the outcomes are significantly different, yet that we have no reason to pronounce one system or its outcomes better than another.

Of course, as experience with these systems grows, the comparison of the consequentially different outputs will increase our level of sensitivity to imperfections in their results. We will begin to object to one set of consequences, once thought quite acceptable, as we come to see that another decision-making system permits us to escape these consequences. Presumably there will be some tendency for judgements to converge on the endorsement of a narrowing range of acceptable decision-making procedures. But the convergence is a very slow process; it will therefore not help us in the immediate task of next steps in the design of decision making procedures; and it may in fact be frustrated by the development of new resources and new medical technologies that increase the variety of possible decision-making systems as fast as the convergence process narrows them.

For the immediate problem at hand of designing appropriate decision-making procedure, I, for example, cannot go much further than this. Beyond recommending any system marked by the platitudinous virtues—and there are countless possibilities of these—I could best bring what I know about decision making to bear on the task of design by studying possible specific defects of existing procedures or engaging in discussion with persons who know the systems and their defects, as well as features of the systems that I might see as defects.

From very preliminary acquaintance with these procedures, I can already guess at some of their most likely defects: In most systems, a close correspondence of decisions with the biases of the medical profession, to the near exclusion of any competing biases; in all systems, including the Seattle arrangement for lay participation in decisions on analysis, a profound bias toward the welfare of conventionally respectable and esteemed people; in all systems, naivete about costs and the economic choices implicit in allocations; in all systems, reliance on highly controversial decision principles, the importance of which to the decision is obscured by the lack of searching discussion of alternative principles; frequent failures to see clearly the feasible range of policy alternatives from which choice is possible; the absence from most decision-making procedures of persons of obviously relevant skills, training or insight, other than M.D.'s; and the like. But that is only a beginning.

In a fundamental sense, a society's task at this point is not to design good new decision procedures for an emerging large category of problems but instead to cope, in the ways I have suggested, with these problems through sequences of decisions which over a long time will begin to define the good. In a new area like this, society will not design decision-making procedures which meet its standards for good decisions, but will instead develop a concept of good relevant to these procedures as a way of endorsing or condemning the procedures it invents. The question is not whether any procedure that may now be designed is or is not a good one so much as it is whether, a generation from now, society will then be able better to define good decisions in this area by reference to the procedures designed in this coming generation.

IV. Big Policy Decisions

We have been discussing decision making on catastrophic diseases in general without any explicit distinction between, at one extreme, big policy decisions made in Congress or state legislature and, at the other extreme, such specific institutional decisions as whose organs can be taken at one time for the benefit of what other person. Many of our examples have had the second kind of decision in mind rather than the first, but the discussion in general has embraced both. Here I want to look briefly into certain aspects of the big-policy-making process.

The structures of contemporary government and of the political process already give us the essential elements for good decision making. Specifically, elections give citizens the possibility of giving at least general direction to policy making, sometimes even on specific major issues on which agreement is high; legislatures and chief executives give us the full-time participation in policy making of people who are sensitive to the interests distributed in the population and who develop some skill in finding ways of reconciling and otherwise aggregating conflicting interests; experts bring their special competences to bear on policy making in a variety of ways—as members of administrative staffs, as consultants brought in from the outside, as staff members for congressional committees, and as advisers to chief executives and high-level administrators; and public administrators bring a combination of technical skills in administration and political skill, often with an admixture as well of special technical competence like that of the professional expert.

There is not much hope of getting a significant improvement in the big decisions on research and treatment of catastrophic diseases without generally altering the mixture and character of these elements in the policy process. To be sure, there are some possibilities of specific administrative and organizational reforms in specific agencies that administer health programs; but the more interesting and probably the more significant improvements depend on improving the general policy-making capacity of government.

Speaking roughly, policy making at these levels is a product of (1) analysis and (2) a play of power. That is to say, some things are settled by fact, analysis and persuasion; others by counting of votes or the exercise of such power as electoral and other procedures give to the participants in the system. More precisely, almost every policy question is settled by a combination of both.

Speaking roughly again, then, in the main there are two avenues toward improving the policy-making capacity of government. The one is through increasing the analytical component in policy making; the other is to change the character of the play of power—most specifically, the distribution of political power.

A number of reforms in American government are repeatedly mentioned as principal ways of achieving these two results, most but not all of the reforms being designed to work on both of these two fronts.

1. *Explicitly authorizing and financing an increase in the analytical component*
One possibility is simply hiring more people to do more studies at appropriate points in the governmental system. Under Presi-

dent Kennedy, Defense Secretary McNamara brought systems analysis and program budgeting into the Department of Defense to a degree never before attempted; and President Johnson, shortly before his retirement from the presidency, asked all government departments to use comparable new analytical procedures in the preparation of their budgets. Another current proposal for increasing the analytical component is for the use of social indicators of welfare to parallel the economic indicators used by the President's Council of Economic Advisers for fiscal and monetary planning. Another development is the ever-growing importance of the Bureau of the Budget as an analytical resource for the President. The apparently growing use of consulting firms and university research teams to explore governmental problems on contract with government agencies is still another example.

Some of these innovations have been attacked. In particular the particular formulas of systems analysis and Program Planning and Budgeting have been attacked as gadgety, as well as dangerous in their over-simplifications. But most of us, including the critics of these particular systems, find it hard to believe that government policy making cannot be greatly improved by a vast expansion of explicit analytical inputs at almost every point in the policy-making process. There is of course no general formula that tells us which of these formalized analytical procedures and other less formalized analytical procedures are best adapted to the particular needs of decision making on treatment of and research on catastrophic diseases. But it is a question well worth investigating in the design of better decision making in these areas.

2. *Legislative reorganization*
Legislative reorganization, especially Congressional reorganization, is widely advocated both as a means of removing from positions of influence a kind of participant in the political process who is hostile to analysis, hence as a method of increasing the analytical component, and also as a method of changing fundamentally the distribution of effective policy-making power in the American political system. A principal obstacle to improvement through either avenue is the committee system in

Congress. The committee system is central to Congressional performance because each committee is a kind of legislature within the legislature. It is to the committee that Congress generally delegates responsibility for acting on policies, though of course the Congress as a whole has to ratify the action of a committee. It is through committee assignments that Congressmen specialize to various areas of policy making. The committee system is thought to be an obstacle to better policy making for at least three reasons: (1) Committees are to a large degree independent of each other, not tied together through any effective coordinating mechanism. Policies in one area are therefore not well coordinated with policies in other areas; and, specifically, allocation of funds in one area are not systematically compared with possible allocations of funds in other areas. (2) By long-standing rule and custom, the chairman of each Congressional committee has been delegated extraordinary powers that give him grossly disproportionate control over the policy decisions his committee will reach. (3) These powerful committee leaders are not appropriately subject to democratic controls either through the votes of their committee members or through votes of those citizens who elect them. They reach their positions of power by seniority rather than election within the Congress, and they tend to achieve seniority over other Congressmen because they come from safe Congressional districts in which their re-election is nearly certain year after year. They come therefore primarily from Congressional districts in which two-party competition is less effective than in other districts, in which voters, therefore, do not have the advantages of close rivalry between parties and candidates. Disproportionately they have come from the Southern states, and they bias the policy-making process heavily toward Southern views.

If Congressional reform seems a long way around to go for improvements in decision making on catastrophic diseases, it is indeed just that. Perhaps Congressional reform is as long overdue as it is because persons concerned with particular areas of policy making are discouraged from so roundabout an approach to their own field. But clearly, Congressional reform would open up major possibilities for improved financial and other high-level decision making of consequence for medical programs; hence discouraging as its prospects seem, it has to be incorporated into any analysis of the design of improved decision making for research and therapy of catastrophic diseases.

3. *Executive leadership*

It is also widely believed by presumably competent analysts that decision making in American government could be greatly improved also by a continuing encouragement of trends toward executive leadership in policy making—trends in American government that increasingly locate the initiative for the design of coordinated national policies in the Presidency rather than in the Congress and cast Congress in a role something like that of the British House of Commons in its relation to the Prime Minister and Cabinet.

Ordinary citizens cannot take time to develop, nor do they wish to take time to develop, all the competences on policy making that are required in a political system. They have to reserve some competences to themselves but delegate others to their representatives. In many countries it has come to be understood that, given the increasing complexity of policy making, the representatives themselves cannot any longer develop all the required competences; and they must therefore in turn reserve only some of them to themselves and delegate others to a cabinet or other organization. Hence a cabinet is to the legislature what a legislature is to the citizenry as a whole. The suggestion, then, is that restructuring the American system to give to the President and his Cabinet or other advisers—perhaps some new kind of cabinet organization—a policy-making responsibility now still being exercised by the Congress would be a substantial improvement in the design of policy-making for the United States.

Again this is a long way around for improvements in medical decision making; but for all the reasons given above, good medical decision making is dependent on good political decision making in general.

There are other possible reforms. Among those I have not discussed, reforms designed to increase party discipline—specifically the responsibility of a party leadership to develop a coordinated policy program and the responsibility of elected members of that party to hold to that program—are often argued to be indispensable to a significant improvement in American policy-making capacity. This reform, like the others I have mentioned, is not easy to achieve. Like the others it would constitute in fact a fundamental alteration in the constitutional structure of American government; and over issues of that profundity and magnitude, agreement is hard to generate, and reform easy to obstruct. I doubt, however, that there are any short cuts to significant improvements in budgetary allocations or more generally in the intelligence brought to bear on major policy questions for medicine or any other field. Either we take the long way around or we do not make the trip.

V. A Market for Organs

A market system of decision making is, of course, out of the question for certain kinds of decisions to which it is simply not relevant—the decisions, for example, on the criteria for death or as to when precisely death occurs in an individual case. But it would be possible to organize a distribution of organs through market arrangements.

Calabresi's paper, I understand, analyzes the possibility and problems of distributing an existing supply or flow of organs through the market. But what of the possibility of stimulating a larger supply of transferable organs through the market, a topic that I understand Calabresi's paper does not look into?

I find that I have less to offer on this question than might be expected from an economist. But the question raises subtle and sensitive questions on which I would welcome an opportunity to participate in a thoughtful discussion. Pending that kind of an interchange, I feel surprisingly uncertain as to the direction of my thinking. I offer only a few suggestions.

To begin with, it seems to me that it would probably be considered intolerable to organize a supply of transplantable organs entirely through market mechanisms (simply leaving it to willing sellers and willing buyers to find each other, with medical personnel doing no more than satisfying themselves that the transfer makes sense medically). Under such a system, if medical researchers wanted organs to do transplanting for research and experimental purposes, they would have to bid for organs against the possible competition of the very wealthy. Or limit their research and experimental transplants to wealthy recipients.

Aside from what such system might do to research, it would, I think, be found intolerable because it would allow the wealthy to buy survival where the poor or even the ordinary well-off could not. Just how serious this problem would be would depend on the relative scarcity of the organ in question and the price that it would have to command. Assuming that the law still prohibited sales that left the seller badly crippled and permitted him to sell only organs of which he in some sense had a surplus, the going price for, say, an eye even if not for a kidney, might create a conspicuously unpardonable concentration of transplants in the very wealthy.

To be sure, it might be proposed that we induce the sale of organs by offering money in exchange for them but then distribute the organs by some criteria other than money. In that case there would be no concentration of transplants to the wealthy. But it would still be the case, as in the earlier hypothetical system of straight sales to any willing buyer, that the force of the financial incentive to part with an eye, a kidney, or some other organ or member, would fall on the low-income groups, who, whatever the price of the organ or member, would presumably respond where the wealthy would not. I should expect that there would be widespread abhorrence to a system in which income inequality was permitted to have so profound an effect on the distribution of sacrifices of organs and members. Only if money incomes and wealth were much more equally distributed would such a system be tolerable, I would guess.

Assuming that thoughtful people agree that we need to induce a larger supply of organs, the only other sure alternative would appear to be a coercive system in which the necessary organs are "drafted" by lot, in some such manner as young men's minds and bodies are drafted for military service. Given common attitudes now, it is hard to believe that such a system could ever be inaugurated in a democratic society; but it is possible that a heightened concern for supply of transferable organs, as transfers become increasingly common, might change that sentiment.

The third alternative, of course, is moral suasion of the type used by the Red Cross to induce blood donations. The limits of success of Red Cross blood collections suggest that moral suasion will not induce enough people to surrender an organ, so that moral suasion may have to work, as it does now for transplants, through the close ties of family and friendship in particular cases of need.

It looks as though for a long time to come we shall have to continue with about the same methods of inducing offers or donations as we now practice. A final objection to permitting even a supplemental use of financial incentives for inducing the required supply is that such a system undermines existing moral inducements. Bequests of organs, for example, would dry up in favor of prearranged sale on death.

11

Still Muddling, Not Yet Through (1979)[1]

For a people weary of their government, Abraham Lincoln asserted "a revolutionary right to dismember and overthrow it." Jefferson at least speculated on the possibility that occasional revolution was healthy for the body politic. It is not to dissent from them that I have been claiming that "muddling through"[2]—or incrementalism as it is more usually labeled— is and ought to be the usual method of policy making. Rather, it is that neither revolution, nor drastic policy change, nor even carefully planned big steps are ordinarily possible.

Perhaps, at this stage in the study and practice of policy making the most common view (it has gradually found its way into textbooks) is that indeed no more than small or incremental steps—no more than muddling—is ordinarily possible. But most people, including many policy analysts and policy makers, want to separate the "ought" from the "is." They think we should try to do better. So do I. What remains as an issue, then? It can be clearly put. Many critics of incrementalism believe that doing better usually means turning away from incrementalism. Incrementalists believe that for complex problem solving it usually means practicing incrementalism more skillfully and turning away from it only rarely.

Of the various ways of turning away from incrementalism, two stand out. One is taking bigger steps in policy—no longer fiddling, say, with our energy problems, but dealing with them as an integrated whole. The other is more complete and scientific

1 My thanks to James W. Fesler, David R. Mayhew, and Edward W. Pauly for their helpful comments on an earlier draft.
2 I now have an opportunity to thank William B. Shore, former managing editor of this journal [*Public Administration Review*], for entitling my article of twenty years ago "The Science of Muddling Through" (19 *Public Administration Review, 1959*), a title that may have contributed as much to the attention the article has received as did its contents.

analysis of policy alternatives than incrementalists attempt.[3] These two—big actions and comprehensive analysis—are obviously closely related, and they come nicely together in conventional notions of "planning." Hence a choice is clearly posed. Is the general formula for better policy making one of more science and more political ambition, or, as I would argue, a new and improved muddling?

I can now analyze the choice better than I did twenty years ago.[4] I begin with an apology for sometimes confusing incremental *politics* with incremental *analysis* and for inadequately distinguishing three versions of incremental analysis. In its core meaning incrementalism *as a political pattern* is easy to specify. It is political change by small steps (regardless of method of analysis). So defined, incrementalism varies by degree. Raising or lowering the discount rate from time to time is extremely incremental. Making the original decision to use the discount rate as a method of monetary control is still modestly though not extremely incremental. Reorganizing the banking system by introducing the Federal Reserve System is still incremental, though less so. Eliminating the use of money, as both the Soviets and the Cubans aspired in their early revolutionary years, is not incremental. Where the line is drawn is not

3 Specifically, the conventional steps, with appropriate refinements to deal with probabilities, are:
a. Identify and organize in some coherent relation the goal and side values pertinent to the policy choice to be made;
b. Identify all important policy alternatives that might realize the values;
c. Analyze all important possible consequences of each of the considered alternative politices;
d. Choose that policy the consequences of which best match the values of step a.

4 The only substantial deepening of the idea of incrementalism that I might be able to claim in the intervening period is an attempt to place incrementalism, as well as partisan mutual adjustment, in intellectual history by showing that it conforms with a long-standing half implicit model of "good" social organization and is challenged by another. See my "Sociology of Planning: Thought and Social Interaction" in Morris Bornstein, ed., *Economic Planning, East and West* (Cambridge, Mass.: Ballinger, 1975), subsequently revised as Chapters 29 and 23 of my *Politics and Markets* (New York: Basic Books, 1977).
In the intervening years, I also spelled out disjointed incrementalism in more detail, including with the extended discussion an analysis of certain problems drawn from philosophic discourse, in David Braybrooke and Lindblom, *The Strategy of Decision* (New York: The Free Press, 1963). I also developed the related analysis of partisan mutual adjustment in *The Intelligence of Democracy* (New York: The Free Press, 1965).

important so long as we understand that size of step in policy making can be arranged on a continuum from small to large.

As for the three meanings of incrementalism as policy *analysis*, it now seems clear that in the literature and even in my own writing each of the following kinds of analysis sometimes takes the name of incrementalism:

1. Analysis that is limited to consideration of alternative policies, all of which are only incrementally different from the status quo.
   Call this *simple incremental analysis.*
2. Analysis marked by a mutually supporting set of simplifying and focusing stratagems of which simple incremental analysis is only one, the others being those listed in my article of twenty years ago:[5] specifically,
   a. limitation of analysis to a few somewhat familiar policy alternatives;
   b. an intertwining of analysis of policy goals and other values with the empirical aspects of the problem;
   c. a greater analytical preoccupation with ills to be remedied than positive goals to be sought;
   d. a sequence of trials, errors, and revised trials;
   e. analysis that explores only some, not all, of the important possible consequences of a considered alternative;
   f. fragmentation of analytical work to many (partisan) participants in policy making.
   This complex method of analysis I have called *disjointed incrementalism.*
3. Analysis limited to any calculated or thoughtfully chosen set of stratagems to simplify complex policy problems, that is, to short-cut the conventionally comprehensive "scientific" analysis.[6]
   Such a practice I have now come to call *strategic analysis.*

Disjointed incrementalism is one of several possible forms of strategic analysis, and simple incremental analysis is one of

5 And more fully in Braybrooke and Lindblom, *op. cit.,* Ch. 5.
6 For illustration, familiar stratagems include trial and error, bottleneck breaking, limitation of analysis to only a few alternatives, routinization of decisions, and focusing decision making on crises, among others.

several elements in disjointed incremental analysis. We can now examine each to see why it should be pursued as an alternative to the pursuit of conventional "scientific" analysis, which I have usually labeled "synoptic" in acknowledgement of its aspiration to be complete.[7] Let us begin with strategic analysis.

I. The Case of Strategic Analysis

The case for strategic analysis as a norm or ideal is simple: No person, committee, or research team, even with all the resources of modern electronic computation, can complete the analysis of a complex problem. Too many interacting values are at stake,[8] too many possible alternatives, too many consequences to be traced through an uncertain future—the best we can do is achieve partial analysis or, in Herbert Simon's term, a "bounded rationality."[9] I need not here review the many familiar reasons by now recorded in the literature of social science for our inability to achieve a synoptic intellectual mastery of complex social problems.

Consider a continuum on which analysis is arrayed according to its *completeness* or synoptic quality. On it, we can indicate both hypothetical and real alternatives.

The continuum suggests several observations. We—policy makers, administrators, policy analysts, and researchers—usually do significantly better than the worst extreme that can be imagined. For complex problems, however, we never approach synopsis but remain instead at great distance. Some of us practice strategic analysis better than others—that is, we employ in an informed and thoughtful way a variety of simplifying stratagems, like skillfully sequenced trial and error.

Granted that, critics may ask: Doesn't the left end of the continuum, complete or synoptic analysis, represent the only defensible ideal? Should we not, therefore, continue to press toward it? To some critics the answers seem obvious, hardly

---

7 In the article of twenty years ago, synopsis was called the *root* method (in contrast to *branch*, which was another term for incrementalism).

8 To which are added all the complications of value analysis arising out of the elusive character of values and their resistance to "scientific" verification.

9 Herbert A. Simon, *Models of Man* (New York: John Wiley and Sons, 1957), p. 198.

worth reflecting on. Consider, however, a simple analogy. Men have always wanted to fly. Was the ambition to undertake unaided flight, devoid of any strategy for achieving it, even a useful norm or ideal? Although the myth of Icarus stimulates the imagination, flying becomes a productive ambition only to those who accept the impossibility of flying without mechanical assistance and who entertain the thought of using fabricated wings and other devices. Achieving impossible feats of synopsis is a bootless, unproductive ideal. Aspiring to improving policy analysis through the use of strategies is a *directing* or *guiding* aspiration. It points to something to be done, something to be studied and learned, and something that can be successfully approximated. What kind of aspiration, norm, or ideal gives direction and other specific guidance to a body builder—his hope to have the strength of a gorilla or his intention to exceed Arnold Schwarzenegger? For a soprano, the impossible aspiration to hit a note six octaves above the highest note ever sung, or the resolve to reach A above high-C? For a person who dislikes telephone directories, to memorize all the telephone numbers he might ever use or to memorize a still difficult smaller set of frequently called numbers? An aspiration to synopsis does not help an analyst choose manageable tasks, while an aspiration to develop improved strategies does.

I suggest that, failing to grasp this point, analysts who think in the older conventional way about problem solving pretend to synopsis; but knowing no way to approximate it, they fall into worse patterns of analysis and decision than those who, with their eyes open, entertain the guiding ideal of strategic analysis. Again through a diagram, I can suggest what actually happens in policy analysis. We can array on the continuum a range of actually possible degrees of completeness of analysis.

For complex problems, tied to an unhelpful aspiration that simply admonishes "Be complete!" an analyst unknowingly or guiltily muddles badly. Or, pursuing a guiding ideal of strategic analysis, he knowingly and openly muddles with some skill. Hence his taking as an ideal the development of better strategic analysis will be far more helpful than his turning away from strategic analysis in an impossible pursuit of approximations to synopsis. Is the appropriate ideal for the commuter miraculously long legs or better bus service? What can actually be done in the pursuit of each of the two?

For complex social problems, even formal analytic techniques—systems analysis, operations research, management by objectives, PERT, for example—need to be developed around strategies rather than as attempts at synopsis. Some theoretical formulations of these techniques and all examples of their successful application to complex problems reflect this important point.

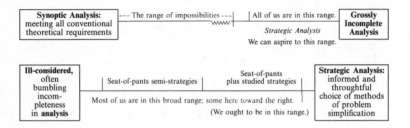

II. The Case for Disjointed Incrementalism

It should now be clear why I endorse not only strategic analysis as a norm but disjointed incrementalism as one kind of it. Disjointed incrementalism is a strategy practiced with variable skill. Taking carefully considered disjointed incrementalism as a norm would improve the analytic efforts of many analysts, for the several now familiar reasons given in the article of twenty years ago. It would set them on a productive course of analysis while turning them away from conventional attempts at formal completeness that always lapse, for complex problems, into ill-defended makeshifts. A conventional synoptic (in aspiration) attempt to choose and justify the location of a new public housing unit by an analysis of the entirety of a city's land needs and potential development patterns always degenerates at least into superficiality if not fraud. A disjointed incremental analysis can do better.

The valid objection to disjointed incrementalism as a *practical analytical method* is that one can find better kinds of strategic analysis, not that one can turn to synopsis as an alternative. The valid objection to disjointed incrementalism as a *norm or ideal* for analysis is that better strategic ideals are available, not that synopsis is a useful ideal.[10] Are there other kinds of strategic analysis, or at least other hypothetic ideals of strategic analysis? More, I would reply, than we have taken the trouble to uncover; hence much exploration remains to be undertaken. A conspicuous early alternative, tapped in a concept with which disjointed incrementalism overlaps, is Simon's "satisficing."[11] Dror and Etzioni have also investigated alternatives.[12] Given the alternative strategies often available, disjointed incrementalism is of course not always necessary in analysis.

All analysis is incomplete, and all incomplete analysis may fail to grasp what turns out to be critical to good policy. But—and this is a "but" that must be given a prominent seat in the halls of controversy over incrementalism—that means that for complex problems all attempts at synopsis are incomplete. The choice between synopsis and disjointed incrementalism—or between synopsis and any form of strategic analysis—is simply between ill-considered, often accidental incompleteness on one hand, and deliberate, designed incompleteness on the other.

Many specific weaknesses have been identified in disjointed incremental analysis: For example, that it will often do no better than to find a "local" optimum, a policy better than its near and only incrementally different neighbors but possibly much inferior to a more distant alternative policy never examined. Disjointed incremental analysis is much flawed, as are all alternative possible or concretely imaginable forms of policy making and policy analysis. I think I have failed to communicate to readers just how bad I think policy analysis and policy making are, even under the best circumstances. Evidence of that failure is Langdon Winner's attribution to me of a "marvelous logic" that promises that "planners can perform effectively" and that "lack of understanding on the broad scale is not a hindrance

10 In addition, an alternative incrementalism as practiced is more skillful incrementalism: for example, more attention to monitoring policies for feedback and correction.

11 Herbert A. Simon, "A Behavioral Model of Rational Choice," 69 *Quarterly Journal of Economics* (February, 1955).

12 Yehezkel Dror, *Public Policymaking Reexamined* (San Francisco: Chandler, 1968), Ch. 14; and Amitai Etzioni, "Mixed-scanning," 27 *Public Administration Review* 1967).

to sound decision making."[13] Of course, it is a hindrance, and a tragic one. And that is why we need analytical strategies like disjointed incrementalism to make the most of our limited abilities to understand.

An aspect of disjointed incrementalism which I filed away years ago as unfinished business and to which I intend shortly to return is the relation between its remedial orientation—its concern with identifiable ills from which to flee rather than abstract ends to be pursued—and what appears to be the mind's need for a broad (and some would say "higher") set of lasting ambitions or ideals. I am myself committed to some such ideals; that is, I make use of them. Yet they are often only distantly and loosely operative in the specific analysis of policy problems. At best they can only be incompletely analyzed—held in the mind loosely where they are beset by internal contradictions. They do not represent, as has been suggested, a distant synoptic guidance of incremental analysis, for synopsis on values remains impossible. Perhaps they enter into our thinking most significantly through posing trade-off problems, in which incremental gains on one front are traded against decrements on others.

III. The Case for Simple Incremental Analysis

Simple incremental analysis—which is analysis of no more than small or incremental possible departures from the status quo—cannot be defended in isolation from the more complex strategies, like disjointed incrementalism, of which it is a part. It is only an aspect of analysis and is or is not useful depending on circumstances and on the stratagem of which it is a part. Insofar, however, as we can speak of one aspect of analysis (bearing in mind its relation to the larger strategy of which it is a part), we can clear up some confusions in the literature. To begin with, the easiest point to make is that, in societies in which actual political change proceeds by incremental steps, it is difficult to deny the frequent relevance of simple incremental analysis. If political decison makers are going to choose among incremental alternatives A, B, and C, it would seem that some analysis of just those alternatives would often be helpful.

13 In Todd R. LaPorte, ed., *Organized Social Complexity* (Princeton, N. J.: Princeton University Press, 1975), p. 70.

The most frequent and basic objection is not to simple incremental analysis of incremental alternatives actually on the political agenda; it is instead to the political practice of change only by increment. That is to say, the objection is not to incremental analysis but to the incremental politics to which incremental analysis is nicely suited.

Let us therefore explicitly digress from the appraisal of incremental analysis to the appraisal of incremental politics. Much can be said both for and against the latter, and I am increasingly impressed with what must be said against those forms of it that are practiced in Western Europe and North America.

A. *Incremental Politics*

Abstractly considered, incremental politics looks very good. It is intelligently exploratory when linked with sequences of trial and error. It reduces the stakes in each political controversy, thus encouraging losers to bear their losses without disrupting the political system. It helps maintain the vague general consensus on basic values (because no specific policy issue ever centrally poses a challenge to them) that many people believe is necessary for widespread voluntary acceptance of democratic government.

Moreover, incrementalism in politics is not, in principle, slow moving. It is not necessarily, therefore, a tactic of conservatism. A fast-moving sequence of small changes can more speedily accomplish a drastic alteration of the *status quo* than can an only infrequent major policy change. If the speed of change is the product of size of step times frequency of step, incremental change patterns are, under ordinary circumstances, the fastest method of change available. One might reply of course that drastic steps in policy need be no more infrequent than incremental steps. We can be reasonably sure, however, that in almost all circumstances that suggestion is false. Incremental steps can be made quickly because they are only incremental. They do not rock the boat, do not stir up great antagonisms and paralyzing schisms as do proposals for more drastic change.

None of this line of argument defuses the deep hostility that many people quite reasonably feel toward political incrementalism. Many people see the U.S., for example, as somehow trapped in an incremental politics that leaves its government incapable of coping effectively with big problems like environmental decay, energy shortage, inflation, and unemployment. I share their concern and would like to clarify its relation to political incrementalism.

American and Western European politics suffer from serious problem-solving disabilities. One, especially pronounced in the U.S., is the dispersion of veto powers throughout the political system. In addition to those veto powers to be found in the Constitution and in legislative procedures are those even more ubiquitous veto powers that reside in property rights. I refer not to rights you and I hold in our personal possessions but to the property rights of business enterprises, which permit, with the help of judicial interpretation, the veto of many forms of government regulation that might otherwise be attempted to cope with our problems. Even business property rights in information throw obstacles in the way of regulators who cannot obtain the necessary facts.

Perhaps a better way to put the point—simultaneously enlarging it somewhat—is to note a fundamental characteristic of politics in market-oriented systems. Having assigned many or most of the great organizing and coordinating tasks of society to business enterprises, then subjecting the managers of these enterprises to market inducements rather than commands (which the constitutional rules of these systems forbid in the main), the only way to get the assigned jobs done is to give businessmen whatever inducements will in fact motivate them to perform. That renders these political systems incapable of following many lines of policy that, however attractive they might look for, say, energy conservation or environmental protection, threaten to undercut business inducements to perform.[14]

This particular structural feature of politics in market-oriented societies, as well as other difficulties in policy making, is often confused with political incrementalism. To see our difficulties clearly, the problem is not incrementalism but a structure of veto powers that makes even incremental moves difficult and insufficiently frequent. (This same structure, moreover, makes

14 Developed more completely in *Politics and Markets,* Part V.

drastic, less-incremental moves even more difficult—ordinarily simply impossible.) If we could imagine an incremental politics without the veto powers that now abound in it, I suggest that we would find incremental politics a suitable instrument for more effectively grappling with our problems. Whether we want to buy that gain at the price we must pay—a reduced role in the system for market enterprises—is another question.

Another source of timidity in American politics is ideological conservatism having its source in the many indoctrinations that grow out of the structure of private enterprise. It is difficult for many political leaders, and for ordinary citizens as well, to open their minds to the possibility that the American Constitution, with its many curbs on the popular will, including the Fourteenth Amendment's guarantees to corporations, is not an adequate set of rules for coping with out current great problems. It is no less difficult for them to let their minds freely explore—and reconsider the traditional justifications of—the extraordinary autonomy of the business corporation and its capacities to obstruct government problem solving.[15] Yet a high degree of homogeneity of timid political opinions is not a consequence of political incrementalism. If there is any relation between the two, political incrementalism is a consequence rather than a cause.

I think these comments rise above the dubious logic that many critics of political incrementalism have employed: U.S. policy making, which is incremental, is inadequate. Let us therefore rid ourselves of incremental politics. My head, which is covered with hair, aches. I ought to shave my scalp.

At this point it would be relevant for a critic of political incrementalism to point out that even if incrementalism is not the source of our problem of widespread vetoes and governmental timidity, nevertheless incremental politics offers us no way out—specifically, no way to reduce the veto powers. To that, several responses might be made. One is that, popular as revolutionary aspiration was among a few of our brightest young people only ten years ago, a revolutionary cause does not have enough advocates and potential activists to warrant much consideration. It is, in any case, always a treacherous

15 See *Politics and Markets,* Chs. 15 and 17.

method of social change that as often disappoints its movers as gratifies them. A potentially revolutionary situation—such as a Lenin, Castro, or Mao, or a Samuel Adams or Jefferson might nurture—is not now in sight.

Perhaps then, short of revolution, we should attempt a comprehensive constitutional reform of American government? Such a proposal, if it could be made effective, falls into a category of big-step policies that strain or pass beyond the limits of incremental politics. Other big step examples would be the realization in actual operation of a comprehensive energy program, to which President Carter and many Americans aspire; or at the local level, a comprehensively planned actual rebuilding of a city, socially as well as physically; or one big integrated implemented solution to environmental decay; or an actually operative development plan for a developing country. For many people these are happy visions, but except in rare circumstances they remain impossibilities. Too many vetoes are cast against them. Too many conflicting interests pull them apart. An operative, integrated solution to a problem is a vast collection of specific commitments all of which are implemented. The odds of agreement among political elites or citizens on these vast collections are extremely slim.

Moreover, among those who draw back from agreement will be many informed and thoughtful leaders and citizens who know that many of the specific elements embraced in the integrated program are bound to be mistaken. They believe that of any large sample of attempts at social problem solving, a large number will always turn out to have missed the mark or to have worsened the situation. They will prefer to see the political system act on the elements one at a time. Not that errors will be avoided, but each element will consequently receive greater attention and will be more carefully watched for feedback and correction.[16] Again, it is because we see reason to expect such big attempts to fail that we move incrementally in politics. It is not that incremental politics is the cause of our not making such attempts.

I suggest, therefore, that poor as it is, incremental politics

16 That I am willing to claim, despite the obvious weaknesses of monitoring of results for feedback and correction that characterize most incremental policy making.

ordinarily offers the best chance of introducing into the political system those changes and those change-producing intermediate changes that a discontented citizen might desire. That holds out no great hope, only as much hope as can be found in any style of American politics. If we live in a system designed by the constitutional fathers to frustrate in large part the popular will, their success in doing so reminds us that even if we attempted a new constitutional convention the same consequences might follow.

Incremental politics is also a way of "smuggling" changes into the political system. Important changes in policy and in the political system often come about quite indirectly and as a surprise to many participants in the system. That life has been heavily bureaucratized by the rise of the corporation and big government is a development that sneaked up on most citizens, who never debated the issues and who did not understand at the time that such a transformation was in process. Incremental changes add up; often more happens than meets the eye. If, on one hand, this is an objection to incremental politics, this feature of it also suggests that a skilled reformer may learn paths of indirection and surprise, thus reaching objectives that would be successfully resisted were his program more fully revealed. This possibility of course raises important issues in political morality.

One last question about incremental politics: Is it true, as often suggested in the literature of political science, that democracies are for the most part committed to change by no more than incremental moves while authoritarian governments can move with bigger steps? It seems clear that authoritarian systems themselves ordinarily move by increments. Indeed, some authoritarian systems are relatively effective in suppressing political change of any kind. The pace of change in the Soviet Union, for example, incremental or other, is not demonstrably faster than in the U.S. and may be slower. On the other hand, authoritarian systems are at least occasionally capable—apparently more often than in democratic systems—of such non-incremental change as the abrupt collectivization of agriculture in the Soviet Union and the Great Leap Forward and the Cultural Revolution in China (as well as the Holocaust and the recent destruction of Cambodia's cities and much of its population).

The most common reason alleged for democratic incapacity to act with comparable vigor on an equal number of occasions is that political change must not challenge the fundamental consensus which exists on the rules of the game and other basic values without which noncoercive democratic government is possible. Small steps do not upset the democratic applecart; big steps do.

Although that argument may be valid, we have no solid evidence on it, and I am increasingly suspicious of it. It is too simple, assigning too much effect to a single cause. Whether a political community will be split in politically dangerous ways when larger issues, posing bigger losses and gains, move onto the political agenda depends, it would seem, on at least one other variable: how rigidly participants are attached to various causes, values, and perceptions of their own interests.

In contemporary societies, political participants are attached less by the flexible or adaptable bindings of reason than by the indoctrinations through which they have been reared: By parents and school and through the ever repeated media endorsements of the American way, private enterprise, the Constitution, and the like. It is easy to imagine a body of citizens more able than ours to cope with big issues because they are less indoctrinated, less habitual, and more thoughtful in their consideration of those issues—and, in particular, more open to alternative ways in which their needs can be met.

Hence, in a very distant future, bigger political steps may be possible—not large without constraint but perhaps significantly less incremental than at present. It is worth our thinking about, even if we cannot predict it.

B. *Simple Incremental Analysis Again*
To return from our digression into incremental politics to the further appraisal of simple incremental analysis, we must meet the objection that simple incremental analysis, like disjointed incremental analysis of which it is a part, encourages political incrementalism. The analytical habit, found as it is in politicians as well as professors, encourages us all to think small, timidly, conservatively about social change. I agree, although the caus-

ation is in both directions, and the phenomenon is something like a vicious circle.

Yet the corrective is not the suppression or neglect of incremental analysis, which remains necessary and useful for all the reasons we have given above, but the supplementation of incremental analysis by broad-ranging, often highly speculative, and sometimes utopian thinking about directions and possible features, near and far in time. Skinner's *Walden Two,* Commoner's *Poverty of Power,* Fromm's *Escape from Freedom,* Shonfield's *Modern Capitalism,* Miliband's *The State in Capitalist Society,* Rawls' *Theory of Justice,* and Rousseau's *Social Contract* illustrate the variety of inputs, great and small, necessary to thinking about policy.

Some features of such analyses are especially pertinent. They are not synoptic—not even the most broadly ambitious of them, like the Platonic dialogues or Hobbes' *Leviathan.* Much is omitted; few issues are pushed to the point of exhaustion; and we take from them not closure but new insight—specifically, powerful fragments of understanding. They are methods that liberate us from both synoptic and incremental methods of analysis.

Moreover, they give us no sound basis for policy choices. They do not seek to make a contribution to policy making by assessing the pros and cons of policy alternatives. But they do greatly raise the level of intellectual sophistication with which we think about policy. Not explicitly directed to problems in policy making, many of them need a substantial interpretation and translation before they become effective, as some do, for millions of participants in policy making.

Some of these liberating analyses have the effect less of giving us information than of making us aware, and in that lies their great effect on our minds. They tell us what we know but did not know we knew; and what we know but had not before been able to make usable.[17]

Of kinds of analysis that are neither synoptic nor incremental in intention, one modest kind frequently makes a highly valu-

---

17 On awareness as one of two forms of knowing, see the illuminating discussion in Alvin G. Gouldner, *The Coming Crisis of Western Sociology* (New York: Basic Books, 1970), pp. 491–95; also in his *Enter Plato* (New York: Basic Books, 1965), pp. 267–272.

able contribution to policy making. It is the analysis of some one or a few pivotal issues or variables critical to policy choices. To research the question, Why Johnny can't read, is to attempt neither synopsis nor incremental analysis. It is simply to try to ferret out some information or develop some understanding essential to good policy making. These modest but critical or pivotal research interventions in policy making perhaps represent professional analysis in one of its most fruitful forms. They make the kind of contribution to which professional research is well suited, and they leave most of the evaluation of policy alternatives in the hands of politicians, administrators, which is perhaps where it belongs.

IV. Partisan Mutual Adjustment and Pluralism

Some critics of incrementalism have failed to catch the distinction between political incrementalism and what in *The Intelligence of Democracy* is labeled and analyzed as *partisan mutual adjustment*. Partisan mutual adjustment, found in varying degrees in all political systems, takes the form of fragmented or greatly decentralized political decision making in which the various somewhat autonomous participants mutually affect one another (as they always do), with the result that policy making displays certain interesting characteristics. One is that policies are resultants of the mutual adjustment; they are better described as happening than as decided upon. Another is that policies are influenced by a broad range of participants and interests (compared to those of more centralized policy making). Another is that the connection between a policy and good reasons for it is obscure, since the many participants will act for diverse reasons.

Another is that, despite the absence or weakness of central coordination of the participants, their mutual adjustments of many kinds (of which bargaining is only one) will to some degree coordinate them as policy makers. In many circumstances their mutual adjustments will achieve a coordination superior to an attempt at central coordination, which is often so complex as to lie beyond any coordinator's competence. Such a proposition does not deny the obvious failures of coordination that mark government and are especially conspicuous in

Washington. It merely claims that such coordination as, with difficulty, our governments achieve will often owe more to partisan mutual adjustment than to attempts at central coordination.

One can imagine a nation practicing political incrementalism without partisan mutual adjustment, or with only a minimum of it. One can also imagine partisan mutual adjustment for nonincremental policy making. In actual fact, the two are closely linked in all national political systems; both have the effect of reducing analytical tasks.

"Partisan mutual adjustment" pins down one meaning of "pluralism." Objections to partisan mutual adjustment, often voiced as objections to pluralism, often begin with the allegation that not all interests are represented by partisans in it, nor are participants influential in proportion to the numbers of citizens for whom they act. Who can deny so obvious a point? It is not, however, a persuasive objection to partisan mutual adjustment unless it can be shown that more centralized political decision making represents a fuller array of interests and does so more consistently with principles of democratic equality. In many cases it does not. For persons committed to democracy, the case for partisan mutual adjustment versus more central forms of policy making thus turns in part on which of the two can best cope with formidable inequalities in politics. A frequent opinion that the inequalities of partisan mutual adjustment are so great that more central decision making can simply be assumed to be an improvement is simply naive. Strong central authority can be—and historically is, in case after case—an instrument for protecting historically inherited inequalities.

A second major objection to partisan mutual adjustment, again expressed ordinarily as an objection to pluralism, is that it is fraudulent. The various participants do not in fact represent the variety of interests and values of the population. Instead they share dominant interests and values, and their relations with each other give the lie to those who claim to find in pluralism a healthy competition of ideas. In the extreme form, critics allege that policy is set by a ruling class with trappings of pluralist diversity.

I find it hard to deny a large core of truth in that criticism. Let us divide policy issues into two categories: Those on the ordinary questions of policy, and those that constitute the grand issues pertaining to the fundamental structure of politico-economic life. The grand issues include those on the distribution of income and wealth, on the distribution of political power, and on corporate prerogatives. On the first set, the ordinary issues, partisan mutual adjustment is active (though not without defects of inequality in participation and disturbing tendencies toward corporatism). On the grand issues, partisan mutual adjustment is weak or absent. The treatment in politics of the grand issues is governed by a high degree of homogeneity of opinion—heavily indoctrinated, I would add. As has often been pointed out, the grand issues are, thanks to a homogeneity of opinion (i.e., the failure of a competition of ideas), simply left off the agenda.[18]

A third objection to partisan mutual adjustment turns out to be an objection to its particular form in many countries, the U.S. included. It is a form in which, though none of the participants can on their own initiate a change, many or all can veto it. That is not essential to partisan mutual adjustment, but it is the way we practice it in the U.S. That fact raises the possibility that a thoughtful response to the imperfections of policy making through partisan mutual adjustment might call for changing its form or its governing rules rather than trying to suppress it. Critics of partisan mutual adjustment sometimes seem to fall into no more careful a logic than: I cannot use my car because it has a flat tire; I had better sell it.

V. Politics and Analysis

Confusing partisan mutual adjustment with incrementalism in its various forms, Charles L. Schultze has incorrectly associated incremental analysis (specifically disjointed incrementalism) with the crudities and irrationalities of "politics" and his more conventional forms of analysis, synoptic in ambition, with "analysis."[19] If he could make that stick—that incrementalism settles issues through power, his methods by brains—it would give

18 Peter Bachrach and Morton S. Baratz, "The Two Faces of Power," 56 *American Political Science Review* (December, 1962).
19 Charles L. Schultze, *The Politics and Economics of Public Spending* (Washington, D.C.: Brookings, 1968), Ch. 3 and *passim*.

him an easy victory in his attack on incrementalism. But he has made at least two mistakes.

First, analytical incrementalism is analysis. It is not simply a substitution of politics for analysis. *Incrementalism* denotes the three kinds of analysis discussed above—more modest methods than he endorses, yet nevertheless methods of analysis. What he should have said is that not incrementalism but partisan mutual adjustment is to some extent a substitution of politics for analysis. The coordination of participants is in some large part left to their political intereactions with each other and, in any case, is not centrally directed analyzed coordination as coordination might be in the mind of a sufficiently cerebral coordinator. This patterns of interaction may be designed—that is, various authorities may be required to interact with each other—or the patterns may have taken form without design. In either case, their coordination arises from their reciprocating political effects on each other, not through a centrally analyzed coordination.

Incrementalism aside, Schultze's second mistake is to miss the significance of the analytical components of partisan mutual adjustment, and indeed of all "politics." In partisan mutual adjustment and all politics, participants make heavy use of persuasion to influence each other; hence they are constantly engaged in analysis designed to find grounds on which their political adversaries or indifferent participants might be converted to allies or acquiescents.

Is that kind of analysis—partisan analysis to achieve influence in mutual adjustment—an adequate way to bring information and intelligence into policy formation? The historical concept of a competition of ideas at least vaguely recognizes its importance. Adversary proceedings in courts of law show our extreme dependence on it for some kinds of decision making. Whatever contribution interest groups make to policy making is largely through partisan analysis. I would like to suggest that partisan analysis is the most characteristic analytical input into politics and also the most productive. It is in a fuller appreciation of how partisan analysis might be improved rather than, as Schultze would seem to have it, curbed, that policy making can be made more intelligent.[20]

Finally I would like to suggest the still insufficiently explored possibilities of intelligent and democratically responsive policy making that lie in improved combinations of incremental analysis (in all of its three forms), incremental politics, and partisan mutual adjustment, including partisan analysis. The possibilities are perceived, though not fully worked out, in John Stuart Mill's *Representative Government* and in other liberal expositions of a competition of ideas linked to political education through political participation. More surprising, they appear in Maoist thought, with its emphasis on achieving economic growth not by a fine-tuning of development from above but by tapping intelligence and incentives broadly through fragmentation of responsibility and the cumulation of fast-moving incremental gains.[21] The same new or refreshed insights now have sprung out of the tradition of orthodox economics, given a new line of development by Harvey Leibenstein and his concept of X-efficiency.[22] Even more significant for skeptics of incrementalism and partisan mutual adjustment are our new insights into how science proceeds. Conventionally synoptic or "scientific" policy making turns out not to be true to science at all.

Michael Polanyi, Lakatos, and Kuhn, among others, have been revealing that in their scientific work scientific communities themselves characteristically practice both incrementalism and partisan mutual adjustment, though by other names.[23] Even

20 For a fuller statement of reasons, see Charles E. Lindblom, *The Policy-Making Process,* 2nd ed. (Englewood Cliffs, N. J.: Prentice–Hall, 1979). Schultze and I agree on at least some of the benefits to be had from one kind of partisan, the research minded "partisan for efficiency." But this very special category, illustrated by the professional economist or systems analyst, is the only category of partisan that Schultze shows much appreciation for.

21 My own thinking is indebted to Albert O. Hirschman for early alerting me to the importance of problem-solving incentives, in addition to intellectual capacity, in complex problem solving. See Albert O. Hirschman and Charles E. Lindblom, "Economic Development, Research and Development, Policy Making: Some Converging Views," Chapter 9 of this text.

22 Harvey Leibenstein, "Allocative Efficiency vs. 'X-Efficiency,'" 56 *American Economic Review* (June, 1966). Also his *Beyond Economic Man* (Cambridge, Mass.: Harvard University Press, 1976).

23 Michael Polanyi, "The Republic of Science," 1 *Minerva* (Autumn, 1962); Imre Lakatos and Alan Musgrave, eds., *Criticism and the Growth of Knowledge* (Cambridge: Cambridge University Press, 1970); Thomas S. Kuhn, *The Structure of Scientific Revolutions,* 2nd ed. (Chicago: University of Chicago Press, 1970). See also, for a detailed empirical study of incrementalism, partisan mutual adjustment, and partisan analysis—especially the latter—Ian Mitroff, *The Subjective Side of Science* (New York: American Elsevier Publishing Company, Inc., 1974).

Kuhn's "scientific revolutions" are the accomplishment of partisan incrementalists. Their reconsiderations of how science is practiced are, I think, conclusive objections to the synoptic ideal.

I have never well understood why incrementalism in its various forms has come to so prominent a place in the policy making literature. The original *PAR* article has been reprinted in roughly forty anthologies. I always thought that, although some purpose was served by clarifying incremental strategies of policy analysis and policy making, to do so was only to add a touch of articulation and organization to ideas already in wide circulation. Nor have I well understood the frequency with which incremental analysis as a norm is resisted. That complex problems cannot be completely analyzed and that we therefore require strategies for skillful incompleteness still seem close to obvious to me.

I thought I ventured into territory not familiar to all social scientists and administrators only when I pointed out that fragmentation of policy making and consequent political interaction among many participants are not only methods for curbing power (as they are seen to be in a long tradition of thought incorporating both Montesquieu and the founding fathers) but are methods, in many circumstances, of raising the level of information and rationality brought to bear on decisions. That led me into examining policy analysis as itself a social process not limited to what goes on in the analyst's mind and thus to the concept of the "intelligence" of partisan mutual adjustment.

I also thought that it was useful to elaborate the ways in which social problems can often be attacked (not well but with some reduction in incompetence) by "resultants" of interaction rather than "decisions" arising out of anyone's understanding of the problem at hand. If coin tossing can settle some problems better than can futile attempts at analysis of the unanalyzable (or futile attempts of analysis when information is wholly lacking), then it is not surprising that various forms of social interaction can sometimes handle problems better than analysis can when analysis at best is grossly incomplete. Understanding a social problem is not always necessary for its amelioration—a simple fact still widely overlooked.[24]

Rather than intending to stimulate a variety of attempts to

question the usefulness of incremental analysis and of partisan mutual adjustment, I had earlier hoped that the *PAR* article and subsequent publications would stimulate attempts of colleagues to articulate other strategies that avoid the impossible aspiration to synopsis, to give a more precise formulation to disjointed incrementalism as one such strategy, and to model partisan mutual adjustment as a mechanism for social "rationality" rather than as, historically, a mechanism for curbing central authority. On the whole, these hopes have been disappointed.

Some of my colleagues tell me they do not understand how—or whether!—I reconcile the benign view of pluralism to be found in my work on incrementalism and partisan mutual adjustment with the skepticism about pluralism expressed in the more recent *Politics and Markets* and its emphasis on an indoctrinated citizenry and the disproportionate political power and influence of business in politics. Do I deceive myself in believing that I have followed a consistent line of thought? As I have already noted, the policy issues that come onto the political agenda in what are called the Western democracies are almost entirely secondary issues on which policy making is indeed pluralistic, though grossly lopsided. On the grand issues that rarely come on the agenda, pluralism is weak to the point of invisibility. It is true that the earlier work emphasizes what works (though badly) in politics, the more recent work what does not work (though it persists). In both phases or steps, I have looked for half-hidden mechanisms. The only thing I see wrong about the two steps is their order. I fear that I became braver only with age, although I should like to deny that interpretation. In any case the subtle influences and pressures of one's academic colleagues are powerful in the development of a scholar's writing and teaching. If we resist yielding to them on what we believe, we often almost unknowingly yield on what we decide to study.

To a disjointed incrementalist, there is never a last word; and these words are not intended to be a "last word in incrementalism," which I have from time to time been asked to attempt. I have only a weak grasp of the concepts here discussed. Having

24 Further developed in Charles E. Lindblom and David K. Cohen, *Usable Knowledge* (New Haven: Yale University Press, 1979), pp. 19–29.

for some years occupied myself with politics and markets and hence subordinated my interest in the further study of incrementalism, I have now returned to the study of knowledge and analysis in policy making and other forms of social problem solving.[25] I hope to muddle through—or along.

25 As a beginning, Lindblom and Cohen, *Usable Knowledge*.

Part Three
Social Science

12

Integration of Economics and the Other Social Sciences through Policy Analysis (1972)

For five reasons, I doubt the wisdom of giving policy analysis the assignment of integrating the social sciences, although the last of the five reasons is simultaneously an argument for giving it a distinctive integrating role for a certain kind of study now part of the social sciences.

I. The Conservative and Superficial Bias of Policy Analysis

Consider some representative policy questions. When an economist studies policies to reduce unemployment, he takes as given an institutional structure which can itself be questioned. When he asks how to improve social security and welfare programs, he takes as given a wages system. When he asks how to facilitate international trade, he takes for granted the existence of a multiplicity of sovereign nations. When he asks how to curb pollution, he takes—in the United States or western Europe—private enterprise as a given. He is correct to take the main structure of society as given. Otherwise his analysis would be irrelevant to the circumstances in which policies are actually made.

The consequence, however, is that as a policy analyst he has to practice a conservative and superficial kind of social science. It is conservative because it does not ask radical questions about fundamental features of the social structure. (Whatever answers a less conservative kind of social science might reach, at least it would ask radical questions.) It is superficial not because it is badly done, for in fact it may be assiduously pursued with first-rate intellectual sophistication, but because it considers only those ways of dealing with policy that are close cousins to existing practices. In this context, I do not make much of the distinction between conservatism and superficiality. Both terms refer to one and the same set of characteristics of policy analysis, but where conservatism emphasizes the political direction of policy analysis, superficiality emphasizes its intellectual direction.

The radical and fundamental kind of analysis from which policy analysis diverts the social sciences is, for example, Plato's question: "What is justice?" Plato's pursuit of that question in *The Republic* leads him into an examination of the fundamentals of social organization, even if his way of posing his question, on one hand, and the authoritarian implications of his analysis, on the other, lead some men to attack him both as superficial and conservative. *The Republic* is a monument to the kind of analysis that advanced by calling into question, step by step, increasingly fundamental aspects of society.

Another example is Hobbes's question: "How can social order be maintained?" Compare it with the Kerner Commission Report, not in pure intellectual distinction, for that would be unfair, but in method. Or compare it with any contemporary analysis addressed to maintaining order on the campus, in the city, or in the ghetto. Hobbes takes as little as he can as given. He keeps pushing back, back, and back to fundamental questions about social organization and human behavior. His answers to his own radical questions were themselves sufficiently radical to give to the world a continuing intellectual tradition that persists, for example, in contemporary political science and that far overshadows the conservative implications of his defense of monarchy.

Adam Smith is another excellent example—there are very few from economics—of fundamental and radical analysis. If, as may have been the case, he began his investigation of economics as an attempt to deal with a practical policy question, specifically, mercantilist constraints on trade, he quickly threw off the conservative and superficial constraints of ordinary policy analysis and went after bigger game. The title of his work describes an intellectual ambition that runs far beyond policy analysis: *An Inquiry into the Nature and Causes of the Wealth of Nations.*

The discipline of economics is the most successful policy science of all the social sciences, with the possible exception of psychology, and at the same time the most conservative and superficial. Since Smith and then the marginalists, one does not often find in economics scholars who pursue radical and fundamental questions to compare with those who do so in other social sciences: for example, Weber, Durkheim, Parsons, Homans, and Merton in sociology; MacIver, Friedrich, Key, Lasswell, Almond, and Dahl in political science; or Radcliffe-Brown, Malinowski, Linton, and Kluckhohn in anthropology. These lists no more than sample the variety of scholars in the social sciences who, quite aside from the great political philosophers of the past, can qualify as asking fundamental and radical questions.

To be sure, the same kind of work is not wholly absent from economics. It is, for example, represented by a stream of work on preference aggregation that has its source in Kenneth Arrow's *Social Choice and Individual Values*. For the most part, however, the most fertile minds in economics have been meticulously and skillfully engaged in refining—that is, making more precise—earlier, rougher insights into processes in the market system for allocating resources, distributing income, improving productive capacity, and regulating the volume of production and employment. It is excellent work, not to be deprecated. But while it pays off handsomely in policy applications, for which it has largely come to be designed, it offers little new fundamental insight into economic or social organization. One evidence of this is that while in the twentieth century the brightest, best educated, and most thoughtful minds are finding exciting new discoveries about the natural world, man, and society in physics, biochemistry, biology, anthropology, psychology, sociology, and political science there has emerged from economics almost nothing to engage these minds. Who reads economics for a new view of the world?

Am I forgetting Keynes? His theoretical innovations took the form of conceptual improvements and a theoretical reconstruction, both of which substantially increased the skill with which economists approached policy analysis. But they did not provide any great new insights into man or social organization. The greatest significance of Keynes is that he provided a set of concepts and a theoretical model that were operational in the specific sense that policy makers could manipulate the variables of his model. For the first time, man had a set of concepts and a theoretical model that could immediately and directly guide policy. Keynesian analysis, taken together with national income accounting, made possible a kind of rational or scientific policy making new to the world.

The impressive accomplishments of economics in tool making, theory building, and in policy analysis are now recognized in the three Nobel prizes that have been awarded to economists. To none of these distinguished economists do we owe much for new answers or hypotheses on fundamental or radical questions about man and society. To each of them we owe an enormous debt in analytical tools and skill in policy analysis and refinements of earlier findings.

I do not wish to criticize economics for its relative inattention to fundamental or radical questions. As a discipline, it developed from strength to strength, that is, along lines that promised fruitful results. It became, therefore, a discipline marked less by its attention to fundamental and radical questions than by its analytical rigor, its inventiveness in methods of analysis, and its skill in handling the narrow range of questions for which its tools and skills gave it a marked advantage. The kinds of questions about economic life that can be called fundamental or radical lie, for the most part, outside the recognized boundaries of the discipline, given its intellectual traditions.

I am not even suggesting that people who call themselves economists should undertake the analysis of these questions. My only point is that a policy orientation for social science as a whole would preclude anyone's picking them up. Someone ought to be asking such questions as what the effect of life in a milieu of exchange relationships is on personality and culture; how defects in popular control (through the market system) over corporate leadership compare with those of popular control (through political processes) over political leadership; what necessary connections there are—logically and empirically, existing and possible—between market systems and governmental systems; whether a Cuban-style moral incentives system can be reconciled with a market system; and whether the economists' traditional identification of market relationships with voluntary or free relationships is, in fact, valid in societies in which necessity compels people to enter into market relationships. There is a weak tradition in economics that accounts for occasional speculative writing on such topics as these, but neither in economics nor in any other social science are they systematically studied. Nor would a policy orientation for social science improve the prospects.

Under some circumstances, of course, policy analysis drives toward fundamental and radical questions. For example, the policy question of whether a developing country should or should not use import controls, industrial licensing, and other administrative substitutes for market forces does push economics toward a more fundamental clarification of the differences between market systems and administrative systems.

A more striking example is the field of psychology where "policy" analysis in the form of practice of individual therapy is a major avenue to fundamental discoveries about the human psyche. Why does the study of "therapy" in public affairs not work the same way? Because, it seems, psychiatric therapy can consider, even experiment with, alternatives entirely unlike those open in public policy making. In therapy, individuals can be asked to make, or at least experiment with, fundamental changes in behavior. They can also be subjected to traumas, as in shock therapy. In short, therapy strikes at fundamentals in ways not permitted to policy makers because of the rigidities of the social order, the limited manipulative ability of the policy maker, and the fragility of the social order. For the society, consequently, even if not for the individual in therapy, the inverse relationship between policy analysis, on the one hand, and fundamental or radical analysis, on the other, seems to hold.

In my own work on incremental analysis, I have wanted from time to time to defend it from the charge that it is a conservative form of policy analysis. Incremental analysis is no more conservative than any other form of policy analysis. There is no contradiction between that position and the one I am taking here. Here I am saying that all policy analysis tends to be conservative—and not in the trivial sense that it is more Tory than Liberal, more Republican than Democratic, but in a sense that it does not ask radical and fundamental questions which are troublesome and irrelevant to policy analysis, however important they may be to man's understanding of himself and his world.

II. Modes of Integration Alternative to a Policy Orientation

Since about the end of World War II, the social sciences have been integrating in a number of fertile ways. The number and richness of these integrations suggest, first, that integration is now proceeding more successfully than it did for many decades; secondly, that the route to integration through policy analysis is only one of a fairly large number of possible alternatives; and, thirdly, that some of the other methods of integration look superior to integration through policy analysis.

Some of the points, areas, or methods of integration are:

A. *Decision Theory*
Economists have brought to the analysis of decision making their experience in the study of rational choice. They have been joined by mathematicians and statisticians in applying probability theory and game theory to cope with problems of risk and uncertainty in rational choice. Psychologists have converged on the field with their studies of perception, cognition, and problem solving. Anthropologists and sociologists have added the study of decision making in observed small groups in the laboratory, and students of public administration and political science have incorporated into decision making studies the analysis of decision making in administrative organizations and in more complex political structures. This summary hardly does justice to all the contributors to the study of decision making, philosophers as well as social scientists, but it suggests how thoroughgoing an integration of the social sciences has been achieved around one fundamental phenomenon.

B. *Organization Theory*
A related and overlapping point of convergence is organizational theory, which has drawn on all the literature of decision

making but has added to it a convergence of anthropological, sociological, social psychological, administrative, and political studies of formal organizations including, from economics, the study of the business enterprise.

C. *Collective Choice*
Within these common areas, there has been a specialized theoretical cultivation of the phenomena of collective as against individual choice. It owes much to Arrow's work on social choice; some to a critique, traditional in economics, of defects in market choice; and some to a growing interest among political scientists in the peculiar characteristics of voting as a method of making collective choices.

D. *Exchange Theory*
The success of economists in explaining a great deal about social organization by reference to acts of exchange among individuals has led both economists and other social scientists to try to explain aspects of society beyond those usually embraced in economics. The earlier work of John R. Commons is now largely forgotten; but Homans and Blau have attempted general explanations of this kind, and the attempt to explain political phenomena by reference to exchange relationships is now attractive to some political scientists including, for example, Curry and Wade in their *Exchange Theory of Politics*. Homans' work, I would guess, owes something to earlier anthropological work on reciprocal and exchange relationships among primitive people. In any case, every social science is represented in this area or focus of integration.

E. *Structural-functional Analysis*
In postulating economic functions to be performed, such as resource allocation and income distribution, and then examining the market system as a structure for discharging the functions, economists have always practiced an unsophisticated kind of structural-functional analysis. But the more explicit theorists and practitioners of structural-functionalism have been anthro-

pologists, like Malinowski and Radcliffe-Brown; sociologists, like Parsons and many of his followers; and political scientists, like Gabriel Almond. Many more names could be added, of course, and one could also incorporate philosophers like Hempel, who has written a now classic critique of the method.

F. *Talcott Parsons*
The work of Parsons has itself been a kind of integration of social science in which many followers have joined him; some, like Levy and Smelser, following the Parsons integrations very closely and others, like Almond or Holt and Turner (*The Political Aspects of Economic Development*), less closely.

G. *Political Culture and Political Socialization*
Some political scientists, like Almond and the authors of the Social Science Research Council's series on development, have turned much of the study of political phenomena away from legal forms to aspects of human behavior on which the political scientists acknowledge a heavy indebtedness to sociology. Others, like Lasswell and Lane, have brought psychology and psychoanalysis to bear on political culture and behavior; and sometimes the mining of psychology by political science is very specific, as in Greenstein's work on political socialization of children.

H. *Political Development*
Taken as a whole, the field of political development is a point of considerable integration in the social sciences, drawing as it does on materials in the study of economic development. Both political scientists and economists are busy these days trying to understand, for example, the relationship between government and market in modernization. The study of political development, however, also draws on the integrations of social science achieved above in the study of political culture and socialization.

I. *Economic Development*

Similarly, the study of economic development in the hands of economists has drawn on political studies of the role of government and administration in developmental tasks. In a few conspicuous cases it has also drawn on psychology, as in Hagen's *Theory of Social Change,* which builds on McClelland's psychological studies of motivation.

It becomes tedious to list all the important integrations that are now occurring in the social sciences. Some lesser but still significant ones spring quickly to mind: role theory, studies of the prerequisites of democracy, attempts to analyze and make power measurable, and studies of authority. In each of these cases, every social science is represented with the possible exception of economics. Not to be forgotten are attempts to anticipate or plan a social science built around cybernetics or communications.

The older tradition of attempting a major integration in order to answer a single fundamental question also ought not be forgotten, even if it has, perhaps, gone out of style. Plato's "What Is Justice?" took him through psychology, political science, economics, sociology and anthropology. So also did Hobbes's "How to Maintain Social Order" or Rousseau's attempt to explain why "man was born free, but is everywhere in bondage."

It seems quite clear that successful integration is a monopoly of no particular mode of integration. In the examples listed, we find cases of integration through common analytical tools, as is true for much of decision theory, in which scholars of various disciplines try to work out the logic of choice under conditions of risk and uncertainty. We also see integration organized around the study of a root phenomenon, as in studies of authority or exchange, or around concepts, where it is not even clear that a common phenomenon is at issue, as in the example of the study of power. Sometimes integration is explicitly itself a major objective, as in the work of Parsons, and sometimes it grows out of a diversified interest in explaining various aspects of very complex empirical trends or developments like modernization. Only some of it develops around policy questions, as has conspicuously been the case for some integration in the study of economic development. Finally, there are some of the greatest integrations, which have been the product of a fruitful question, such as those of the political philosophers.

III. Integration through Graduate Academic Training

To the extent that the various modes of integration now being practiced are inadequate so that we might consequently seek a way to give an additional impetus to integration, there is no apparent reason for choosing policy analysis over the other methods; and, in fact, one can think of at least one alternative method that might well be superior to policy analysis if one is looking for a feasible, practical program. It is simply to alter the character of the Ph.D. program in the social sciences.

Using training in economics as an example, while it is true that many graduate economics students are content to cultivate economics to the exclusion of other social sciences, a significant and perhaps growing number of others find that such convergences as have just been listed greatly attract them. There is today, among graduate students in economics and the other social sciences, a powerful incentive toward integration as well as enough examples of successful integration to leave them untroubled as to its feasibility.

But graduate training throws obstacles in their paths. By the testimony of a number of graduate students, it seems clear that many Ph.D. programs compel a student to pursue a finely honed, technical competence in formal economic theory at the expense of frutiful ventures into neighboring disciplines. To be sure, some graduate departments have moved a great deal toward incorporating training in related social sciences, but in this respect I believe that economic departments are well behind departments of political science, psychology, sociology, and anthropology. For many graduate students in economics, whatever training they obtain around existing integrations comes, as in the example of decision theory, from instruction by faculty in their own departments much more than from courses permitted them in other departments.

Some decades ago one would have hesitated to propose changes in the structure of graduate education to achieve integration, for graduate instruction was then more informally organized than it is now. One could be reasonably confident that a sufficiently enterprising student would find his way to whatever faculty he needed. But graduate education has had to accommodate larger numbers and has, for this and other reasons, become bureaucratized. Its requirements and its options have come to be somewhat more rigidly defined than earlier. At Yale, for example, as at many other universities, the last decade has seen a growing pressure for completing course work in two years and the dissertation in two more. In Yale's case, pressure was stimulated by a desire to economize on the new large funds invested in graduate fellowships. That source of pressure is symptomatic of the kind of force that has routinized graduate education.

In short, a sufficient number of young scholars want to do integrative work. There is no dearth of fruitful modes. To accelerate integration, then, one ought simply to break the bottleneck of graduate education. It is not necessary, if this argument is correct, to be much concerned about which of the various modes of integration is the most fruitful.

IV. Architectonic Integration?

One might argue that the kinds of integration now to be found in the social sciences are, with an occasional exception, too fragmentary or incomplete. One might hope for some method of integration, like policy analysis, that would bring together *all* of social science.

The objection to such an argument is that an architectonic integration of social science, an all-embracing structure of social science knowledge, is a premature aspiration. Premature at least, and possibly forever impossible of achievement. The social sciences are still in a state—they may forever be—in which the disciplines taken together do not embrace the whole of the social world and in which each one taken singly by no means encompasses, in the range of its accomplishments, all that is by intellectual tradition assigned to it.

Take economics again as an example. Its highly skilled preoccupation with resource allocation in the market system leaves economics still underdeveloped on the economics of nonmarket economies. More than that, it has left unattended such questions as some of those mentioned above, like the question concerning the effect of life in a market milieu on personality and culture. To be sure, that illustrative question happens to be one that calls for some integration of social science. But a particular integration is required to answer it. It will be a long time before work on that and other questions now neglected can be seen as part of an architectonic whole.

But perhaps, one might reply, the way to complete the unfinished work of each of the disciplines is to map the whole of social science, divide up assignments, and encourage each scholar to work at his own specialized assignment in the cooperative construction of a great structure. If this were to have the effect of turning scholars away from such effective foci of integration as they have already found, it might turn them from fruitful work into jejune system-building. Aside from that, it is to be doubted that social science yet has captured enough pieces of a grand structure to infer from them what the design of the grand structure should look like. There have been impressive intellectual achievements in architectonic integration—much of Lasswell's work in the last two decades, for example, or Kuhn's *Study of Society*. But they remain, so far, more idiosyncratic than syncretic.

On several specific counts, social science seems a long way from an architectonic integration. First, most of the social sciences—including those closest to public policy—have so far produced few nomothetic propositions. Instead their propositions are true or valid only for particular times, particular places, particular cultures, particular nations. Even the maxims of rational choice in economics that give rise to such propositions as that entrepreneurs maximize profits assume certain culture patterns, specifically certain choice patterns between money, on one hand, and leisure and other kinds of satisfaction, on the other. Empirical propositions about corporate behavior are very much the product of observation of twentieth-century institutional development. The same is true for propositions on unions and wage determination, and so on.

In political science, to take another example, what the discipline has to tell us about the behavior of parties, interest groups, or even about voting, which is the most splendidly cultivated area of empirical research in political science, gives us propositions that are true for only limited domains.

Secondly, social science faces a problem that, for the most part, does not plague natural scientists. Societies learn. They change their ways. A society's experience with forms of economic behavior and economic organization teaches it to change those forms, as also for parties, interest groups, and other political institutions. So far, social science has done very little more than to try to analyze systematically a contemporary cross-section picture of behavior rather than the learning process itself. An architectonic social science is an impossibility until social science turns to the learning process and develops the capacity to say something about sequences of social behavior and institutional organization, in addition to describing correctly a series of cross-sections.

Obviously social science has not even begun such a task, except for an occasional Marx whose very ambitions on this score tend to disqualify him as a social *scientist* in the eyes of less ambitious scholars. It is, of course, possible that what I call social learning is a dynamic process that will always—forever and inevitably—leave emerging patterns of behavior beyond the competence of an always-lagging social science. In that case, the architectonic social science will always elude us.

Finally, it is certainly of some significance to our plans for integration that the physical and biological sciences, which are much less ambitious in scope than the social sciences and which are not plagued by a counterpart process to social learning, are themselves not integrated, despite their greater degree of maturity or comprehensiveness when compared to the social sciences.

V. The Need for Policy Analysis

But if policy analysis is not the way to integrate social science, perhaps it is a way of integrating pieces of social science and other studies which, though useful for the guidance of policy, may fall short of what we call social *scientific*.

Presumably, enormously larger informational and analytical input into policy making would be desirable. I do not propose an unlimited new input, since at some point the cost of the input is worth more than the benefits produced. Still, a much larger input would seem almost certainly to promise benefits. Much of the required new input, however, takes the form of information on particular configurations of events and the analysis of relationships there displayed. It is not the kind of information collection and analysis that contributes greatly to a cumulating body of knowledge, even though there is, of course, a good deal of spillover from policy analysis to a cumulating body of knowledge. For example, to develop better policy on irrigation in India, which is a good example of a major policy problem, the policy maker needs to know a great deal more than he does about the state of the arts in the practice of irrigation by Indian peasants. He also needs to know more than he does about the way in which present seed strains respond to water and how seed strains to be developed in the foreseeable future will respond to water. He also needs to know—I am choosing only a few examples—about the costs of different irrigation technologies. It is information that will quickly become obsolete and which has only limited fruitfulness for cumulating science.

It looks as though we do, indeed, need an enriched policy analysis and one that is integrated in that it does not much respect disciplinary boundaries. But it ought not to be confused with social science. Should it not bear something of the same relationship to the social sciences that medicine bears to the natural and biological sciences? And should we not systematically train people in it as former President Harry Rowan of The Rand Corporation proposed to do at Rand? Should we not dignify an integrated, analytically sophisticated, continuing, professionalized study of policy with some such status as the study of medicine enjoys?

If factoring out of contemporary social science a recognized integrated profession of social "medicine" or social "engineering" might greatly improve society's skill in policy making, a subsidiary advantage might be a great improvement in social *science* itself. For it would make clear, as it is now not clear, that there is a difference between social science and the highly professional study of policy problems. It would give social scientists, or young people who want to be social scientists, a clear conscience about what their scholarly responsibilities might best be. It might turn the social sciences toward more ambitious attempts at nomothetic propositions. In the case of economics, it might arrest what seems to be an increasingly rapid flight of that discipline from the pursuit of significant scientific aspiration. For, thanks to its elegance, its tools, and its analytic investiveness, economics has itself become the core of policy analysis—a point of integration in the analysis of policy. Recognizing this accomplishment and giving it an institutional status might free other economists to pursue the relatively neglected *science* of economics, which remains a worthy aspiration, now too timidly pursued.

13

Another State of Mind (1982)[1]

About liberal democracy, V. O. Key, Jr. wrote: "Political parties are basic institutions for the translation of mass preferences into public policy."[2] He did not write that they obstruct the translation of mass preferences into public policy. Although his formulation may be the correct one, it is not justified by any evidence and argument.

Karl Deutsch wrote that "...politics has the function of coordinating the learning processes of the whole society."[3] He did not say "indoctrinating"—his was the kinder word "learning." Nor did he write "obstruct" or "distort" the learning processes; his word was "coordinate." How does he know his words are more accurate than these alternatives? Again, his statement is introduced as a preface to subsequent analysis, all of which simply assumes it to be true.

David Easton and Robert Hess[4] wrote—and Richard E. Dawson and Kenneth Prewitt[5] wrote that they agree—that a political community is "a group of persons who seek to solve their problems in common through a shared political structure." They did not write that the phenomenon they sought to describe was that of prevailing over adversaries—their phrase was the more benign "solve their problems *in common*." Again, how do

1 For spirited thoughtful comment and correction, I am much indebted to Gabriel Almond, Robert Dahl, Robert E. Lane, Adam Przeworski, Douglas Rae, and Michael Sabia, especially the last named, with whom I several times discussed the paper at length. This work was supported in part by grants from the Ford Foundation.
2 In *Public Opinion and American Democracy* (New York: Alfred A. Knopf, 1967), p. 432.
3 In *Politics and Government* (Boston: Houghton Mifflin, 1980), p. 19.
4 In "The Child's Political World," 6 *Midwest Journal of Political Science* (1962), p. 233.
5 In *Political Socialization* (Boston: Little Brown, 1969), p. 45n.

they know that their formulation is more accurate than the alternatives they did not choose? They do not say.

Let me interrupt this illustrative procession of witnesses, though I shall resume it shortly with younger authors. My concern is that when we political scientists make gratuitous claims like these, we leave mainstream American political science vulnerable—vulnerable to the charge from radical political science that we have without evidence fallen into a complacent view of the liberal democratic political process, government, and state and that we do not even bother to debate it.[6] It is, I think largely an American problem. European political theory has in recent years been greatly reconstructed by the incorporation of much radical thought. If these European developments can be taken as leading, American thought is a decade or two behind.[7]

I. Two Views of Liberal Democracy

To see whether there is any merit to so brusing a charge, let me first lay out—very briefly because it is familiar—the simplest elements of the democratic political system and state as they have often appeared since World War II in respectable circles in much of theoretically oriented American political science.[8]I shall also lay out a simple synthetic dissenting view that captures much of the radical concept of the democratic state. They will

6 These vulnerable views can be and are sometimes attacked from within a broad mainline tradition, going back to Madison in the *Federalist Papers* and even earlier. My primary interest is in their vulnerability from any source of attack. I give special attention, however, to the radical attack for several reasons: the magnitude of the assault, the sharpness of issues posed, and a concern that radical thought is likely to be undervalued as a corrective to the problem.

The argument that this intellectual tradition is vulnerable is an argument about the specific content of the tradition and is quite different from the familiar argument that political scientists fail to and cannot keep fact and value separate, as among others, Charles Taylor (1969) has effectively argued.

7 Have I misrepresented these scholars by excessively brief quotations? I think not. More evidence is yet to come in this paper. I will grant, however, that I can find in the same authors other statements that contradict what I have quoted. And many political scientists go about their work more concretely, avoiding such sweeping generalizations as I have quoted. Those who do write such generalizations often implicitly deny them when they turn to more concrete studies. Yet such generalizations as just quoted, and many more yet to be cited as testimony, document a common prevailing habit of mind.

be two views of what democracy is, not what it ought to be. After laying them out, I propose to appraise basic elements of the conventional view that I have chosen to discuss.

A. *A Conventional Intellectual Tradition in American Political Science*

According to views common in theoretical circles of the profession in which broad generalization is attempted—and for which I shall offer further documentation—the political system called democratic in the West is best understood as a distinctive kind of mutual-benefit society. However, imperfect, it provides some degree of social order, as well as widespread benefits beyond that. In Deutsch's term, it "coordinates the learning processes." In Easton and Hess's, it attacks "problems in common." In Key's, it "translates mass preferences into public policy."[9]

Conflict abounds, however, in this view of the democratic state, running in all directions. The state is therefore also seen as a conflict-resolving system—a theme so common as hardly to require documentation. The theme can be traced back to Hobbes, and earlier; and among contemporary voices that sounds it is Dahl's in the opening pages of his *Democracy in the United States* (1972). It also opens the analysis of politics in Prewitt and Verba's *Introduction to American Government* (1977).

The concept of the state or government as a common-benefit

8 There are, of course, other mainstream traditions. I am tryting to capture an intellectual tradition in mainstream theory construction, one of recent unchallenged prominence in American political science. I think it has already lost much of its earlier vitality, for two different reasons. On the one hand, its persuasiveness has already declined among some political scientists. On the other hand, it is less vital because it is taken for granted in many circles. It remains strong, as I see it, sometimes all the stronger for being taken for granted, for therefore remaining only implicit, and for directing research attention down some avenues rather than others without explanation or justification. 9 In mainstream political science, the existence of a common good is probably more often denied than asserted. What is denied, specifically, is that there exists a common good that is well-enough defined and agreed upon to serve as a criterion for public policy. That denial is consistent with a belief that almost everyone wants and benefits from the state's pursuit of a number of common efforts like law and order, national defense, a prosperous economy, or education of the young. It is this belief that I find in the conventional view.

organization has to be reconciled with the concept of the state as conflict resolver. The reconciliation is easy. Everyone is seen as wanting a core of much the same fundamental services or benefits: law and order, national defense, and a prosperous economy, among others. Ordinarily, only secondary conflict develops within such an agreed fundamental set of desires. Class conflict is only one important conflict among many.[10]

The specialized political machineries of these systems (elections and legislative representation, for example) are seen as necessary instruments for holding government or the state responsible to society as a whole by placing important powers in the hands of all—with some approximation to equality in the distribution of these powers. It is believed that some consequential approach to equality, even if distant, is achieved and justifies interpretation of the system as benefiting, however unequally, almost everyone.

In this conventional intellectual tradition, the disproportionate political influence or power of elites is recognized. But their disproportion does not deny any of the above characteristics of democracy; all that is required is that elites be held accountable. Some political scientists, David Truman[11] among them, go further to make elites the guardians of democracy, on the grounds that they are more committed to it than are non-elites.

Pluralism is not a necessary feature of this picture. It is at most secondary and is absent from some versions.

B. *A Synthesis of Dissent*
An alternative view captures the most basic features of dissenting Marxist and other radical thought on liberal or bourgeois democracy. A transitional form, liberal democracy can be

---

10 In anthropological and sociological writing, the distinction between conflict models and integration models of social processes is conspicuous. (See, for instance, Ralph Dahrendorf, *Class and Class Conflict in Industrial Society* [Stanford: Stanford University Press, 1959], Ch. 5; Ronald Cohen and Elman R. Service, eds., *Origins of the State* [Philadelphia, 1978], Introduction.) The intellectual tradition I am describing has a foot in both camps. It is integrationist in seeing the political system as serving common purposes for the good of all. It is conflictual in its attention to pervasive conflict in political life.
11 In "The American System in Crisis," 74 *Political Science Quarterly* (1959), pp. 481–497.

understood only in light of where it came from. If we cut into the historical process at a stage at which humankind has already developed a complex social structure marked by substantial specialization of function, we see that some subsets of the population at that time rule others and enjoy various advantages denied to other subsets. Once such a degree of complexity is realized, a high degree of political inequality and resultant conflict thereafter become universal historical phenomena—in all places and at all times, though less in some circumstances than in others.

There is some cohesion or cooperation, much though not all of it unintended and without self-awareness, among the advantaged on one hand and the disadvantaged on the other. Most radicals would say that it is the distribution of property rights that has for the last few centuries marked off the two loose, somewhat cohesive, aggregates. That the disadvantaged and the advantaged each cohere loosely is critical to the model, and the usual word for each of the aggregates is *class*. Within, between, and jointly among the advantaged and disadvantaged aggregates are conflicting subgroups. But the most critical conflict is between the two aggregates, even if it is suppressed and consequently not recognizable as a conflict by such mainstream political scientists as I am summarizing.[12]

The liberal democratic political systems of the world have to be understood as the present institutionalized form of that struggle. Democratic institutions represent the present alignment, strengths, and formal authority of advantaged and disadvantaged groups. Democracy did not come about through any agreement between advantaged and disadvantaged groups that henceforth the political system should be operated for the benefit of all. These systems represent social machinery for converting the age-old struggle into a more peaceful one than it would otherwise often be, but not for terminating the struggle.[13]

For the advantaged groups in these systems, the principal effort is to keep such advantages as they have, even if it has become impolite for them to say so. For the disadvantaged groups, the principal effort is to reduce the degree of inequality,

12 Some neo-Marxists have moved substantially to acknowledge that the *manifest* struggle is a multifaceted struggle like that in the dominant model.

or exploitation, or dominance—the dissenters do not all use the same terms. A principal weapon of the advantaged groups, which have always been more educated and have had instruments of communication available to them (ranging from the Church in times past to the mass media today), is indoctrination of the disadvantaged groups to induce them to believe in the rightness of their disadvantaged position and of the difficulty, in any case, of doing anything about it. Hence, the principal purpose of most members of the disadvantaged groups is no more than to protect such gains as are already won and to pursue others only timidly and fitfully.

It is then argued that the political systems of the West are, as a consequence, not mainly mutual-benefit or common-purpose systems. Both sides share an interest in some common purposes, such as in some degree of social order and organized economic production. But many interests are shared only in the sense that two nations at war have shared interests in methods of communication between them and in the exchange of prisoners. Their common interests are usually best understood as serving more fundamental conflicting interests. Some of the common interests of the advantaged and disadvantaged are best understood as no more than common interests in keeping the struggle from escalating.

Finally, specific mechanisms of government, like mass elections and broad legislative representation, are concessions (wrung from a bourgeoisie that earlier won these gains for itself) that have grown out of historical struggle. For the disadvantaged, the gains are significant. They are, however, so far from perfect instruments of popular control and political equality that they leave many opportunities for the advantaged to con-

13 Not only Marxists and other Left radicals hold to a fundamental distinction between advantaged and disadvantaged. So also did Mosca, Pareto, and Michels. Yet if they are read to allege only a kind of technical difficulty in governing without elites whose interests come to conflict with mass interests, they are perhaps more mainstream than radical. If, however, they are read to allege a more fundamental exploitation of mass by elite, they are more radical than mainstream though far removed on many points from Left radicals. Reading them the second way makes their interpretation of democratic politics inconsistent with our quoted statements above and others to follow. Mainstream political science sometimes claims to have absorbed at least Michels and Mosca, but the absorption is not evident in the dominant view of democratic politics that we document.

tinue their predominance of control and other advantages. If, in the eyes of the disadvantaged, the purpose of these mechanisms is or ought to be the establishment of popular control and political equality, in the eyes of the advantaged the point of establishing them was to make no more than necessary concessions, sometimes of more apparent than genuine significance.

The relation between polity and economy is a key issue in the dissenters' model. Orthodox Marxism often tended toward a conspiratorial model of dominance by property, yet those at the frontiers of current Marxist though have moved far from such a position. They are now exploring more carefully qualified and specific hypotheses. I attribute to contemporary radical thought a concept of the state as much more autnomous than that in traditional Marxism.

In some formulations, the state achieves autonomy because of the existence of competing capitalist factions, to no single one of which the state is subordinate. In other formulations, the state to a degree responds to demands from the working class and is therefore not wholly subordinate to property. Or the state has to provide welfare benefits to all classes because they each provide an input necessary to the productive system. In still another formulation, the state responds to all interests within a set of constraints that protect the survival of capitalism. Some Marxists have also introduced explicit elements of pluralism into their analyses.[14]

The dissenting view draws no great number of adherents in the American political science profession. But many of us are aware that some of our students, including many of the brightest, are exploring it independent of our tutelage. They claim to be finding intellectual nourishment in such sources as Habermas, Poulantzas (1973), Miliband (1969), Offe, O'Connor, Lukes, Mandel, and Gough, among others who are being widely cited in a new literature on the state. The hold of the conventional theory on political science is indicated by a striking fact that, although scholars like those just named write about politics, they come to it from sociology, philosophy, economics, and history, as well as disproportionately from European intel-

---

14 These fresh currents are identified and briefly appraised in Crouch, Holloway and Picciotto, and Mouzelis.

lectual traditions to which American political science is cool. Very few come from American political science—and of this particular list, none. Radicals do not see political science as a well-designed discipline; its very defintion is an obstruction, they will say, to necessary research. Our discipline itself is a formidable difficulty in the way of some of our younger colleagues.

C. *The Nondissenting Dissenter*

In their choice between these two pictures of democratic politics, a wider array of political scientists than first appears holds to the conventional one. So persuasive is the conventional picture that even some forms of dissent among political scientists do not break with it. Lowi's polemic (to use his own term) against interest-group liberalism in *The End of Liberalism* (1979) makes no sense if the radical picture of the political system is correct. Only on the assumption that the political system might be and should be evaluated as a mutual-benefit organization, a problem-solving mechanism for the good of all, can he be indignant that it has drifted off course.[15]

Dye and Zeigler set out to attack pluralist interpretations of democratic systems. Yet they propose an alternative in which the political system is still a mutual-benefit association whose elites "may be very 'public-regarding' and deeply concerned with the welfare of the masses."[16] If the elites normally turn policy making in directions that advantage themselves, they nevertheless maintain a kind of stewardship of the system. The Dye–Ziegler picture moves away from conventional theory to a degree, but it remains far from the radical model.

Similarly, Dolbeare and Edelman, who desire in their textbook to give full hearing both to the conventional and what they call the challengers' models of the American political system, categorically declare by way of introduction that people "erect

15 In his textbook, *American Government* (1976), however, Lowi breaks more boldly from conventional theory by introducing, as an alternative to both the dominant and the radical models as he sees them, his own model of the state as institutionalized conquest.
16 In *The Irony of Democracy* (Belmont: Wadsworth, 1970), pp. 1–2.

governments to maintain order, further mutual goals, and promote general well-being."[17]

I am suggesting that scholars of a wide range of ages, tem-
peraments, and schools of thought are largely committed to the
conventional view and give little sustained analytical attention
to the radical model. My list of samples above is illustrative of
the variety.

D. *An Incomplete Breakaway*

In recent decades, some significant attempts have been made
by members of the conventional school to break out of its
confines with frames of reference or theories that would then
permit an eyes-open choice among existing or yet-to-be-
developed theories. A monumental attempt of this kind—of a
functional framework—has been that of Almond and Powell[18]
on foundations they attribute, in part, to Easton. It is worth
our examining because its explicit features do not seem to make
the arbitrary choices that separate the conventional view from
the radical model. Almond and Powell explicitly acknowledge,
for example, the possibility that the advantaged (but not the
disadvantaged) effectively articulate their values and that the
values aggregated might be those of the advantaged to the
exclusion of those of the disadvantaged. Their analysis of the
political process is worked out with such extraordinary care
that it can accommodate both the dominant and the radical
pictures.

For their discussions of democratic politics, however, they
choose, without any explicit defense of their choice, the conventional view. For example, although interest aggregation might,
according to their framework, largely neglect the interests of
the disadvantaged, they appear to take it for granted that in
democratic politics it does not. Having developed a framework
that will work for either the conventional or radical view of
democracy, they work it for the conventional one.

In addition, their framework seems to have been designed
with an eye on variables that best fit the conventional view. For

17 In *American Politics,* 3rd ed., rev. (Lexington: D.C. Heath, 1981), p. 7.
18 In *Comparative Politics* (Boston: Little Brown, 1966).

one thing, the framework is structural-functional with debt to Parsons; it therefore habitually identifies functions served for the whole society rather than some functions for the advantaged and others for the disadvantaged. Although fundamental and continuing struggle between the two groups is neither denied in the framework nor impossible to place in it, it is difficult to fit the struggle in. To fit it would require that a strained interpretation be given to such society-wide functional categories as interest articulation and interest aggregation. It is possible to consider the advantaged group's interest in exploiting the disadvantaged as just another interest to be articulated and aggregated, but one cannot help wondering about the usefulness of these terms—articulation and aggregation—for describing such a situation. To make the point vividly by analogy, though with some exaggeration: If a racketeer shakes down a tradesman for monthly protection payments, we could say that in so doing he is both articulating his own interests and aggregating his and the tradesman's. But the concepts would seem strained.

II. Do We Know That the Dominant Model Is Superior?

At this point, the questions are: How solid, verified, or even thoughtful is the conventional tradition? Why do we think our picture is more useful for political science than the radical picture? Let us examine some of the differences between the two. I propose to do so without any appeals to the vocabulary of radical thought and without any radical methodological stances; nor shall I ascend to the philosophy of science. I shall stay with the language and habits of thought of the dominant tradition. The approach biases the analysis against the radical model, but doing so may reassure mainstream political scientists. In the mainstream myself, I cannot pretend in any case to do justice to the radical model; indeed, I think it is badly flawed. Nevertheless, I want to ask some questions about the simplest elements of the conventional view in the light of its vulnerability.

A. *Common Purposes Versus Struggle*
Is it known—is it settled—that the primary motivation among leaders and ordinary citizens is the pursuit of those benefits they

share in common? Clearly not. Empirical evidence does not establish even a thin case that, on this point, the conventional view is correct.

Those who hold the conventional view do not really mean that participants themselves are mainly concerned with the pursuit of certain common purposes. What they really might mean is that a sophisticated observer will see that the state nevertheless pursues certain common purposes. But how does an observer see any purposes in so sprawling an organization as the state unless they are the actual purposes of at least some participants in it? To assign a purpose to the political system independent of the purposes of any significant number of participants requires careful formulation and justification.

What do we actually observe when we observe political life? We observe millions of ordinary people pursuing a variety of objectives. Even to an experienced observer, it is not at all clear that certain objectives common to all occupy much of their energies. On the other hand, neither is it obvious that the various partisans cohere either deliberately, tacitly, or unintentionally into two loose coalitions, the advantaged and the disadvantaged, each pursuing distinctive conflicting objectives. In short, we actually observe forms of behavior that the dominant view wants to construe one way and the radical the other. A principal task of a scientific political science might be to research the issue. Conventional political science has no grounds for simply holding to its present view to the neglect of the radical one.

There seems to be a way to escape making such a concession to the radical model. We can argue as many do—Dolbeare and Edelman (1981) most explicitly among those cited above—that a political system, government, or state is necessary for law and order. We simply cannot imagine doing without it—all people need it whether they know it or not. Hence, it makes a certain kind of sense to say that fundamentally the state's purpose is (for the benefit of all) law and order and other necessary benefits. In an earlier analogy, however, we noted that to carry on international warfare seems to require that some system of communications between the warring nations be kept open and that they thus can be seen as joining in pursuit of that common purpose. But it would confuse our understanding of war if we called it a common-purpose activity. We would do better to see it as a struggle moderated by some common concerns. Similarly, perhaps, the democratic state is an institutionalized form of a struggle to which such necessary common purposes as observers see are secondary. Until that possibility is more carefully examined, the conventional view is not persuasive.

More important, by what logic does a purpose rather than any other important variable dictate how we should build analytic models? Suppose a river flows through an isolated community, providing essential water without which the inhabitants would die. Suppose also the river annually floods with consequent loss of life and constantly carries pollutants into the community. If we talk the language of purpose, I take it that we would say the purpose of the river is to provide necessary water to the community. But a good model or theory of the river would not play up that effect on the community to the relative neglect of the adverse effects. The argument that the community needs, must have, cannot live without the river does not justify, in the model or theory of the river, denying prominent place to floods and pollution. As a guide to what goes into models or theories, there is no logical imperative that requires that an essential social purpose must be made the centerpiece.

Perhaps we are still missing something. Perhaps the emphasis in the conventional view on certain common purposes rather than on struggle between advantaged and disadvantaged is not meant to assert or imply any *fact*, historical or contemporary. Perhaps it is only intended to lay out a fruitful strategy, thus to imply a judgement about method—that we shall get more results if we study the state in the light of certain necessary functions than if we study it as though it were an institutionalized form of a long-standing struggle. If this is so, perhaps all variants of the conventional view represent a commitment to structural-functionalism, though only a few are explicitly so labelled.

I do not want to undertake as this point a survey of the pros and cons of structural-functional analysis. But if structural-functionalism is a requirement of good social science—which is not obvious at all—note that the radical model is often put in structural-functional terms.[19] Some advocates of the radical model subscribe to such propositions as that the state's function is to preserve the advantages of the advantaged. I take it that they mean that the state is a structure serving such a function for the ruling class, whether members of the ruling class know it or not. Similarly, many Marxist statements about the working class attribute functions to it. We do not often recognize structural-functionalism in radical thought because the functions postulated are not for the whole society but instead for either the advantaged or the disadvantaged or for an abstraction like "the development of the productive forces."

Have we any reason to assume that the nation-state society is the correct social group for which functions and structures are to be analyzed? Or that the functions explored should be stabilizing functions? Do we have any reason to say we know that structural-functional analysis is inappropriate when used to analyze the functions performed for subgroups or for social change rather than for stability? Must structural analysis be limited to its particular formulation in conventional theory?

Thus we come to the end of our first line of inquiry into analyzing the state of government as a kind of mutual-benefit organization versus analyzing it as an institutional form of struggle between advantaged and disadvantaged. If neither position is wholly satisfactory, as I believe to be the case, we have nevertheless found no solid ground for choosing the first approach over the second. The radical model begins with what may be a historical fact, a struggle, while conventional theory begins with allegations about necessity without connecting that necessity to facts about participants' behavior. There is, consequently, a slightly stronger a priori or question-begging tone to conventional than to radical thought. But our purpose is not to evaluate the relative merits of the two models but only to try to understand the grounds on which the advocates of the dominant model might be justified in holding confidently to it. So far, we have found no grounds,[20]

B. *Diversified Conflict: Second Line of Defense*

Perhaps I am giving too much attention to the "common benefits" theme in conventional theory. A mainstream political scien-

19 "There is no well-stated alternative to the view that major Marxian explanatory claims are functional in character" (Ronald Cohen and Elman R. Service, eds., *Origins of the State* [Philadelphia, 1978], p. 279).

tist might want to play it down, arguing instead that the critical point of difference between the two views is that one asserts diversified conflict in all directions, the other asserts a more fundamental conflict between advantaged and disadvantaged, each as loosely cohesive groups.

As a defense for conventional theory, the tactic will not quite do. For one thing, as my quotations have shown, the assertion of common benefits and of their central importance to the understanding of democratic politics is hardly an only seconday feature of conventional theory.

Second, the conventional emphasis on diversified conflict to the near exclusion of attention to conflict between advantaged and disadvantaged is, I shall argue below, an intellectual habit of focusing on manifest conflict rather than an emphasis warranted by empirical comparison of the two patterns of conflict which are not equally manifest. What I say may seem to be denied by such efforts as Dahl's to categorize different kinds of political conflict in his *Democracy in the United States* (1972). But his types do not admit the pattern characteristic of the radical model except in unusual circumstances or when class conflict is reduced to only one of several conflicts.

I do not have to show that the radical view of the pattern or conflict is correct, the mainstream view wrong. All I must do is show that the mainstream view is unsubstantiated and that there is an issue between the two views that has not been carefully investigated. On whether the conflict is dichotomous or not, consider the distribution of wealth. It is not conclusive evidence that the advantaged cohere in the perpetuation of their advantages, but it is a phenomenon of such striking character as to make such an hypothesis worthy of investigation. So also are patterns in the perpetuation of educational inequality that

20 So far, I say. I have not, however, looked into possible disqualifying weaknesses in the radical model. The asymmetry in my treatment of the two models is deliberate. I do not want to argue that the radical model is better than the conventional. I only want to show that the conventional model is extremely weak, is vulnerable to easy radical attacks, and is without obvious advantage over the radical model on the main features under discussion. I believe that those features are the ones to which mainstream political scientists refer in justification of their model in preference to the radical. How comparative study of and experimentation with the two models, sustained and dispassionate, would turn out, I would not guess. I suggest that it is high-priority work for the profession.

persist despite public education and state universities. So also is the frequency with which government subsidies turn out to be for the benefit of the well-off rather than for the disadvantaged for whom they are ostensibly designed. So also are differences in teachers' treatment of children of different socioeconomic class. All of these examples, and many more easily listed, should stir our curiosity about the radical model of conflict. Proving nothing but suggesting much to which much mainstream political science has been indifferent, they undercut confidence in the conventional picture of diversified conflict.

The ordinary or daily business of politics, it might be replied, is resolution of conflicts of a highly diversified sort. What we can observe on the political agenda is diversified conflict. That, consequently, is what democratic politics is all about. What we can see is what is really happening. What we cannot see, or cannot see very clearly, we must not only doubt, but we must also entertain a strong presumption against its existence. In one formulation in the mainstream literature that caught my eye, it is said that, so long as men have liberty to express their views, conflicts will exist—as though conflict does not exist unless made so conspicuously manifest. Indeed, I think one of the misunderstandings separating mainstream and radical political science is that the one often identifies conflict with such expressions of it as liberty permits while the other is sensitive to repressed conflict.

Let me further examine this "politics is what we see" argument in defense of the conventional view of diversified conflict—in three steps.

The first possible point of vulnerability in the argument is the counter argument that what we do not see can be seen if we look harder. Radical political science often argues hypotheses about those parts of the social world, such as indoctrination, most difficult to see. It also warns us against imputing to the unseen the same characteristics as mark the seen. Some mainstream political scientists consequently allege that radicals hold a conspiracy theory of political life. Some radicals do, but that is not characteristics of radical political science. The unseen that interests them is no more conspiratorial than, and is in many ways comparable to, Smith's hidden hand, though a less benign hidden hand—perhaps a hidden fist. Their hypotheses, like earlier hypotheses about the once unseen backside of the moon, are not to be discretdited solely because of formidable difficulties in proof so long as they are willing, as at least some are, to specify what phenomena they would seek to observe if they actually became observable.

The second point of vulnerability in the "politics is what we see" defense of conventional theory is the possibility that, as good scientists, we have to explain both what exists and what does not exist. Radicals believe so—that nonoccurrences require explanation. Sherlock Holmes had to explain why the dog did not bark. If people do not have liberty to express their conflicts, we must often explain why. John Gaventa, our Woodrow Wilson prizewinner for this year, says he had to turn traditional political science around—to ask why rebellion in Appalachia does not occur.[21] That is no less a scientific question than why rebillions occur when they do. That many conflicts between advantaged and disadvantaged, which radicals think are fundamental, *do not appear* on the political agenda is a good scientific hypothesis. And if they exist and do not so appear, why they do not is a good scientific question.

The third point of vulnerability of the "politics is what we see" defense of conventional theory is that all the statement means is that "we"—we political scientists—do *not* see and that it is for other kinds of social scientists to observe. Sometimes I hear the opinion that although some of the phenomena in the radical model may exist (indoctrination of the disadvantaged by the advantaged, for example), they are not part of the political process. They are prepolitical, or at least nonpolitical; and they deserve investigation not by our discipline but by sociologists, social psychologists, and anthropologists. For, again, politics is what goes on in the political process, not what does not go on in it.

Such an argument is not a good reason for rejecting the radical model. It is only an argument about disciplinary lines, and it throws some light on why radicals usually find the lines that define political science unacceptable.

I would conclude that for these three reasons the "politics is

21 In *Power and Powerlessness* (Urbana: University of Illinois Press, 1980), p. vi.

what we see" defense of conventional theory is extremely weak and the radical criticism of that defense is highly plausible.

I grant, however, that radical political scientists have been short on empirical research into the unseen. That fact cannot be used to deny the inadequacies of the conventional thought; it points, however, to a potential available to radical thought to verify its model. Researchers might challenge both the conventional picture and their own if they could bring into sight elements of political life now less manifest than the easily observable turbulence of pluralist politics.[22]

C. Scientific Neutrality: Third Line of Defense

A third line of defense for conventional theory is that its propositions are more neutral—they commit you to less—than those of the racial model. To assert, even with historical evidence, a fundamental struggle in politics between advantaged and disadvantaged seems to assert a highly questionable proposition. To study the political system as a system into which we are all drawn because of a common concern for law and order seems safer scientifically.

It is not a very good argument. Even if the state does provide law and order and certain other shared benefits, one takes a position—with no satisfactory evidence—if one asserts that participants are drawn into politics and motivated by those functions of the state. There is nothing neutral at all about such a position. It may seem to be a colorless, nonprovocative kind of position to hold; but it is nevertheless an exposed, unproved position, no less so than the belief in struggle between advantaged and disadvantaged.

I shall go further in showing that conventional theory is far from neutral, whatever "neutral" might be defined to be. It departs from neutrality in the specific sense that it claims that democratic politics are at root benign. It grants, of course, that democratic governments make mistakes, are sometimes harsh, and occasionally sink into violence or repression. But its fundamental characterization of these systems is as benign.

22 Examples of doing so are in G. William Domhoff, *Power Structure Research* (Beverly Hills: Sage, 1980), although some are unconvincing.

We have already seen benignity in Deutsch's[23] reference to its coordination of learning, in repeated quoted references to communities pursuing common purposes, and (to take a specific example) in Dolbeare and Edelman[24] on promoting general well-being. Benignity appears again in Apter's description of moral purposes coalescing with other variables "generating a healthier climate in which individuals can make decisions." When Dahl finds the origin of the state in the need for conflict resolution, he says, ". . . communities search for ways of adjusting conflicts so that cooperation and community life will be possible and tolerable."[26] He might have said, "adjusting conflicts so that subordination of groups to other groups, or repression, or stratification will be possible." That he instead uses happier terms like "cooperation and community life" expresses what I mean by a view of politics as benign.

V. O. Key, Jr., takes an equally benign view: "Legitimization of the view that the preferences of the governed shall be accorded weight by governnors constitutes the moral basis of popular government, an ethical imperative that in mature democracies is converted into consistent habits and patterns of action among those in places of authority and leadership."[27] The quoted sentence characterizes democracy as so benign that it sounds like the statement of an ideal, but he writes it as a statement of fact.[28]

The benign view is missing from the radical model, in which

23 *Politics and Government, op. cit.* p. 19.
24 *American Politics, op. cit.,* p. 7.
25 In *Introduction to Political Analysis* (Cambridge: Winthrop, 1977), p. 5.
26 In *Democracy in the United States* (Chicago: Rand McNally, 1972), p. 5.
27 In *Public Opinion and American Democracy, op. cit.,* p. 412.
28 A frequently quoted statement from David Truman is an example of a different kind, but again it is evidence of democratic politics as benign. He writes of elites: "Being more influential, they are privileged; and, being privileged, they have, with few exceptions, a special stake in the political system on which their privileges rest" ("The American System in Crisis," 74 *Political Science Quarterly* [1959], p. 489). I first saw this statement out of context, and I took it for granted that he was pointing to a flaw in the system: inequalities arising out of privilege. When I went to the article from which it was excerpted, I found that his argument was that privileged elites could be counted on to protect democracy. He may be right, but it is an example of putting benign interpretation on an ambiguous phenomenon. I can think of some comparable passages in my own work in which apparent defects of democratic politics are construed as advantages.

politics is a struggle between adversaries. In some older and contemporary Marxist versions of the radical model, the state is malevolent rather than benign; but usually the model depicts the political process as a mixture of benignity and malevolence unless, more neutrally, it is simply described by reference to historical causation. We cannot categorically say that the radical view is superior, but we clearly have no grounds for declaring the dominant benign view to be the more neutral. Hence, the second line of defense of the dominant model will not hold.

D. *The Wrong Questions: Fourth Line of Defense*

A fourth line of defense is this: Perhaps the trouble with the radical model is that people who use it ask the wrong questions. I suggest that the very questions that radicals have long raised about democratic politics are being raised belatedly by mainstream political scientists in acknowledgment of their importance. Among others, they are questions about political indoctrination, about rising expectations and other sources of new popular demands on government, about corporatism, and about increasingly tense conflict between popular demands and the needs of business (a conflict highlighted in the Reagan administration's declared position that the economy cannot prosper without a reduction in popular demands for regulation and entitlements). These questions include, consequently, new interests in the politics of inflation growing out of possible connections between inflation and magnitude of demands made on government.[29]

These questions connect with even larger questions about the viability and efficacy of democracy, questions that radical thought has long approached with a useful skepticism that is free of certain defects of mainstream thought.[30]

29 Some examples of the radical literature on these issues are to be found in Lindberg et al., Crouch and O'Connor.

30 Examples are Miliband (1969), Holloway and Picciotto, Littlejohn et al., and Skocpol. In much radical thought, skepticism about democracy went so far as to construct defenses for despotism.

The tendency of radicals to turn every apparent strength in democratic politics into a weakness has not gone any further than the mainstream tendency to convert every apparent defect into a strength. Berelson made apathy a strength; Truman made elite privilege a bulwark of democracy, and some of you have read Lindblom on the blessings of fragmentation.

For attacking these questions, it is not at all obvious that conventional theory is superior to the theory of struggle between advantaged and disadvantaged. The literature on these questions is clearly greatly enriched by the radical contribution, the best of which is of a quality that warrants the attention of all mainstream political scientists (despite their habit of regarding contributions from that quarter as falling outside the essential literature of the profession). The fourth line of defense, in short, is no defense at all.

III. A Brief Case Study

I now propose a case study: The literature on political socialization. In it, we can find concrete examples of the weaknesses of conventional theory to solidify the foregoing analysis.

To begin with, in their view of the democratic political process as benign, many conventional scholars see political socialization as a life-long process, even if especially critical in childhood, in which citizens "mature." Socialization helps the citizen to "comprehend" and to "evaluate." It gives him "cognitive growth" and "increasing grasp."[31] Such a view slights the possibility that socialization is intellectually confining, is sometimes crippling, may reduce understanding, and may obstruct the development of skill in evaluation. But which of these it does, or in what mixture, is as important a question for political science as can be imagined. To begin analysis of socialization, as some studies do, with exclusive reference to its benign effects and never to turn to its more questionable effects is, by any scholarly standard, dubious if not unacceptable.

Curiously, in many contributions to the literature, there arises a dual interpretation with no attention to the possible inconsistency between the two. Socialization is maturing, liberating, skill developing. It is simultaneously a way of inducing the citizen to accept the norms of his society. Under what circumstances can or cannot the two be reconciled? That is a question to which the conventional literature remains largely inattentive.

The widely used concept of "learning" helps to obscure the possible contradiction between crippling the mind and fitting

31 Richard E. Dawson and Kenneth Prewitt, *op. cit.*, pp. 16–17 and 56.

the citizen into society. The term *learning* runs through much of the literature. Thus, in one formulation, socialization is "an individual's learning from others in his environment, the social patterns and values of his culture.[32] In another formulation, political socialization is simply equated, for purposes of analysis, with political learning.[33]

An analytic problem arises because *learning,* like *socialization,* can refer to developmental or other processes through which persons improve their grasp of reality, improve the accuracy of their perceptions, and develop skills in perception, analysis, and evaluation. Or it can refer to the effect of influences on the mind that reduce these very competences, as when a person learns that he is destined to fail in anything he attempts or learns from an abusive parent to trust no one. These two kinds or effects of learning—one benign, the other not—are simply not separated in much mainstream political science. And thus both terms *socialization* and *learning*—against which radical thought would pose such a term as *indoctrination*—though pretending to scientific neutrality, take a position: Specifically, that learning and socialization are to be viewed as bringing people into society rather than as obstructing their social capacities.[34]

That this process, which might variably be called *socialization, learning,* or *indoctrination,* goes by the benign name of socialization in the literature of political science illustrates the

32 Kenneth P. Langton, *Political Socialization* (New York: Oxford University Press, 1969), p. 3. Recall also above "learning" in Deutsch's conception of politics in *Politics and Government* (Boston: Houghton Mifflin, 1980), p. 19.
33 See Richard G. Niemi, "Political Socialization," in Jeanne N. Knutson, ed., *Handbook of Political Psychology* (San Francisco: Jossey-Bass, 1973), p. 118.
34 Some methodological rules practiced in the mainstream seem to deny any scientific method for distinguishing between learning and indoctrination unless the existence of objective interests can be established. And the establishment of objective interests is then argued to be beyond the grasp of methods acceptable to mainstream political scientists. On those issues, there exists a gap between scholars holding such a position on one side and other mainstream and radical scholars on the other. I believe that most mainstream political scientists believe that such questions as the following are significant and can be investigated: Are some political communications more truthful than some others? Do some communications stimulate political thought while some others discourage it? Do some communications obfuscate and some others clarify? Can choice-encouraging communications sometimes be distinguished from those that attempt to deny the possibility of choice? If so, then I infer that they can find and study at least some important differences between learning considered as a benign process and as indoctrination.

disposition of the dominant model to find benefits for all in political processes, thus benefits for the abstraction called *society.* That disposition confuses the study of socialization in other ways too. Easton and Dennis are an example. They are much too careful to fall into the trap of associating socialization with maintenance of the status quo; it may also be an agent of change, they say. Notwithstanding, they finally work toward what they consider to be the theoretical significance of socialization, which is its effects on system persistence. They conceive of these effects as the capacity of sets of behavior that allow institutions of value to persist even when their specific forms change.[35] System persistence is, again, a benefit for society, a benefit for all. It renders Easton and Dennis unable to examine the extent to which the process they study, whether called socialization or indoctrination, is an instrument through which the advantaged, with their advantages in the control of communications, teach the disadvantaged to accept their disadvantages. Again, I do not have to argue that the latter interpretation of the process would be the correct one, only that users of the dominant model formulate their inquiries so that they do not investigate it as a possibility.

Easton and Dennis subsequently take note of the possibilities that the process they call socialization teaches citizens to curb their demands. Here one might expect them to see indoctrination as the other face of socialization and plunge into an examination of its potential adverse consequences for fully democratic choice. Instead, intent as they are on social benefits for all, they observe that these taught self-restraints help to prevent system overload.[36] No doubt they do, but the other side of the coin is no less important. The process of constraining demands is a process which on some counts seems to make democracy more viable, yet on other counts argues that democracy is much less democratic than we have supposed. In such a benign view of demand constraint as Easton's and Dennis's, this great issue is missed.[37]

35 See David Easton and Jack Dennis, *Children in the Political System* (New York: McGraw–Hill, 1969), pp. 36–38 and 47–48.
36 Easton and Dennis, *op. cit.,* pp. 55, 66.
37 In the same way, a benign view of socialization misses important issues in Dennis's later "Major Problems of Political Socialization Research" in Jack Dennis, ed., *Socialization to Politics* (New York: John Wiley and Sons, 1973).

Another example of a distorting preoccupation with benefits for all is a comment in Langton about findings that working-class children accept the norms of their class superiors: "The social scientist would suggest, on the basis of the preceding findings, that there is a potential for introducing 'modernizing' norms to the lower classes by way of heterogeneous class environments.[38] No doubt there is. But it seems arbitrary to single out the benign potential for modernizing norms to the exclusion of some other obvious potentials, such as teaching the disadvantaged to be satisfied with their disadvantages.

Greenstein's views on socialization avoid many of the traps into which the dominant model seems to have lured political scientists, but consider the following benign picture: "The long-run effect of media attention is probably to build up, gradually and inadvertently, an awareness of basic elements in the political system."[39] Suppose that I reverse the meaning of the sentence, rewriting it to read that the effects are to reduce awareness of the most basic elements. How could he claim that his sentence is any better than mine?

In the same article, Greenstein moves from *socialization* to *learning*, and then, without explanation to the term *education*. He might have moved, but did not, toward the term *indoctrination* instead of *education*. With that word *education* he chooses, perhaps with little self-awareness, to put the best possible interpretation on a two-faced process. We must turn to the radical model if we are to see the other side.

To the dominant model may perhaps also be attributed a gap in socialization studies. Users of the model are familiar with widely circulating propositions that democracy is impossible without some degree of agreement on fundamentals, at least on rules of the game and among elites. Believing that such agreement is functional for society, they have invested little effort in explaining how it comes about. They can of course point to the socialization mechanisms—family, school, peer groups, the media—which pass the agreed beliefs of one generation on to the next. That approach leaves wholly unexplained the agree-

38 Langton, *op. cit.,* p. 138.
39 In "Socialization: Political Socialization," David L. Sills, ed., *International Encyclopedia of the Social Sciences* (New York: The Macmillan Company and The Free Press, 1968), pp. 551–555.

ment that is already formed when transmitted.[40] How does it come about that certain transmitted beliefs and values are agreed rather than diverse? That we do not understand.

We fall into a bad habit of simply taking for granted that people in any society will think alike, as though agreement were a natural phenomenon that requires no explanation. Even natural phenomena require explanation. Moreover, on some beliefs and values, people differ greatly; only on some do they cluster. Agreement on political fundamentals cries for an explanation. Why, how, through which mechanisms do people come to think alike about political fundamentals?

Sometimes that question is thought to be answered by reference to tradition. But to point to tradition is merely to acknowledge that something has passed through many generations; it is again to point to transmission and to leave the transmitted agreement wholly unexplained.

Or it is suggested that agreement develops spontaneously. Again, that is no explanation at all. At most it says that no large organized effort brings about the agreement; it somehow happens through a variety of communications, many of which may not have been intended to produce the effects they in fact produced. But we do not know how.

One might argue that people living with each other, all in much the same circumstances, will converge on agreed beliefs about the fundamentals of politics.[41] In fact, people in the same society or nation live in markedly differing circumstances: some rich, some poor; some ruling, some ruled; among other differences. We do not know that even those who live in similar circumstances will necessarily, for that reason alone, come to such a degree of agreement on fundamentals as we find among political elites, especially in the United States. It looks as though we confront a phenomenon for which we have no explanation

40 A separate question is how and why some beliefs or values are transmitted and others are not. The socialization literature helps very little on that question. For example, how did we in America transmit to each succeeding generation a resistance to many forms of constitutional and other structural change yet transmit hardly any resistance at all to the bureaucratization—both of governments and corporations—of American life? The extraordinary selectivity of transmission of political beliefs and values is itself a research gap.
41 Such an argument is in R. Weissberg, *Political Learning, Political Choice and Democratic Citizenship* (New Jersey: Prentice-Hall, 1974), pp. 2–3.

in our mainstream literature except that earlier generations passed on their agreement. The agreement remains unexplained.

While conventional theorists are on the whole satisfied merely to note that agreement of certain kinds is necessary and therefore to turn off the search for how it is in fact accomplished, radical theorists have at least some hypotheses to offer. The hypotheses derive from the first feature of their model that we identified above—that political democracy is a transitional phase in a long-standing struggle between advantaged and disadvantaged. The democratic political system has a history; it cannot be understood without reference to its historical origins. If we then look for an explanation of political agreement, we shall find it not in studies of contemporary socialization, though they may give us new chapters for an old story, but in a history in which, as Marx said, the ruling ideas have been the ideas of the ruling class. We shall find it in tendencies toward agreement that were set in motion many centuries ago through such instruments of indoctrination of the disadvantaged by the advantaged as the shaman and later the priest of the Middle Ages. The mechanisms include, through processes of cultural diffusion not well researched, the permeation in more recent history of entire societies with such doctrines as were codified by John Locke and Adam Smith.

Attempting to understand this history, Gramsci in both of his articles,[42] offers propositions, which we may regard as hypotheses well worth study, on cultural hegemony and on the role of intellectuals. In recent years, Habermas and Marcuse have grappled, though not lucidly, with some hypotheses based on Weber on how technology and markets bring about a pervasive purposiveness in human relations that induce acquiescent likemindedness.

We do not know whether the radical hypotheses are true, but they are meaty. They are also sophisticated in their understanding that in opinion formation, just as Adam Smith asserted for the market, much is accomplished through social life without organized intent—often with no intent at all to produce the

---

42 "The Formation of Intellectuals" and "The Study of Philosophy and of Historical Materialism," in Gramsci, *The Modern Prince and Other Writings* (New York: International Publishers, 1968), pp. 118–125.

results actually effected. The hypotheses are an advance over no hypothesis at all from mainstream study of socialization.

IV. Conclusion

Neither in our four lines of defense nor in our brief case study of the socialization literature have we found any grounds for confidence in the conventional theory on democratic politics. I have not, however, argued the superiority of radical over conventional theory. The conclusion is not that the radical is superior but only that mainstream political science ought to bring it in from the cold. The conventional theory creaks and on the evidence here leads political scientists to say silly things.

We cannot, in a final desperate move, reject the radical model because radicals practice questionable methods. My argument has been that, on its own terms, conventional theory is seriously defective and that, presented in mainstream language and concept and without acceptance of any but the most familiar methodology, the radical model is not obviously inferior.

Radical political scientists, however, annoy many of us with their excursions into phenomenology, hermeneutics, interpretive theory, and critical theory. Yet, so many in the mainstream join in certain of these exursions that we can no longer afford to deprecate them. The radicals' use of these new methods as well as the older habits of Marxist method does, I grant, create a chasm between radical and most mainstream thought. And many mainstream scholars, myself included, have made little attempt to cross it. We are also rebuffed by what we are fairly confident are serious shortcomings in much radical writing. It is sometimes insular and arrogant, sometimes humorlessly incapable of self-criticism. Its terms sometimes defy association with any observable real-world process. It begs questions. And its authors, themselves feeling rebuffed, sometimes make no attempt to communicate beyond a privileged radical circle with its private language—thus also excusing themselves from demands for evidence. But the clichés of some radical thought are no more relevant to my argument than the fatuities of some mainstream thought. My argument has not been that radical thought is a model for all of us. It has been instead, to say it once more, that conventional theory is embarrassingly defective. It greatly needs to call more heavily on radical thought.

14

Who Needs What Social Research for Policy Making? (1984)

We have in common this morning an interest in how best to bring social research to the aid of public policy making, or, to put it in even larger terms, an interest in how best to use professional fact gathering, inquiry, and analysis to help us solve our society's problems. For some decades, only professional social scientists and researchers themselves took any great interest in this question. They had a stake in pushing their product, enlarging their market, satisfying themselves and at least a few clients that they had a valuable product to offer. Today the question engages a wider audience, for social research has become a sizeable—and expensive—industry, and institutions have sprung up to train policy analysts. The cost and payoff of professional social inquiry are now anybody's concern in the same sense that the performance of the medical or legal profession, the Supreme Court, the bureaucracy, or the National Football League is of concern to millions of people.

More important, we hear with increasing frequency a message—full of promise to some people, ominous to others who hear it—that power in contemporary society is passing from those who hold conventional sources of authority, like arms, public office, or wealth, to those who *know*. The rising new elite, it is said, consist of the knowledgeable. And the more complex a society, the more specialized its division of labor, the more its reliance on technology, then the more its affairs fall into the hands—or the powers—of those who have the skills, the time, and the funds for analyzing the society's problems. Only professional social researchers and social scientists have the time, skills, and funds for analyzing the larger social problems of society. As Daniel Bell says, "What counts is information."

And, he says, that the new great political struggle is between the professional and the populace.[1] In short, the professional analysis of social problems is worth our examining with meticulous care because of the possibility that professional inquiry is changing the very structure of politics and society.

I. The Conventional Rules of Good Policy Research

Let us begin an examination of how best to use professional social inquiry by setting out in our minds some familiar bedrock principles of how in general orientation a social scientist or researcher should proceed. They are frequently violated in practice, yet they remain prized principles in the theory and textbooks of policy analysis. In discussion of *social* practices, nothing really is bedrock: Some interesting minds always stand ready to dispute even the simplest propositions. But let's try anyway, try for such a set of guiding principles as are to be found in the teaching of policy analysis.

The science-for-its-own-sake social scientist who ignores practical problems and simply follows his or her own curiosity, we shall ignore this morning. We shall attend only to professionals who intend to make a contribution to public policy. What general guidelines are appropriate for them?

1. The first principle, I suggest, is that in a democratic society the best professional researchers, social scientists, analysts—-whatever the label—ought normally to be concerned in a non-partisan way with the values or interests of the whole society. They should analyze problems with an eye on the public interest rather than the interests of some segment of society. Since we are all sufficiently sophisticated these days to deny that there exists any one objective public interest, we are wiser to say that—some exceptions aside—they must be motivated and governed by some all-embracing version—of which there will be several or many from which they might thoughtfully choose—of

---

1 "Labor in the Post-Industrial Society" in Irving Howe ed., *The World of the Blue-Collar Worker* (New York: Quadrangle Books, 1972), pp. 164ff. As Galbraith argues it, power is shifting to people with knowledge, experience and talent who are bound together in organizations (J. K. Galbraith, *The New Industrial State,* 3rd ed. (Boston: Houghton Mifflin, 1978), p. 61.

the interests of all, or some concept, among several or many, of the public good, or society's welfare, or the commonweal. Their responsibility is to avoid partisanship, thus somehow to take every legitimate value or interest into account.

An example of this aspiration toward capturing every aspect of the public interest in a nonpartisan way is in cost-benefit analysis. As one advocate of it prescribes: "Isolate the full set of impacts which [a proposed policy] generates." Then "attach a value to each input and output." Then "choose that policy for which the excess of benefits over cost is as great as possible."[2] Another illustrative prescription is that good policy analysis "obligates the policy analyst to take the larger view. ... It minimizes the opportunity for the intrusion of the analyst's own values ..."[3]

Analysts who are not independent scholars but who are attached closely to government agencies often acknowledge that they take a partisan position. The power of the principle that analysis should pursue a nonpartisan public interest is indicated in the loss of status in the eyes of other analysts and scholars that attends such an acknowledgement.

2. A second principle is that professional inquiry intended to aid public policy should usually avoid the irrelevance of investigating policy alternatives that are simply infeasible—infeasible, for example, because too costly, or too discordant with society's practices and institutions, or without hope of political support, or at odds with fundamental values in that society, or impossible to inaugurate or administer without wholesale social transformation.

This second principle meets with some dissent—more so than does the first principle on the public interest. But its weight is evidenced by the character of instruction in the public policy schools that have been springing up in recent years. They train for the analysis of policies for the here and now, for practical policies that have some chance of winning political support,

---

2 Robert H. Haveman and Julius Margolis eds., *Public Expenditure and Policy Analysis* (Chicago: Markham, 1970), pp. 7ff.
3 George J. Graham, Jr., and Scarlett G. Graham, "Evaluating Drift in Policy Systems," in Phillip M. Gregg ed., *Problems of Theory in Policy Analysis* (Lexington: Lexington Books, 1976), p. 86.

that respect the society's values, and that fit into other existing policies and institutions. In coping, say, with the problem of inflation or with problems of industrial relations, one would not expect a trained policy analyst to give a moment's thought to so unidiomatic a solution as in the Marxian slogan, "Abolish the wages system!"

3. A third principle might better be called an understanding, habit, or obvious rule of thumb rather than be dignified as a principle. It is that professional inquiry speaks to the people who have to make the policy decisions, as in Wildavsky's book title, *Speaking Truth to Power*. Who needs profesional inquiry? The president, the prime minister, senators, congressmen, mayors, aldermen, chairmen of commissions, high-level civil servants, union leaders, corporate executives, party leaders, and political bosses. Professional analysts should not simply write for each other; and often they will need to take special pains to formulate issues and construct analyses—as well as use prose—so as to meet the decision maker at least half way. This means that the professional has to understand the problem as the decision maker sees it, which may not be at all the way the academic mind sees it. A National Research Council report tells us: "From the point of view of participants, policy-relevant research is research that helps them carry out their roles and achieve goals they consider important." Who are the participants? They are the policy makers, public officals.[4]

4. A fourth principle applies only to those analysts who are very close to the decision maker: for example, a staff analyst in the Department of Agriculture, or a research team on contract with the Department of Transportation to work on transport problems in the Northeast Corridor, or any graduate of any of the public policy analyst training schools who has moved into the kind of position for which these schools prepare him. The principle is that policy analysis takes the form of examination of a question of policy, often requiring problem reformulation, in any case requiring some canvassing of possible solutions, and

4 Laurence E. Lynn ed., *Knowledge and Policy* (Washington, DC: National Academy of Sciences, 1978), p. 16.

normally culminating in some recommendations as to what the decision maker ought to do.

Because actual policy analysis does not follow this prescription—specifically, does not culminate in recommendations—I might be faulted for listing it as a widely shared principle. Again, however, its weight is indicated by textbooks and curricula, as well as by the emergence in recent times of an academic theory of policy analysis, all of which cast policy analysis in this form: some kind of attempt at problem reformulation, together with a canvass of some possible alternatives, culminating in advice to the decision maker on what to do or on which few vetted alternatives are worth his final consideration.[5]

The four guiding principles for making professional inquiry helpful to public policy are, then: nonpartisan pursuit of the public interest, a practical concern with feasible policies, meeting the needs of public officials, and, in particular, providing them with recommendations. I wonder if they do not seem so obvious as to have raised in your minds a question about why I bother to discuss them. It has been dull, hasn't it?

II. Public Interest and Partisanship

But there is more in these principles than meets the eye. Let's look further now at the first one: the nonpartisan pursuit of the public interest.

Unless there is some yet undiscovered harmony in the universe, we know that what is good for General Motors is not on all points good for Chrysler. We know that what is good for organized labor is often achieved at the expense of unorganized labor; that if you win a promotion, I do not; that if the so-called pro-life groups win, the so-called pro-choice groups lose; or that conservationists and mining companies get in each other's way.

Some of these conflicts can be settled by a formula; for example, by majority rule. But neither majority rule nor any other formula is applicable to most cases of conflict. For the thousands of important policy decisions that must be made

5 In Phillip M. Gregg ed., *Problems of Theory in Policy Analysis* (Lexington: D. C. Heath, 1976). Nine of the papers comment on this principle. Eight endorse it; only one questions it.

each year by federal, state, and local governments, we do not know what the majority would want if informed on the issues, nor can the public be expected to take time to inform itself on each. Nor would we want a majority decision on those thousands of decisions which—like setting interest rates for the economy—require special competences rather than expressions of popular preference however informed.

How is it then to be decided that in the resolution of conflict the interests of farmers should yield to those of the urban workforce? And if so, to what degree? How is it to be decided how heavily to weigh the interests of those who look for jobs in a proposed new shopping mall against the interests of the local residents who want no further commercial development in their neighborhood?

To answer such questions, one has to first understand that the problem is not of knowing a right answer but of deciding on, or willing, a defensible outcome. Given the conflict, there is no one correct solution. Any benefit sought will be at cost to someone. Some substantial groups will always be hurt. It is not possible, consequently, to *know* an answer; indeed there is no *answer*. There is only a choice to be made, a decision to be taken, an outcome to be achieved by commitments or acts of will. Up to a point, knowledge will help form the commitment; for example, by helping to rule out the worst of possible solutions. Beyond some point, however, there is nothing more to know that will resolve the conflict. Indeed, knowledge may exacerbate. It is time for will, commitment, choice rather than knowledge.

A professional analyst can sometimes be useful in situations in which there are elements of common interest to be uncovered and elements of solution that will suit everyone. Or a good analyst can sometimes discover solutions that ought to be avoided because they suit no one. In academic language, he can find a Pareto efficient solution; specifically, a solution that is to the advantage of some persons and disadvantages to no one.[6] If such a solution exists, *knowledge* that it exists can make a contribution to good policy making.

6 Edith Stokey and Richard Zeckhauser, *A Primer for Policy Analysis* (New York: Norton, 1978), pp. 270–272.

But even in these cases, there remains conflict. Economists often blunder into the conclusion that policy makers should choose Pareto efficient solutions because they help some persons and hurt no others. Not so. If, as is typically the case—and perhaps always the case—there are still other solutions that bring substantial advantages to large numbers of persons and these advantages are worth seeking even at loss to other persons—for example, protecting civil liberties of minorities even if doing so is greatly irritating and obstructive to others—then, there remains a conflict as to what is to be done. The Pareto efficient solution is not necessarily the best choice. The appropriate choice is, again, not something that can be known. It must be chosen, willed, decided upon; and doing so passes far beyond the competence of a professional knower—that is, of a researcher or social scientist.

When we ask a social scientist or researcher to formulate a version of the public interest and pursue his analysis in the light of it, we are asking him or her to go beyond knowledge to choice or commitment. But his special competence, if any, is knowledge. His special training and professional qualifications do not fit him for the task. Do you really believe that a monetary expert has a sufficient competence to give a policy maker good advice on weighing the interests of the unemployed against those of the employed? Do you believe that a professionally trained policy analyst has, by reason of his training, a sufficient competence to advise a policy maker on the degree to which the values of pro-choice advocates should prevail over those of pro-life advocates? From where or what might he ever have developed these remarkable competences?[7]

Who, then, is to be considered competent on such weighings, evaluations, and choices? No one. Beyond some point, as I have just said, it is not a question of competence. Who, then,

7 Leaving aside the very long run, most analysts and social researchers, of course, acknowledge that policies typically help some groups and hurt others. My point is that they are not competent to go on to find, invent, or propose a resolution of that conflict, as though there existed some intellectual ground for sacrificing one group's interests to another's and as though they as analysts possessed some *professional* competence to make such judgements. When agreed rules for resolution are absent, in the face of gains to some at the expense of other groups, social scientists, researchers, and analysts reach the limit of their competence (if not before).

competent or not, ought to make such choices or give advice on them? The only defensible answer, I believe, is the political officials, elected or appointed (aside, of course, from some very few weighings and choices that citizens might make directly). Politicians do indeed sometimes develop some unusual skills in reconciling conflicting values and interests; but my claim that the job is theirs rests less on their demonstration of competence than on the argument that, again, competence is not the issue. The issue is who is to make a choice that cannot be justified as correct or as competent but which nevertheless must be made. The politician is the person to do it for two reasons. First, he understands better than does a social scientist that the decision to be made cannot be *known* to be appropriate, and that it calls for will and commitment, for which he has authority. Secondly, you and I know that, by definition, a politician in a democracy is a role player who can be removed from his role if, taking many things into account and on balance, we are distressed by his performance.

In short, there is a place for knowledge, on one hand, and for commitment or choice, on the other, in the making of public policy. The two aspects ought not to be confused; and professional social inquire should not confuse the two.

Not so fast, many of you will respond. This principle—the dispassionate pursuit of the public interest—does not propose that social researchers usurp a political function. They only *advise* the decision maker on how to weigh the interests of one group against another. It remains for the decision maker, who is an elected or appointed public official, to accept or reject the advice. True enough. My point, however, is that the professional researchers or social scientists have no special competence even to advise on the reconciliation of interests in conflict. Whether one group should prevail over or be asked to give way to another is not something on which he has knowledge—and knowledge is all he has to offer professionally. Again, the issue on which the policy maker needs advice when faced with the conflict is not finally an issue on which knowledge is decisive. Again, one cannot *know* what is to be done in such a situation. What is required is an act of choice, commitment, or will.

Give the researcher or analyst, then, tasks more suited to his special training and abilities. What might they be? Before I suggest an answer, I want to describe briefly an additional particular damage the professional researchers do in their attempts to hold to the principle of nonpartisan pursuit of the public interest. It will throw light on what needs to be done to replace that principle and assign new tasks.

According to Jefferson, Lincoln, Jesus and Plato, among others, one major legitimate interest in every society, one often limited, however, to no more than a small number of people, is an interest in either gradual or rapid transformation of the society—an interest in drastic, radical change. It is, I suggest, impossible for a dispassionate policy analyst or researcher to weigh that interest heavily. Nor can he weigh heavily any sharply dissenting small-group interest, one that seems bizarre, out of touch, or utopian to the great mass of people in society. His version of the public interest must always—if it is to be accepted as relevant—hold closer to conventional values and conventional weights among them. It has to move toward a kind of modal version of the public interest.

Now this tendency for the public interest to be defined around conventional values and weights offers some advantages to the society. It means that social researchers, because their versions are all much alike, can talk easily with each other; and in turn they can talk easily to political leaders, who in turn can talk easily with each other. They all find themselves thinking very much alike. In addition, their easy agreements may make a contribution to political stability.

But another result is that dissident interests are disproportionately deprived of the services of social scientists and researchers. Dissidents stand for odd sets of values that social researchers reject as not in the public interest but instead in the interests of no more than one or more small minorities. Is that regrettable? On the ground that most dissidents are foolish people, it is not. On the ground that all major social reforms, all great improvements in the welfare of humankind come from dissidents, to deprive them disproportionately of the services of professional social inquiry would seem to be a gross mistake, perhaps better characterized by a word like *tragedy*. When Eugene Debs and Norman Thomas dissented to advocate old-age pensions and other forms of social security in the late nineteenth and early twentieth centuries, social scientists disregarded them—they were socialists and hence irrelevant to American public affairs. If they had been listened to, we might not have been among the last industrial nations to design and inaugurate such programs, which everyone today recognizes as essential in a humane society. Because dissidents, however irrelevant on the average, are an indispensable source of our future, they, above all, might be argued to need helpful professional social analysis.

On this point, mine is a simple kind of logic. We need brains at the growing points of society, for guiding the dissidents, who are our innovators. The public interest notion of social science and research frustrates such an allocation. At an extreme, it labels a radical social scientist an eccentric and bestows the accolade of "soundness" only on those social scientists whose concept of the public good is unexceptional.

At this point, I now offer a replacement for the first principle. It will be a principle that will excuse the professional social researcher from tasks in reconciling conflict that go beyond his competence and that will also attend to the need to bring social research to the innovating points in society.

Scratch the principle of the impartial pursuit of the public interest. Put in its place the principle of thoughtful partisanship. (But let me explain the concept of partisanship before you let your possible hostility to partisanship distort the concept.) I mean by a partisan social scientist or researcher one who acknowledges that his work is guided by a selection of some among other possible interests and values; who so far as feasible reveals his selection; who makes no claims that his values or interests are good for everyone; who, in other words, acknowledges that they are to a degree injurious to some people; and who believes that it is impossible for him to do otherwise without deceiving himself and those who use his work. I do not mean someone who lies, conceals evidence, or violates conventional standards of scientific integrity except as just stated.

Some of you will be piqued by the phrase I used: the partisan "so far as feasible reveals" his values. All of you, at one time or another, have run across prescriptions that advise social scientists to reveal their values (which are, of course, supposed to be those that define the public interest). But it cannot be done explicitly. The task is endless, for there are too many values at stake in public policy, too many subtleties of priority ranking and trade-offs. And as an analyst moves more deeply into any project he continues to uncover values earlier thought irrelevant. Disclosure of values is always therefore in large part ony tacit or implicit and inescapably incomplete. My partisan will push disclosure very far, and he will want his choices of values understood rather than swept under the rug because, unlike a would-be nonpartisan analyst, he does not pretend. But he will understand that he cannot achieve full disclosure.

Among a number of reasons for recommending partisanship to all social scientists and researchers, the first is that everyone is in fact a partisan, whether he knows it or not. Obviously, a member of the National Rifle Association is. So also is a member of Common Cause or the League of Women Voters. I do not call them partisans because they are narrow minded, bigoted, ignorant, or opinionated, which they may or may not be. They are partisans because they wish to advance certain values over others and thus the interests and preferences of some people over those of others. And my point is that everyone does so.

Like any president, President Eisenhower recognized an obligation to pursue the public interest and to respond to all legitimate interests, needs, and values in society. He went further than most presidents in a deliberate effort to "stay above the fray," to rise or appear to rise above party partisanship. But he could not avoid taking sides, no more than anyone else can. For example, he had at some point to stand for those monetary and fiscal policies that would respond to the interests of the unemployed or those that would respond to the interest of employed and propertied groups that feared inflation. He of course wholly neglected the interests of neither group. But, on the other hand, he had to choose, for he could not find a set of monetary and fiscal policies that fully met the interests of both groups. He used a rhetoric of public interest or common good, perhaps himself believed it. But he had to take a position for some people and against others. In doing so he became, as we all do, a partisan: *for* some values, interests and groups; *against* others.

Highly educated people who find their political antecedents in the Enlightenment and in the English liberal tradition often deplore what they see as the narrowness of partisanship of benighted persons who appear to fasten on some single issue, like guns, abortion, or godlessness. But these allegedly single-issue partisans usually in fact take a broad view of values and interests. Passionate members of the National Rifle Association, for example, endorse a complex set of interlocked values, embracing guns, to be sure, but also personal independence, civil liberty, family autonomy, and patriotism. They are committed to a complex ideology or political philosophy. The same can be said for most or all of the other allegedly narrow partisan groups. They are not necessarily any more narrow in their partisanship than highly educated persons who fasten on the environmental issue or agitate for an equal rights amendment.[8]

I make this point to suggest that most partisans, including both those you like because you are one of them and those you do not because you are not, try to fit their most distinctive concerns into a broad picture of the public interest. For their desires are varied and broad. Moreover, to win influence they usually must place their interests within a package of interests that will win allies. Most, then, label their package of the common good or the public interest.

What I am proposing, then, is not that we neglect the public interest but that we recognize that out versions of it are partisan. In particular, I am proposing that professional scholars, analysts, and researchers acknowledge and display their selection of values and interests—in short, their partisanship—and give up any pretense or appearance of speaking from Olympus, or as neutrals, or as representing a nonpartisan integration of interests that is for the good of all and injurious to none. An analyst should let his work be guided by a set of partisan values either because he or she believes in them or because he or she accepts, for purposes of a research project, values of a client.

Examples of social scientists who are thoughtfully partisan, openly and honestly so? They are almost all Marxists who confess a commitment to the working class and acknowledge that their preferred policies would be injurious to propertied groups in society. Among mainstream social scientists and social researchers are many who are often called partisan—Milton

8 For supporting evidence, see Sylvia Tesh, "Upholding Principles: A Note in Support of 'Single' Issue Politics," Yale University Institution for Social and Policy Studies, Working Paper No. CHS–54, September, 1983.

Friedman, for example. But almost all of them, Friedman included, see themselves as nonpartisan, as speaking for everyone's best interests. If my argument is correct, they are deceiving themselves, and, if we believe them, they are also deceiving you and me. They are also distorting their research. If there are many partisan non-Marxist social scientists and social researchers who are trying to follow such a prescription as mine for thoughtfully acknowledged partisanship, not many of them have yet come out of the closet.[9]

Aside from the virtues of disclosure of what professional analysts are up to, one benefit of acknowledged partisanship is that it would free professionals to work for the full variety of groups who have legitimate interests in policy, including dissident groups. So long as professionals hide beyond a myth of nonpartisanship they can bring their analytic services to governmental agencies without losing their reputations for scholarly integrity and excellence, but they cannot do so for either the National Rifle Association or for the dissident or radical groups on which our future depends, just as they could not do so for Eugene Debs. Under present self-deceiving formulas on nonpartisan pursuit of public interest, ordinary professionals, by which I mean genius aside, can best keep their reputations by offering their services only to central tendencies, established values, mainline interests, common denominators, or conventional formulas. They forget the long-standing view that the purpose of new knowledge in all fields is subversion.

We sometimes characterize democracy as, in Lord Bryce's phrase, government by discussion. What is the character of that discussion? Theorists sometimes idealize it as a cooperative

---

9 One reasonable interpretation of Marxist thought is that it is partisan in the short- and middle-run but is directed by a concern for the good of all, with injury to none, in a distant classless and harmonious future. And many non-Marxists may regard their appearances of partisanship as illusory, for they, too, pursue a distant good for all. To this attempt to turn partisans into nonpartisans, I would offer two replies. First, no social scientist or researcher can tightly derive short-run and the middle-run interim steps from a model of a far distant, wholly harmonious society; instead he must take some partisan positions for the interim, positions that cannot be defended by reference to the distant future. Second, that there exists a model of society in the distant future in which gains impose no losses on anyone is not persuasively argued, even by Marxists.

search for solutions in the light of agreed values.[10] But how does discussion actually proceed—face-to-face, through political negotiation, or through publications—when people are in conflict, as we have been arguing is always an element in public policy making. The basic form or paradigm of discussion is this: You try to persuade me that the policies that you want (because you think they suit your values) would in fact also suit my values. You as a partisan appeal to my partisan values. That is about as far as discussion can go.

Democratic political discussion is overwhelmingly partisan discussion. Its effectiveness lies in the frequency with which it turns out to be the case that your partisan values and mine, though different, can both be satisfied by one and the same policy. If social science and social research are to be made more fully helpful to public policy, they must enter into that partisan discussion rather than obscure it with a pretense of neutrality. Again, that is not to suggest that researchers conceal or misrepresent. It is only to ask them to bring their inevitable partisanship into the open, thus take the wraps off it, and make their work maximally useful. The potential quality of partisan analysis is illustrated by *The Federalist Papers,* designed to make the case for the new Constitution and still today a magniticent piece of political analysis.

I can put this line of argument into even more familiar context. Many thoughtful people in liberal societies like ours have long celebrated the virtues of a competition of ideas for guiding social change. Accordingly they have protected and even stimulated a diversity of groups, each encouraged to defend and advance values precious to it. They have claimed that the outcome of civilized contention among such groups, each bringing some special insight to public affairs, would be better for us than the solutions to our problems that would be proposed by a political, even if also intellectual, elite. All liberal democratic states have been greatly influenced by this line of thought, which bears the name of pluralism.

In the last two decades pluralist thought has been heavily attacked and with success. The main criticism has been, how-

10 For example, in Frank Knight, *Freedom and Reform* (New York: Harper and Brothers, 1947), pp. 185 and 190.

ever, not that pluralist diversity is not a good thing but that the liberal democratic states have not sufficiently practiced it.[11] Central tendencies in politics, a dominant ideology, and interests in protecting the *status quo* overwhelm the touted diversity. The competition of ideas is rigged, as in the nearly complete absence from television of radical politics and economic thought, or as in the narrow range of difference between the Republican and Democratic parties, both of which hold close to their sides of the center.

In social research, the principle of nonpartisan pursuit of the public interest is one of the betrayals of pluralism. For reasons I have explained, it puts the influence of social science and research at the service of central, conventional, established interests and values. It sabotages a competition of ideas. It starves the growing or innovating points of desirable social change. By contrast, the principle of partisanship moves in the direction of allying social research with still unrealized pluralist aspiration.

Perhaps one reason that professional analysts have betrayed pluralism with their principle of nonpartisan pursuit of the public interest is that they took their training not amidst the competition of ideas in politics but through term papers and dissertations. Their trainers, having been mistrained by their trainers, put them under obligation to pretend to a role of neutrality and to treat problems as though solutions could be *known*. To believe that a solution to a problem calls at some point not for further knowledge but for a partisan commitment or act of will would require that many term papers and dissertations be left unfinished.

A similar misconception of what social problem solving is all about persists in professional life in the myth or pedagogic assumption that there exists for each problem "the decision maker" to whom the professional brings advice. "Our perspective is that of a unitary decision maker" say the authors of a leading text in policy analysis.[12] Since the obligation of "the decision maker" is to achieve an integration of interests of benefit to all while disdaining partisanship, his professional

11 For a summary of criticism, see William E. Connolly, "The Challenge to Pluralist Theory," in Connolly ed., *The Bias of Pluralism* (New York: Atherton, 1969).
12 Edith Stokey and Richard Zeckhauser, *op. cit.,* p. 23.

adviser must do likewise in advising him. But the palpable fact about politics is that there is no "the decision maker." There are many, and they are always to some degree in conflict—all partisans.

most national policy problems in the U.S., the conflicting many decision makers include at the very least congressmen and senators, civil servants at the policy-making level, and members of the White House staff, often with close-at-hand participation by interest-group leaders. The professional analyst feeds what he has to say into the process through one or more of these multiple conflicting participants in problem solving, either by serving on his staff, or by consultation with some participants, or by writing books, articles, and reports that directly or indirectly reach the mind of a participant. All participants need—and most of them want—help in the gathering of information and analysis of problems. A candid professional researcher or social scientist either accepts as guidelines the partisan interests of the participants to whom he most wishes to speak or, often with their happy consent, tries to persuade them they do not well understand their own interests. If he does the latter, he does so as exponent of other partisan values than theirs.

If pluralism flourished, the results would be that every participant in policy making could call on professional help in finding solutions consistent with his values and of professional help in reconsidering them. In partisan contention with each other, the considerations and arguments advanced by one partisan or by his partisan researcher would be challenged by others. No one would labor under the misapprehension that any participant or any professional researcher had come close to grasping the whole truth or spoke for everyone's and all values.

The competition of ideas I am describing, which many social researchers betray, is often described by the betrayers in such words as I here take from James Q. Wilson when he described one common form of it. "When [organizations] use social science at all, it will be on an *ad hoc*, improvised, quick-and-dirty basis. A key official, needing to take a position, respond to a crisis, or support a view that is under challenge, will ask an assistant to 'get me some facts.' ... social science is used as ammunition, not as a method, and the official's oponents will also use similar ammunition." And, then, he comes to his punch line. He says "there will be many shots fired, but few casualties except the truth."[13] His generalization is false. I find it hard to understand what he would like in the place of the competition of ideas he has characterized with hostility. Of course, social research has to be tied to positions; of course it is ammunition. But it is through the resulting challenge and counterchallenge that usable truth often emerges; and, imperfect as the process is, indeed there is no feasible better alternative way of reaching an approximation to truth for social problem solving.

Wilson is, of course, lamenting not merely the *competition* of ideas, which is the issue I am raising with you, but also—to digress for a moment—the lack of sustained, serious research, lamenting the tendency of officials to wish to grab whatever social research results are already at hand. But that tendency is not to be lamented. For any problem you can imagine, the cumulation of past study will be a better guide than any *one* further study. We solve problems with cumulated intellectual capital. It is both inevitable and economical that we do so.

The competition of ideas requires this kind of degree of thoughtful partisanship—and vigorous partisanship—that I am describing if the competition is to advance a society's capacity to cope with its problems. I would add that we have more to fear by an inadequate or rigged competition such as we now practice than by an excess of challenge and counterchallenge among informed advocates of competing values and interests.

Do I hear a voice anxiously asking, "If partisans abound, who will look after the common interest"? The answer is that, if there are genuinely common interests, they are the shared interests of all partisans, all of whom will consequently pursue them. If they are hidden, the possibility of discovering them lies in interchange among partisans, each of whom is motivated to find common ground in order to turn adversaries into allies. The more important answer to the anxious question is that, as already noted, partisans tend to develop alternative versions of the public interest rather than ignore it. That is often the best

13 James Q. Wilson, "Social Science and Public Policy," in Laurence E. Lynn, Jr. ed., *Knowledge and Policy* (Washington, DC: National Academy of Sciences, 1978), p. 92.

a society can do: acknowledge conflicting versions and work out—politically not analytically—a resolution.

And do not forget the noncommon and uncommon good. We are not all exactly alike, and no thoughtful person recommends that we should suppress all differences. Hence a diversity of interests and subgroup goods ought to be pursued along with versions of what we have or ought to have in common.

Or do you now ask: If there are, as always, conflicting partisan versions of the public good, how do we resolve the conflict? How is an outcome achieved? We all know the answer, even if theorists on policy analysis seem sometimes to forget it in their desire to find an excessively large role for analysis in the resolution. Usually the outcome is not analyzed and decided upon, *for beyond some point it is not analyzable*, as we have seen. Instead, it is brought about by political acts or some other form of action or interaction, not analysis. Some outcomes are decided by voting, some by negotiation, some by other forms of mutual influence of partisans on each other.

Remembering this helps us understand that research and analysis can at best be no more than a part of social problem solving and that the shortcomings you fear from partisan analysis are really inevitable limitations on any and every attempt to reach an outcome through research and analysis.

III. Research for Officials and Other Decision Makers

Let us now look into the third principle, skipping the second for the moment. The third was that research intended to be helpful to public policy usually be designed to meet the needs of government officials and other key decision makers. The public policy analysis textbooks take this prescription for granted. Perhaps you do too. Our government officials make the decisions; obviously it is they who need the information and analysis that research can offer. Who else?

Who else? How about you, and you, and you, and me? Millions of us, all of us, "we, the people." In a democracy, as in all other forms of government, officials are the immediate or proximate decision makers. But in a democracy, they make decisions within constraints, even if loose ones, laid down by public opinion. And to a degree at least, they respond to popular agitation. Ranges of possible policy choice are walled off by certain public rejection and cannot be attempted by political leaders even if they were innovative enough to offer them. The "public," even the ignorant and apathetic public, is a force in policy making in the democracies.

So who most needs such enlightenment on social problems as research and social science can sometimes offer? Leaders or ordinary citizens? It is not at all clear. By what argument has the research community come to fasten on leadership as its audience? By no argument at all. By thoughtless habit, by simple assumption that leadership is more worth talking to than mass.

One might suggest that the issue itself makes a good public policy question: Who, leadership or citizenry, most needs the help of social science and social research? One might then expect that social scientists and researchers would study the question before jumping to an answer. They have not. Aside from Marxist and other radical thought, the literature of social science and research is almost wholly silent on the issue. A curious state of affairs for a profession that believes in studying policy issues!

Because the question is large and endlessly complex, I shall have to be highly selective and inconclusive. I shall go only so far as to develop one line of argument: That the ordinary citizen's need for help from social science and social research is enormous and that great gains are to be had from a drastic redirection of social science and policy research to meet that need. That would be enough to destroy the third principle.

My argument will be roundabout. It will strike some of you as odd, and on that count alone you will be deeply suspicious of it. It will irritate, perhaps enrage, some of you. But I believe it is of the greatest consequence; and I ask you to take it home with you, mull it over, and put yourself under an obligation not to reject it without good reason. I am audacious enough at this point to estimate that you will not find a good reason.

The argument that ordinary citizens need much more help from social science and research turns on the phenomenon of widespread social agreement on many big political and economic issues. Although not unanimously, Americans widely agree, for example, on the merits of the American Constitution, on a presidential rather than parliamentary system, on private enterprise, on loyalty to country, on family solidarity, on improving one's condition through personal responsibility rather than changing the structure of society, on cooperation or going along rather than criticizing or agitation, on playing the game instead of complaining "foul!"[14]

Most of us prize that agreement. It seems to make for social stability and social cooperation. Anthropologists tell us that without agreement on some fundamentals a group of people cannot live peaceably together, cannot constitute a society.[15] In political science, it is frequently argued—in the words of Brzezinski and Huntington—that "a political system is effective to the extent that the history behind it has brought about an underlying consensus."[16] And it is often taken as not needing supporting argument that democracy can exist only when such agreement exists, for only then are disputes small enough so that losers are willing to bear their losses rather than subvert the government in order to dominate their adversaries.

That such vast agreement as characterizes American and Western society ought to be prized is dubious. Empirical evidence is lacking. The brief argument I have just given fails to take account of the possibility that citizens might be sufficiently flexible, even if in disagreement on fundamentals, if their attachment to their fundamental values were reasoned rather than dogmatic. That is to say, the argument for democratic agreement perhaps applies to ideologically rigid citizens rather than to a more enlightened electorate.

But set aside the question of whether agreement is desirable. I want to ask you to put a question to yourself: How does such agreement come about? Prize it or not, how do you *explain* it? Would we not expect widespread differences of opinion on such complex questions as the Constitution or private enterprise, for example?

For agreement on many kinds of belief, explanation is easy—beliefs, for example, that the world is round, that battered children are often the children of parents battered in their

14 An insightful review and comment on the character of political agreement and disagreement is Michael Mann, "The Social Cohesion of Liberal Democracy," 35 *American Sociological Review*, (June, 1970).

15 Ralph Linton, *The Study of Man* (New York: Appleton–Century–Crofts, 1936).

16 Zbegniew Brzezinski and Samuel P. Huntington, *Political Power: USA/USSR* (New York: Viking, 1965), p. 5.

childhood, or that some judges take bribes and some do not. We agree on many issues because we know. We have evidence. Competent people have inquired into the issue and found grounds for one belief rather than a diversity. Knowledge is a great source of agreement.

But we do not *know*, we only believe, that the U.S. Constitution is superior to other constitutions that might be written, that private enterprise is best for us, that a parliamentary system would not suit us, that loyalty to country is better than a more cosmopolitan loyalty to humankind, and so on. No one can *know* that these beliefs are correct. Sufficient evidence is not available. Moreover—now consider this—those who inquire most deeply into these complex issues disagree more than do those who do not inquire. That is to say, knowledge on these issues creates diversity of belief rather than agreement.

Some of you may reply: But I know that ours is a superb constitution. My reply is that I can find at least a few persons as informed and thoughtful as you who believe that they know it is not. You believe that you know; but the fact that other equally qualified people believe that they know otherwise tells us that none of you know; you only fervently and confidently believe. Knowledge cannot possibly explain your conviction on such complex issues of political belief as I cited as examples of widespread agreement.

That leaves us in a quandary. Why do so many Americans venerate the Constitution, free enterprise, the family, patriotism, and the like? There is plenty of room for disagreement; and, to repeat, the more knowing the persons the more likely they are to disagree. How, then, to repeat my question, can we explain widespread social agreement on these fundamental values? Would we not expect a great variety of minds to come to a variety of conclusions, so complex are these questions, so inconclusive our information?

Not at all, do you reply? You will say that tradition passes down agreed beliefs from generation to generation. The schools, our parents, political oratory, the press—all of them pass down much the same set of beliefs on fundamentals to all of us. If you take that position, you must ask why tradition passes down agreement instead of a variety of beliefs. *Tradition* is a word referring to transfer from generation to generation; but family, school, and religious traditions can, and on some issue do, transfer a diversity not a homogeneity. Look at it another way. If you believe that one generation's homogeneity is sufficient to explain the next generation's, how do you explain the earlier generation's? Somehow, somewhere along the line a possible diversity was converted into agreement. For example, somewhere the idea of the democratic nation state, once an entirely new idea to most people, and then an issue of controversy, came gradually to mark a point of at least rhetorical consensus in many Western societies. How did that agreement first come about, the agreement which tradition now passes on? We need an explanation. Tradition fails to explain. It only explains how, if an agreement is formed, it is continued.

I can find no possible explanation of why people agree on complex issues on which the absence of sufficient knowledge leaves room for thoughtful diversity of belief except for one. It is that we have thoughtlessly accepted an indoctrination. Our agreement is the result of our not exercising our critical faculties. Had we exercised them, we would disagree much more than we do.

We are an insufficiently thoughtful, we are a careless body of citizens. We fasten on formulas. We do not explore the variety of possibilities to which we might turn to solve our problems. We are mired in conventional thought, restricted to a narrow range of possibilities. The evidence that all this is the case is, again, that we agree on matters on which critical thought could not possibly agree. And even if the Constitution is superb and even if the private enterprise system is superior to all others, since we cannot—at least yet—*know* either to be true, then agreeing either to be true is evidence of our thoughtlessness. For, again, lacking sufficient evidence to constitute knowledge, our critical faculties would produce diversity of belief among us on such issues.

Of course, we might conceivably be thoughtlessly diverse rather than homogeneous. So we must ask why our thoughtlessness is a source of agreement rather than careless diversity. On this point, the idea of tradition at least points us in the right direction. We cannot explain the thoughtless and indoctrinated agreement simply by looking at contemporary social processes. This generation inherited through tradition a homogeneity of belief on such issues as I listed. An earlier generation also inherited much the same body of belief. We must find much of the explanation in still earlier history.

In most of the world and in all of Western Europe, small ruling groups long ago organized the rest of mankind to maintain social order, to organize production, and to permit themselves to practice various forms of exploitation. As far back as we can trace our social origins, we consequently find small dominant groups teaching obedience, loyalty, faith, respect for authority, thus respect for wealth and property, political quiescence, inequality—and, over and over again, veneration for existing political and economic institutions.[17] In the Middle Ages lord and priest taught these lessons. In more recent times, earlier agreements are modified but nevertheless perpetuated—no longer through feudal authority but through the influence of property, wealth, and business enterprise. The continuity of association of obedience, authority, inequality, and property is illustrated in the contemporary word *landlord*.

Patterns of belief in obedience, authority, deference to wealth, veneration for existing institutions, inequality and the like having been established, they are now easily maintained through many channels of indoctrination: the public schools, for example. Parents themselves do much of the work of indoctrination, especially working class parents who stress obedience and docility over critical independence of thought.[18] And of course, we are flooded with corporate communications that explicitly and implicitly teach the virtues of private enterprise, the Constitution, and our other fundamental institutions. So great is the disproportion of business oriented communication—for no other group has even a fraction of the funds available to business for indoctrination—that the ordinary citizen is crippled in his ability to think straight about public policy. Most ordinary citizens in the United States, for example, cannot even distinguish between political democracy and private enterprise, so often have the two been treated as identical in commerical, public school, and other indoctrinations. Even a recent Presi-

17 Among many other sources, see Alexander Rustow, *Freedom and Domination* (Princeton: Princeton University Press, 1980).
18 Robert D. Hess and Judith V. Torney, *The Development of Political Attitudes in Children* (Chicago: Aldine, 1967).

dent of Harvard appeared to suffer from the same difficulty when, in replying to critics of his economics department, he assured them that his economics faculty supported the American way of life, for—he said—they are all trying to make the private enterprise system continue to work.[19]

My conclusion, then, is that the existence of social agreement on many complex issues on which free minds would be expected to disagree is itself sufficient evidence that the minds of ordinary citizens are greatly impaired and are in desperate need of help from social science and social research for solving their problems. The great body of citizens in the democracies—to say nothing of less liberated citizens elsewhere—have hardly begun to explore the possibilities for solving their problems, thus for improving their prospects. Our minds are impaired, we remain in substantial ignorance of the alternatives.

The impairment, of course, afflicts our political leaders as well as the whole citizenry. But what is required to right it is not policy analysis directed largely to the special needs of political leadership, but analysis that constitutes an education and an enlightenment and liberation for leader and citizen alike. A tradition of policy analysis and research on social problems that is inattentive to the task of enlightenment of citizens is a gross inefficiency and misallocation in a democratic society, quite likely a tragedy, and an always potential source of catastrophe, especially in a nuclear age.

IV. What Does the Citizen Need?

Social science has given so little attention to the informational and analytic needs of the ordinary citizen that precisely what he needs has not yet been clarified. Sometimes the citizen is dismissed as a largely passive participant in politics—it is pointed out, for example, that only a few citizens ever go to political meetings or write their representatives.[20] Producing knowledge for the ordinary citizen, then, appears to be a waste of time and effort. That knowledge of the right kind in the right channels

19 Nathan M. Pusey, *The Age of the Scholar* (Cambridge: Harvard, 1963), p. 171.
20 Sidney Verba and Norman H. Nie, *Participation in America* (New York: Harper and Row, 1972), p. 31.

at the right time might turn him into an active citizen is not much speculated about, except for some political leaders and social scientists, like those on the Trilateral Commission Task Force on the Governability of Democracy, who seem to prefer to keep him passive.[21]

Perhaps one reason for neglecting the citizen's need for information is that many of us picture democratic politics as a process in which political leaders do all the work. And just what is the work to be done? It is to discover or invent policies that will respond to citizen preferences. All the citizen has to do is to reveal those preferences. What the preferences are might of course itself be made a task for social research. If so, it could be turned over to political leadership to commission and use the research. But, fearful of letting anyone but the citizen himself say what his preferences are, most of us have apparently taken the position that the best authority on what A's preferences are is A himself. And he needs no research help: On reflection he knows what he wants, not perfectly but well enough.

From where did the notion come that a citizen can know what he wants in politics by simple reflection and without any helpful study? In social science circles, it comes, I suggest, from economic theory, in which the concept of preferences is a workhorse. The successes of economics in theory construction have given prestige to that discipline in the eyes of the other social sciences. The others are eager to borrow concepts from economics. Preferences is such a concept, and it has been easy for political scientists to give political preferences the same formulation and role in political analysis as in economic analysis. Thus, the citizen's preference for private enterprise or for the Constitution is treated like his preference for bananas. I like what I like, and I know what I like. My preferences do not require study.

I find it impossible to describe this state of affairs in social science without finding it ludicrous. Your attitude toward the Constitution is not at all like your taste for bananas. Your preference for most goods and services is fairly simply construct-

21 Michael Crozier, Samuel P. Huntington, and Joji Watanuki, *The Crisis of Democracy* (New York: New York University Press, 1975). See, for example, their "Introduction."

ed in your mind. You either do or do not like vanilla, either because you were built that way or because you have been reared in a vanilla-appreciating society. Whether you like vanilla or not is a fairly simple fact. It is not a moral choice. It is relatively independent of other preferences. It does not require prolonged investigation of consequences or implications.

For some more complicated market preferences and for all political choices, the economist's concept of preferences is wildly inappropriate. Do you have a *preference* for a constitutional prohibition of abortion? It is a silly question. Making up your mind on abortion issues calls up a variety of tasks. You must grapple empirically with questions of fact, ranging from facts about the reproductive process to facts about the feasibility of administering any public policy. With moral or ethical questions, ranging from those of life itself to those pertaining to the rights of your fellow citizens. With prudential questions: questions, for example, about practical rules for social cooperation and decisions. All these questions are extraordinarily complex for many reasons, one among them being that whatever choice is made now will produce indirect and subtle consequences into a future no one can predict. You cannot exhaustively pursue any of these many aspects of making up your mind, but almost everyone exercises his mind to some degree on each of them.

Your position on abortion, then, is no preference. Nor is it anything to be discovered. It is not a fact that you must ascertain. It is something you make, form, create. Whatever thinking you do culminates not in fact about you that is disclosed but in a commitment upon which you decide by your, to some degree, considered choice. It is a volition, far removed from what we call preference. Indeed you may—and often do—form a volition for an outcome or policy that at the simpler level of preferences you do not prefer. "I don't like what I have to do, but I think I ought" is familiar to us all.[22]

Like all important words, both *preferences* and *volitions* carry a load, in this case a political load. If I think about preferences I am encouraged to believe that I am what I am. If I think about volitions I am encouraged to think that I am not yet what I might like to become.

If, rather than uncovering preferences, citizens are engaged in the construction of volitions, then they need helpful empirical, prudential, and moral analysis and must themselves engage in it through discussion. In instructing and constraining leadership, citizens need such studies as, among others, of the range of possible social institutions and practices, of the competences and incompetences of government and of alternative social machinery like the market system, of how to train and organize themselves for political participation, of the history of constraints on their own habits of thought (a subject hardly touched in contemporary social science). We have no ground for believing that studies of this kind would make a smaller contribution to better public policy than would conventional policy analysis. The effects of such studies would be slow to realize but of potential highest order of consequences.

It may throw light on some of the help citizens need—and in this case their leaders no less—to consider the frequent distinction between the substance or merits of an issue, on one hand, and the "politics" of the issue, on the other. It is often believed that research should attend to substance or merit.

One of the greatest issues a citizen has to face is this: How far am I willing to go or how far ought I prudentially or morally go in order to meet other citizens halfway—to find a possibility for agreement? For civilized humankind, that is a substance question *par excellence*. But it is also a basic political question. What citizens and leaders need is help in the exploration of bending volitions in a search for specific solutions and the development of a continually reshaped political community. Politics is substance.

22 A related argument: "Although preferences are important for the understanding of welfare, their proper place in the scheme of things must not be exaggerated, as a not inconsiderable sector of modern economics has been inclined to do. ... the road from preference to welfare is too long and winding. A man's welfare may, indeed standardly does, bear *some* relationship to his preferences, but that does not result in their mutual assimilation. Preference is too gross an instrument to capture the subtle nuances of welfare. If Jones prefers apples to oranges—be it in general or in point of, say, appearance or flavor—this does not go far to indicate what his welfare consists in. Welfare is a thing of stability and solidity; preferences can be things of the fleeting moment, and indeed things that fly in the race of consciously reckoned benefits." (Nicholas Rescher, "The Role of Values in Social Science Research," in Charles Frankel ed., *Controversies and Decisions* [New York: Russell Sage Foundation, 1976] pp. 36–37.)

I do not suggest that all that citizens need is research and social science. The political and interactive part of policy making is a necessary stimulus to forming better volitions. An analogy: Suppose you and I had to submit annual lists of all consumer goods and services we desired for the next twelve months and could not test our consumer preferences by facing a specific and concrete decision to buy or not to buy or by changing our purchases repeatedly in response to satisfaction and dissatisfaction with recent purchases. Would we not finally conclude that being an informed and thoughtful consumer requires participation in market interactions?

Similarly, to form our volitions, we need the specific experience of political life: discussion, agitation, voting and the like.

Note that I have only suggested the main outlines of what citizens need from social research, if policy making is to be significantly improved. Within these main outlines, you might like to consider more specific research priorities. But the thoughtful consideration of such priorities—to say nothing of research on priorities themselves—is in its infancy. Mainline social science hardly acknowledges that a problem exists, so set in its ways is it.

V. Practical Research and Problem Solutions

In the light of rejection of our first and third principles, let us now look at the second and fourth.

The second prescribed that social research intended to be helpful to public policy be limited to the consideration of feasible policy alternatives, alternatives that fit into existing institutions and politics. If there is any validity to what I have just been saying, that principle has to be rejected as too constraining. It would deny the appropriateness of the very variety of studies I have just described.[23]

In particular, it would continue to turn citizens and leaders alike away from a pivotal question the neglect of which has already done enough damage. The pivotal question is this: Are there some problem areas for which no satisfactory solutions can be found that are consistent with existing institutions? Or, to put it another way, does headway in some problem areas require fundamental, even if gradual and tentative, institutional change? One of the blindnesses of much contemporary research is its assumption that all problems have solutions within the existing institutional order. Perhaps they do; but the possibility that they do seems to strain credulity. In any case, the question needs study by anyone who is concerned about better public policy.

The fourth principle is that analysis close to the decision maker, analysis intended to have relatively immediate application to a decision, should be designed to culminate in a recommendation to a decision maker. That the foregoing analysis, if valid, destroys that principle too, is perhaps less obvious. Clearly, if the foregoing is valid, citizens need a variety of studies and only rarely need recommendations about specific solutions to specific problems. So also for officials and other leaders who, we point out, suffer from the same indoctrinations and impairment of critical faculties. Hence, all need a variety of kinds of analyses. It is striking that empirical studies of what officials say they need from social science often report that they, the officials, say they want no recommendations but want challenges to their ways of thinking, new orientations of their thought, or enlightenment rather than social engineering.[24]

23 There is a good deal of discontent with "practical" studies. For example, "The amount of really useful [research in support of] analysis relevant to major defense decisions has been limited ... [w]hile hundreds or possibly thousands of studies are turned out each year, few of them are of any real use for decisions at the Secretary of Defense level. ... This is not necessarily a criticism of the individuals participating in these studies, many of whom are highly capable. Nor do we believe that the problems addressed by these studies are so complex that they can never be understood. In part the problem stems in our judgment from the fact that nearly all such studies are oriented to near term program decisions. Few, if any, ever attempt any 'basic research' on underlying areas where data and knowledge are lacking."

The quotation is from a highly experienced analyst, Alain Enthoven, in Walter Williams, *Social Policy Research and Analysis* (New York: American Elsevier Publishing Company, Inc., 1971), p. 57.

24 See for example, Carol H. Weiss, "Research for Policy's Sake: The Enlightenment Function of Social Research," 3 *Policy Analysis* (Fall 1977). Other interesting evidence comes from a study of educational policy making in Sweden, where the frequent use of study commissions (assisted by researchers) to develop policy recommendations would seem to imply the use of researchers for just that specific purpose. Their actual usefulness to the commissions is of a different kind, closer to "enlightenment." See Rune Prefors, "Research and Policy-Making in Swedish Higher Education," University of Stockholm Group for the Study of Higher Education and Research Policy, Report 24 (October 1982), pp. 95–96.

If we go back to the beginning of the discussion on partisanship, we find still another reason for rejecting the fourth principle. If it is correct that social researchers go beyond their
capacity in proposing resolutions of conflicts of interest and
values, and if that resolution is a political rather than scholarly
task, calling not finally for knowledge but for a commitment
or act of will, then social researchers should usually not be
called on for recommendations. As for officials, they should ask
researchers for critical facts and pieces of analysis that will
enable political leadership to perform its task of conflict resolution. Faced with an urgent choice to be made, political leadership needs—depending on the situation—one or more of many
specialized contributions available from social research. The
political official may need a missing fact. Or a sustained piece
of analysis on interconnections he has not been able to work
out in his own mind. Or a challenge to a conclusion tentatively
reached on which he feels vulnerable. Or a hypothesis to stimulate his thinking. Or a checklist of variables that he must take
into account. Or an array of possible solutions. The list of
possible social research contributions is a long one; and the
theory of policy analysis that tries to push policy research into
a specialization in making recommendations is both excessively
constraining and mistaken in principle.

An example. Years ago in India while working for the Agency
for International Development, I encountered a situation that
still remains vivid to me. Indian officials had reached a tentative
conclusion that to increase foodgrain production it would be
necessary to guarantee farmers a minimum price to be announced before planting so that farmers could be confident that
it would be profitable to plant and to use fertilizer, insecticides
and improved seed. Before reaching a final decision, the officials
had to answer many questions. For example, in an illiterate
rural society, could they get the announcement of the program
and the promised minimum price communicated to the farmers?
Would the farmers believe the promise? If, in the coming harvest
season, foodgrain prices threatened to fall below the announced
minimum, could the civil service get grain purchasers out in the
field to buy up the grain at the minimum? If they bought grain,
was there warehouse capacity for its storage? Among their
various questions was another of particular interest: Do Indian

small farmers plant by tradition the same amount of seed in the same way every year, or would they plant more and better if they could count on a good price?

The Indian officials asked for some research help from the American aid mission. They did not ask, however, for a rec- ommendation from us, from their researchers, or from any other researchers. Nor did they even ask for research help on whether they could make an announcement effective, whether farmers would believe, whether the government could actually make millions of purchases in the field if necessary, and whether they could store their purchase. On each such question, they knew that good enough research could not be conducted in the time available. Moreover, they thought—correctly, I would guess—that their political and administrative judgement on answers to these questions was more competent than research was likely to be.

The one question that troubled them was whether farmers would plant the same regardless of their price expectations or would respond to price. On this they thought—correctly—that some research had been done; and they wanted its results. They got the results—findings that price mattered to farmers. Answering their other questions favorably, they went ahead with their program. Social research had been of great help because it has been focussed on a specific critical need, not because it had made any recommendation. In another situation, the critical need might have been entirely different; but critical need rather than recommendation was the key to useful social research. It was, and it is.

I can recapitulate the analysis in a few words about the four principles with which we began:

1. Instead of the pursuit of the public interest, partisanship;
2. Instead of a preoccupation with feasible solutions, a variety of studies to free the mind from its impairments;
3. Instead of serving the needs of officials alone, help for the ordinary citizen; and
4. Instead of recommendations, a tailoring of research to meet varying specific critical needs.

References

Almond, Gabriel A. and C. Bingham Powell, Jr. *Comparative Politics*. Boston: Little Brown, 1966.

Anderson, Charles W. "The Political Economy of Charles E. Lindblom." *American Political Science Review*. 72 (September 1978).

Apter, David. *Introductions to Political Analysis*. Cambridge, Massachusetts: Winthrop, 1977.

Bachrach, Peter and Morton S. Baratz. "The Two Faces of Power," *American Political Science Review*. 56 (December, 1962).

Beer, Samuel H. "New Structures of Democracy," in William N. Chambers and Robert H. Salisbury, eds. *Democracy Today*. New York: Collier Books, 1960.

Bell, Daniel. "Labor in the Post-Industrial Society." In Irving Howe, ed., *The World of the Blue-Collar Worker*. New York: Quadrangle Books, 1972, 164f.

Berelson, Bernard R., Paul F. Lazarsfeld, and William N. McPhee. *Voting*. Chicago: Univ. of Chicago Press, 1954.

Bowles, Samuel and Herbert Gintis. "The Power of Capital: On the Inadequacy of the Conception of the Capitalist Economy as 'Private.'" *Philosophical Forum*. 14 (Spring–Summer, 1983).

Braybrooke, David and Charles E. Lindblom. *The Strategy of Decision*. New York: The Free Press, 1963.

Brzezinski, Zbegniew and Samuel P. Huntington. *Political Power: USA/USSR*. New York: Viking, 1965.

Burnham, James. *The Managerial Revolution*. New York: John Day, 1941.

Chomsky, Noam and Edward Herman. *Political Economy of Human Rights*, Boston: South End Press, 1979.

Churchman, C. W., R. L. Ackoff, and E. L. Arnoff. *Introduction to Operations Research*. New York: John Wiley and Sons, 1957.

Cohen, G. A. *Karl Marx's Theory of History*. Princeton, New Jersey: Princeton University Press, 1978.

Cohen, Ronald and Elman R. Service, eds. *Origins of the State*. Philadelphia: Institute for the Study of Human Issues, 1978.

Connolly, William E. "The Challenge to Pluralist Theory." In William E. Connolly, ed., *The Bias of Pluralism*. New York: Atherton, 1969.

Crouch, Colin. "The State, Capital, and Liberal Democracy." In Colin Crouch, ed., *State and Economy in Contemporary Capitalism*. London: Croom Helm, 1979.

Crozier, Michael, Samuel P. Huntington, and Joji Watanuki. *The Crisis of Democracy*. New York: New York University Press, 1975.

Dahl, Robert A. *Democracy in the United States*. Chicago: Rand McNally, 1972.

Dahl, Robert A and Charles E. Lindblom. *Politics, Economics and Welfare.* New York: Harpers, 1953.

Dahl, Robert A. *A Preface to Democratic Theory.* Chicago: Univ. of Chicago Press, 1956.

Dahrendorf, Ralph. *Class and Class Conflict in Industrial Society.* Stanford, California: Stanford University Press, 1959.

Dawson, Richard E. and Kenneth Prewitt. *Political Socialization.* Boston: Little Brown, 1969.

de Jouvenel, Bertrand. *The Ethics of Redistribution.* Cambridge, England: Cambridge Univ. Press, 1951.

Dennis, Jack. "Major Problems of Political Socialization Research." In Jack Dennis, ed., *Socialization to Politics.* New York: John Wiley and Sons, 1973.

Deutsch, Karl. *Politics and Government.* Boston: Houghton Mifflin, 1980.

Dolbeare, Kenneth M. and Murray J. Edelman. *American Politics,* 3rd ed., rev. Lexington, Massachusetts: D. C. Heath, 1981.

Domhoff, G. William, ed. *Power Structure Research.* Beverly Hills, California: Sage, 1980.

Dror, Yehezkel. *Public Policymaking Reexamined.* San Francisco: Chandler, 1968.

Dye, Thomas R. and L. Harmon Ziegler. *The Irony of Democracy.* Belmont, California: Wadsworth, 1970.

Easton, David and Jack Dennis. *Children in the Political System.* New York: McGraw–Hill, 1969.

Easton, David and Robert D. Hess. "The Child's Political World." *Midwest Journal of Political Science.* 6 (1962), 229–246.

Etzioni, Amitai. "Mixed-Scanning." *Public Administration Review.* 27 (1967).

Frank, Andrew Gunder. "Goal Ambiguity and Conflicting Standards: An Approach to the Study of Organization." *Human Organization.* 17 (1959) 8–13.

Frank, Andrew Gunder and R. Cohen. "Conflicting Standards and Selective Enforcement in Social Organization and Social Change: A Cross-Cultural Test." Paper read at American Anthropological Association Meeting, Mexico City, December, 1959.

Galbraith, J. K. *The New Industrial State.* 3rd ed. Boston: Houghton Mifflin, 1978.

Gaventa, John. *Power and Powerlessness.* Urbana, Illinois: University of Illinois Press, 1980.

Golden, Clinton S. and Harold J. Ruttenberg. *The Dynamics of Industrial Democracy.* New York: Harper & Brothers, 1942.

Goldstein, Joseph. *The Government of British Trade Unions.* Glencoe, Illinois: Free Press, 1952.

Gough, Ian. "State Expenditure in Advanced Capitalism." *New Left Review.* 92 (1975) 53–92.

Gouldner, Alvin G. *The Coming Crisis of Western Sociology.* New York: Basic Books, 1970.

Gouldner, Alvin G. *Enter Plato.* New York: Basic Books, 1965.

Graham, George J. and Scarlett G. Graham. "Evaluating Drift in Policy Systems." In Phillip M. Gregg, ed., *Problems of Theory in Policy Analysis.* Lexington, Massachusetts: D. C. Heath, 1976, 86.

Gramsci, Antonio. "The Formation of Intellectuals." In Antonio Gramsci, *The*

Modern Prince and Other Writings. Translated by Louis Marks. New York: International Publishers, 1968, 118–125.

Gramsci, Antonio. "The Study of Philosophy and of Historical Materialism." In Antonio Gramsci, *The Modern Prince and Other Writings*. Translated by Louis Marks. New York: International Publishers, 1968, 58–75.

Greenstein, Fred I. "Socialization: Political Socialization." In David L. Sills, ed., *International Encyclopedia of the Social Sciences*. New York: The Macmillan Company and The Free Press, 14 (1968) 551–555.

Gulick, Luther and Lyndall Urwick, eds. *Papers on the Science of Administration*. New York: Institute of Public Administration, Columbia Univ., 1937.

Habermas, Jürgen. *Legitimation Crisis*. London: Heinemann, 1976.

Harris, Joseph P. "The Future of Administrative Management," in L. D. White, ed., *The Future of Government in the United States*. Chicago, Ill.: Univ. of Chicago, 1942.

Hartz, Louis. "Democracy: Image and Reality," in William N. Chambers and Robert H. Salisbury, eds. *Democracy Today*. New York: Collier Books, 1960.

Haveman, Robert H. and Julius Margolis, eds. *Public Expenditure and Policy Analysis*. Chicago: Markham, 1970.

Herring, E. Pendleton. *The Politics of Democracy*. New York: Rinehart and Co., 1940.

Herring, E. Pendleton. *Public Administration and Public Interest*. New York: McGraw-Hill, 1936.

Hess, Robert D. and Judith V. Torney. *The Development of Political Attitudes in Children*. Chicago: Aldine, 1967.

Hickman, C. Addison and Manford H. Kuhn. *Individuals, Groups, and Economic Behavior*. New York: Dryden Press, 1956.

Hirschman, Albert O. *The Strategy of Economic Development*. New Haven, Connecticut: Yale University Press, 1958.

Hirschman, Albert O. and Charles E. Lindblom. "Economic Development, Research and Development, Policy Making: Some Converging Views." Paper No. P–1982, Santa Monica, California: The RAND Corporation, May 4, 1960.

Hitch, Charles. "Operations Research and National Planning—A Dissent." *Operations Research*. 5 (October, 1957) 718.

Holloway, John and Sol Picciotto. "Towards a Materialist Theory of the State." In John Holloway and Sol Picciotto, eds., *State and Capital: A Marxist Debate*. Austin, Texas: University of Texas Press, 1978.

Kerr, Clark. "Wage Relationships—the Comparative Impact of Market and Power Forces." Reprint of Institute of Industrial Relations, University of California at Berkeley. Reprinted from John T. Dunlop, ed., *The Theory of Wage Determination*. New York: St. Martin's Press, 1957.

Key, V. O. in L. D. White, ed., *The Future of Government in the United States,* Chicago: Univ. of Chicago Press, 1942, 145–163.

Key, V. O., Jr. *Public Opinion and American Democracy*. New York: Alfred A. Knopf, 1967.

Kingsley, John D. *Representative Bureaucracy*. Yellow Springs, Ohio: Antioch Press, 1944.

Klein, B. "The Decision-Making Problem in Development." Paper No. P–1916. Santa Monica, California: The RAND Corporation. February 19, 1960.

Klein, B. "A Radical Proposal for R and D." *Fortune*. (May, 1958), 112.

Klein, B. and W. Meckling. "Application of Operations Research to Development Decisions." *Operations Research.* 6 (1958) 352–363.

Knight, Frank. "The Ethics of Competition." *Quarterly Journal of Economics.* (May 1922).

Knight, Frank. "The Meaning of Democracy." In Frank Knight, *Freedom and Reform.* New York: Harper and Brothers, 1947.

Kuhn, Thomas S. *The Structure of Scientific Revolutions,* 2nd ed. Chicago: University of Chicago Press, 1970.

Lakatos, Imre and Alan Musgrave, eds. *Criticism and Growth of Knowledge.* Cambridge, England: Cambridge University Press, 1970.

Landsberger, Henry A. *Hawthorne Revisited.* Ithaca, New York: Cornell Univ. Press, 1958.

Langton, Kenneth P. *Political Socialization.* New York: Oxford University Press, 1969.

LaPorte, Todd R., ed. *Organized Social Complexity.* Princeton, New Jersey: Princeton University Press, 1975.

Latham, Earl. *The Group Basis of Politics.* Ithaca, New York: Cornell Univ. Press, 1952.

Leibenstein, Harvey. "Allocative Efficiency vs. 'X-Efficiency.'" *American Economic Review.* 56 (June, 1966).

Leibenstein, Harvey. *Beyond Economic Man.* Cambridge, Massachusetts: Harvard University Press, 1976.

Lindberg, Leon, et al., eds. *Stress and Contradiction in Modern Capitalism: Public Policy and the Theory of the State.* Lexington, Massachusetts: D. C. Heath, 1975.

Lindblom, Charles E. *Bargaining: The Hidden Hand in Government.* Santa Monica, California: The Rand Corporation, 1955.

Lindblom, Charles E. "Decision Making in Taxation and Expenditure." In Universities—National Bureau of Economic Research, *Public Finances; Needs, Sources, and Utilizations.* Princeton, New Jersey: Princeton University Press, 1961.

Lindblom, Charles E. "The Handling of Norms in Policy Analysis." In M. Abramovitz, ed., *Allocation of Economic Resources,* Stanford, California: Stanford University Press, 1958.

Lindblom, Charles E. "In Praise of Political Science." *World Politics.* 9 (January, 1957), 240–253.

Lindblom, Charles E. *The Intelligence of Democracy.* New York: The Free Press, 1965.

Lindblom, Charles E. "Policy Analysis." *American Economic Review.* 48 (June, 1958) 298–312.

Lindblom, Charles E. *Politics and Markets.* New York: Basic Books, 1977.

Lindblom, Charles E. *The Policy-Making Process,* 2nd ed. Englewood Cliffs, New Jersey: Prentice–Hall, 1979.

Lindblom, Charles E. "The Science of Muddling Through." *Public Administration Review.* 19 (1959) 78–88.

Lindblom, Charles E. "Sociology of Planning: Thought and Social Interaction." In Morris Bornstein, ed., *Economic Planning, East and West.* Cambridge, Massachusetts: Ballinger, 1975.

Lindblom, Charles E. "Tinbergen on Policy Making." *Journal of Political Economics.* 66 (1958) 531–538.

Lindblom, Charles E. and David K. Cohen. *Usable Knowledge.* New Haven, Connecticut: Yale University Press, 1979.

Lindblom, Charles E. and Robert A. Dahl. *Politics, Economics, and Welfare.* New York: Harpers, 1953.

Linton, Ralph. *The Study of Man.* New York: Appleton-Century-Crofts, 1936.

Lipset, Seymour M., Martin A. Trow, and James S. Coleman. *Union Democracy.* Glencoe, Illinois: Free Press, 1956.

Littlejohn, Gary, Barry Smart, John Walkford, Nira Yuval-Davis, eds. *Power and the State.* New York: St. Martin's Press, 1978.

Lowi, Theodore J. *American Government.* Hinsdale, Illinois: The Dryden Press, 1976.

Lowi, Theodore J. *The End of Liberalism,* 2nd ed. New York: W. W. Norton & Company, 1979.

Lukes, S. *Power: A Radical View.* London: Macmillan, 1974.

Lynn, Laurence E., Jr., ed. *Knowledge and Policy.* Washington, D.C.: National Academy of Sciences, 1978.

Mandel, Ernest. *Late Capitalism.* London: New Left Books, 1974.

Mann, Michael. "The Social Cohesion of Liberal Democracy." *American Sociological Review.* 35 (June, 1970).

March, James G. and Herbert A. Simon. *Organizations.* New York: John Wiley and Sons, 1958.

McCloskey, J. F. and J. M. Coppinger, eds. *Operations Research for Management,* Vol. II. Baltimore, Maryland: The Johns Hopkins University Press, 1956.

Meyerson, Martin and Edward C. Banfield. *Politics, Planning and the Public Interest.* New York: The Free Press, 1955.

Miliband, Ralph. *New Left Review.* 59 (January–February, 1969).

Miliband, Ralph. *The State in Capitalist Society.* New York: Basic Books, 1969.

Mills, C. Wright. *The Power Elite.* New York: Oxford Univ. Press, 1956.

Mitroff, Ian. *The Subjective Side of Science.* New York: American Elsevier Publishing Company, Inc., 1974.

Mouzelis, Nicos. "Reductionism in Marxist Theory." *Telos.* 45 (1980) 173–185.

Niemi, Richard G. "Political Socialization," in Jeanne N. Knutson, ed. *Handbook of Political Psychology.* San Francisco: Jossey–Bass, 1973.

O'Connor, James. *The Fiscal Crisis of the State.* New York: St. Martin's Press, 1973.

Offe, C. "Political Authority and Class Structure." In P. Conneton, ed., *Critical Sociology.* Harmondsworth, Middlesex, England: Penguin Books, 1976.

Parsons, Talcott. "The Distribution of Power in American Society." *World Politics.* 10 (October, 1957) 123–143.

Pateman, Carole. *Participation and Democratic Theory.* Cambridge, England: Cambridge University Press, 1970.

Pennock, J. Roland. "Democracy and Leadership," in William N. Chambers and Robert H. Salisbury, eds. *Democracy Today.* New York: Collier Books, 1960.

Polanyi, Michael. "The Republic of Science." *Minerva.* 1 (Autumn, 1962).

Polsby, Nelson W. *Community Power and Social Theory.* New Haven, Connecticut: Yale University Press, 1980.

Poulantzas, Nicos. *Political Power and Social Classes.* London: New Left Review Books, 1973.

Poulantzas, Nicos. "The Problem of the Capitalist State." *New Left Review*. 58 (November–December, 1969).

Premfors, Rune. "Research and Policy-Making in the Study of Higher Education." University of Stockholm Group for the Study of Higher Education and Research Policy, Report 24. October, 1982.

Prewitt, Kenneth and Sidney Verba. *Introduction to American Government*. New York: Harper and Row, 1977.

Pusey, Nathan M. *The Age of the Scholar*. Cambridge, Massachusetts: Harvard University Press, 1963.

Rescher, Nicholas. "The Role of Values in Social Science Research." In Charles Frankel, ed., *Controversies and Decisions*. New York: Russell Sage Foundation, 1976, 36–37.

Rogow, Arnold A. *The Labour Government and British Industry 1945–1951*. Ithaca, New York: Cornell Univ. Press, 1955.

Rustow, Alexander. *Freedom and Domination*. Princeton, New Jersey: Princeton University Press, 1980.

Schattschneider, E. E. *Party Government*. New York: Holt, Rinehart and Winston, 1942.

Schultze, Charles L. *The Politics and Economics of Public Spending*. Washington, D.C.: Brookings, 1968.

Simon, Herbert A. "A Behavorial Model of Rational Choice." *Quarterly Journal of Economics*. 69 (February, 1955).

Simon, Herbert A. *Models of Man*. New York: John Wiley and Sons, 1957.

Simon, Herbert A., Donald W. Smithburg and Victor A. Thompson. *Public Administration*. New York: Alfred A. Knopf, 1950.

Skocpol, Theda. "Political Response to Capitalist Crisis: Neo-Marxist Theories of the State and the Case of the New Deal." *Politics and Society*. 10 (1980) 155–201.

Stokley, Edith and Richard Zeckhauser. *A Primer for Policy Analysis*. New York: Norton, 1978.

Sturmthal, Adolf. *The Tragedy of European Labour 1918–1939*. New York: Columbia Univ. Press, 1943.

Taylor, Charles. "Neutrality in Political Science." In Peter Laslett and W. G. Runciman, eds., *Philosophy, Politics and Society,* 3rd ed. Oxford: Blackwell, 1969.

Tesh, Sylvia. "Upholding Principles: A Note in Support of 'Single' Issue Politics." Working Paper No. CHS–54. Yale University Institute for Social and Policy Studies. September, 1983.

Tobin, James. "The Eisenhower Economy and National Security: Two Views, Dollars, Defense, and Doctrines." *The Yale Review*. 47 (1958) 321–334.

Townsend, William. *Dissertation on the Poor Laws*. 1785.

Truman, David B. "The American System in Crisis." *Political Science Quarterly*. 74 (1959) 481–497.

Truman, David B. *The Governmental Process*. New York: Knopf, 1951.

Verba, Sidney and Norman H. Nie. *Participation in America*. New York: Harper and Row, 1972.

von Hayek, Friedrich. *The Constitution of Liberty*. Chicago: University of Chicago, 1960.

Waldo, Dwight. *The Administrative State.* New York: Ronald Press, 1948.

Weiss, Carol H. "Research for Policy's Sake: The Enlightenment Function of Social Research." *Policy Analysis.* 3 (Fall, 1977).

Weissberg, R. *Political Learning, Political Choice and Democratic Citizenship.* Englewood Cliffs, New Jersey: Prentice-Hall, 1974.

Wilensky, Harold L. "Human Relations in the Work-place: An Appraisal of Some Recent Research." In C. M. Arensberg et al., eds. *Research in Industrial Human Relations.* New York: Harper, 1957.

Williams, Walter. *Social Policy Research and Analysis.* New York: American Elsevier Publishing Company, Inc., 1971.

Wilson, James Q. "Social Science and Public Policy." In Laurence E. Lynn, Jr., ed. *Knowledge and Policy.* Washington, D.C.: National Academy of Sciences, 1978, 82.

Whyte, William H. *The Organization Man.* New York: Simon and Schuster, 1956.

Index